400 *letters from my mother*

Joseph Oubelkas

Foreword by
Stedman Graham

FOREWORD

The relationship Joseph has with his mother is pure poetry. Beyond the letters referenced in this literary work, I have witnessed it personally. It is beautiful. And, with the love, will and perseverance she bestowed upon and within him, he overcame the difficulties of being incarcerated for crimes he did not commit. He is a remarkable person because of her influence, and the influence he now bestows on others.

As with Nelson Mandela, Joseph's hero, he did not let his circumstances stop him. Those circumstances did, however, change him – to become even better. Joseph's mother states it best, *"Life has many barriers we must cross.... It is then that you must stand up and move on and see past the darkest clouds to a heavenly blue, with flowers blooming in all of their beauty."*

Joseph Oubelkas is a man who has chosen to share his message and his fortitude. He is a man who knows the power of forgiveness, and who understands that managing his perspective and his thoughts are paramount in living a good life. He is a man who decided to leave a legacy of good and to pay forward his learning. He is a man that acknowledges that he cannot change what is past, but who can carve his future.

His ultimate choice is to pass on that knowledge to others. He offers hope, strength, purpose and ultimately love to those who will read this book, who will be intrigued and inspired by his message, and who will decide to utilize determination to live a life according to their will, not the will of others.

One of the biggest blessings in life is to know thy self. In life, we can control who we are – our identity – and how we choose to show up each day. Joseph has chosen well and I applaud him. Joseph's future is rich with promise and possibility. We are very fortunate to learn from him and his experiences, and to have an example of not only making the best of the conditions we face, but making the most of them in the form of caring to impact each other.

Thank you, Joseph, for who you are, what you do, and all that I know you will be.

Stedman Graham
Author, Speaker and Entrepreneur

Title: *400 LETTERS FROM MY MOTHER*

Author: Joseph Oubelkas

www.josephoubelkas.com

Produced by: Galilee Media
www.galileemedia.com

Portrait photo: José Donatz
Interior design: Galilee Media

Translated by: Anne Marie Westra-Nijhuis
Edited by: Paul Ruffolo / Joyce Garritano

Koninklijke Bibliotheek reg.nr: 020-14249
ISBN: 978-90-77607-831
NUR: 402

Life, my child, has many barriers you must cross.
Most of the time, you will be warned.
But everyone stumbles once in their life
on an invisible barrier.
Then, my son, you must stand up and
move on for you will see a heavenly blue
between the darkest clouds and
flowers blooming in their full beauty.
Lots of love, mom.

CONTENT

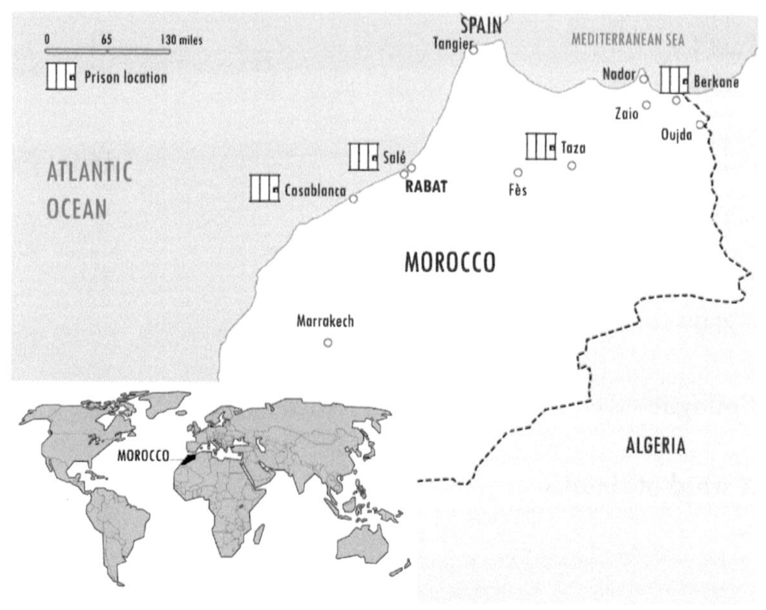

0
65
130 miles
Prison location
SPAIN
Tangier
MEDITERRANEAN SEA
Nador
Berkane
Zaio
Oujda
Salé
Taza
ATLANTIC
OCEAN
Casablanca
RABAT
Fès
MOROCCO
Marrakech
ALGERIA
MOROCCO

PROLOGUE

The cars were parked in a strange way, almost like the blades of a fan spread around the gate. When I stepped out of my car and walked up, it soon became clear that something was wrong. There were many people crying and dozens of men in uniform. The men, whom I recognized as customs officers, were canvassing the area with shotguns in their hands. No matter where I turned, all I could hear were people screaming as I saw the terrified glances on their faces.

What's going on here?

As I got to the gate, I waved several times trying to draw the attention of one of the customs officers. One of them finally came up to me and asked sternly: "Who are you and what do you want?"

"Uh, my name is Joseph and I work for a Dutch company," I replied. I watched the officer looking at me with his eyes growing larger. "What is going on?" I asked.

"Follow me!" the officer snapped.

And that was how my nightmare began...

PART I

2004, 2005

1

My name is Joseph Oubelkas – my friends call me "Sef" or "Joe" – and until the end of 2004, I was fortunate enough to live my life free from any real setbacks.

I was born in the Netherlands in 1980 on the 10th of September, in a small village called Raamsdonksveer. It was an active village in the Province of Brabant, where sand turns into clay. In this village I had a wonderful youth; a caring mother and father, many friends and a lovely girlfriend.

At the age of sixteen, I began studying Computer Science in the city of Breda, also in the Province of Brabant. Four years later, I graduated as one of the Netherlands' youngest IT engineers and I made the decision to start my own company, which was a success from the very beginning.

Study, work, love, everything in my life was running perfectly. But then, in December of 2004, it all went wrong.

Something happened that turned my comfortable life completely upside down. Something that apparently can happen to anyone.

It all started with a routine business trip to Morocco, which would prove to have unimaginable consequences...

2

Monday, December 20, 2004.

My mom was sitting on the couch in the living room and I noticed her restlessly staring around. She was obviously worried. "Mom? Are you okay?"

"I don't know, Joseph. I don't know what it is, but I'm so nervous..."

"Don't worry, mom," I said trying to comfort her. "There's nothing to be afraid of."

I had just packed my bags and was about to leave for another week on business in Morocco. This trip wasn't planned, but one of my colleagues couldn't make it. My client, "Sword fruits"– a major import and export company of fruit and vegetables – had asked me to replace him.

I looked at my watch and saw that my plane would be leaving soon from Schiphol Airport in Amsterdam. I was late again.

"Mom, don't worry, okay? Nothing will happen to me..."

I paused and looked at her with a big smile. "I'm looking forward to Christmas! I really have to get going, but I will see you on Friday!"

My mom walked me to the door. "Be safe, my child," she said in the doorway.

"I'll be fine!" I was smiling on the garden path, holding my red suitcase. My mom smiled back at me, all the while keeping the serious look on her face.

"Bye, mom! Love you!" I looked at my watch again and quickly walked down the path. What I didn't know back then and never could have known, was that my life would never look the same again from that moment on - and that I would never return to the house I had just left.

3

The winter sun was shining brightly, low in a cloudless blue sky. It was busy on the highway for a late Monday morning.

As I always do when traveling on business, I brought my CDs and listened to familiar songs from Lenny Kravitz and Bruce Springsteen, to Pearl Jam and Nickelback. I skipped the house and R&B music, because I wasn't in the mood. Of course I would take the music CDs to Morocco. At Schiphol Airport, I parked my car in the 'Long Term Parking' lot, I took my red suitcase from the back of the car and headed for the terminal.

I looked again at my watch, for the thousandth time. Surprisingly, I was on schedule.

At least that's what I thought. I arrived at the check-in desk where a lady in uniform kindly informed me that I had just missed my flight's final call.

"Okay, but could you still check in my suitcase?" I asked as nicely as I could.

"Yes, I will weigh your suitcase," she answered me with a modest smile. "You have to go to Gate 9B."

"Thanks!"

As I arrived, people were already boarding the plane. I noticed head scarves and djellabas[1] and knew I was in the right place. Nearly three hours later I was at Oujda[2] Airport in Morocco. There I was again, in my father's country. I've always felt at home here, although I never looked forward to the grumpy faces of the Moroccan customs officers.

My watch said it was half past five, but during winter in Morocco, the clocks were set back two hours. So it was actually only half past three in the afternoon.

The driver of one of Sword fruits' many contacts was waiting for me. He was a nice guy, but more importantly, he drove safely, which is rare in Morocco.

It would take about forty minutes to travel from Oujda to my destination: a small city called Berkane.

In Morocco, the highways are almost always empty.
However, the city is full of cars, taxis, buses, cyclists, pedestrians,

1. A djellaba is a long, loose robe with long sleeves and a sort of hood.
2. Oujda is pronounced as "Woozjdah". This town is situated in northeastern Morocco, near the Algerian border.

donkeys, horses and hand-carts. Accidents happen easily here.

After arriving at the house that was rented by Sword fruits, I threw my suitcase on the bed and quickly freshened up. The driver then took me to one of the packing stations so I could pick up my company car. My workweek had started.

4

When I try to explain what I was doing in Morocco, I often joke that I was there to hold people's hands and assist them in getting the job done. Actually, it's not a joke, because I really did support them. Sword fruits had purchased a large number of mandarin fields in the region of Berkane. The company came to know me through a reference from my former employer and immediately expressed interest in hiring me for the project in Morocco. According to them, hiring me had its advantages: I'm Dutch, my father is Moroccan, I speak French, and in my teenage years I worked in the vegetable department of a supermarket and my former employer told them that I am a good and serious worker. In fact, the work I performed for Sword fruits had nothing to do with my background as an IT engineer, but I enjoyed making the extra money on top of my income from my own company. I also loved the idea of working abroad, especially in my father's country.

One of the major problems Sword fruits coped with was that in the Moroccan (work) culture, time is not of the essence. Today, tomorrow, the day after, none of it really mattered. This was completely opposite of the way in which we are used to working in the Netherlands. Time is money. Therefore, we do our best to accomplish every task on time. That's why the company chose me to guide the entire process, from harvesting to export.

Another issue was the fruit packing stations. For some reason, no matter how many times the workers claimed to be following instructions, the fruit was never packed correctly and I never found out why.

The packing stations are large halls, where hundreds of people are busy sorting and packing the mandarins. To ensure the quality of the packed fruit, I visited the various stations every day with a checklist of items. The pallets had to be manufactured solidly and properly numbered, according to the requirements. I also had to meet with the directors of each plant. I would discuss what went right and what went wrong, and then report back to Sword fruits.

After the fruit was packed on pallets, it was then transported by trucks to the port of Nador, a city about fifty miles west of Berkane, near the Mediterranean Sea. I visited the port regularly to check the condition of the pallets and make sure they were shipped properly. When the vessel was moored, I had to ensure that the pallets with the right numbers were loaded in the corresponding cargo compartments. Once the vessel left, we began preparing for the next shipment.

5

Thursday, December 23, 2004.

The days flew by. It was Thursday, early in the morning. Everyone has those days, days that are etched in your memory for the rest of your life. Days with a certain date. Days that you will always remember as if it were yesterday.

I remember how I woke up in a very good mood. At six o'clock in the morning, my alarm went off. It would be my final busy day. I had everything well prepared and planned.

It was very cold in the house. After getting up, I walked on my toes to the stereo to put on one of my CDs. It was a CD with hits from Lenny Kravitz. *Are You Gonna Go My Way* and *Fly Away* jumped out of the speakers. I quickly hit the shower and started to wash myself while singing and beat boxing. The bathroom floor quickly turned into another Atlantic Ocean. I was in such an euphoric mood, that I didn't care about the mess. I usually kept everything tidy, even though a cleaning maid came to the house every day.

Most of my belongings were already packed and I was looking forward to Christmas. The next day, early in the morning, I would fly back home for a long weekend of eating, having fun and unpacking presents.

I left the house whistling and headed toward one of the cafes on the main boulevard. I ate breakfast there every morning. Then, as most other days, I started my rounds at the packing station Melika Fruits. In the company car, no Lenny or Bruce, but tapes with Moroccan and Algerian music. Not my favorite kind, but I did hum along with the funny tunes as I drove the long straight road just outside of Berkane toward Melika Fruits. My euphoria was reaching its peak, until I arrived at the main entrance of the packing station. I saw that the gate was blocked by a number of cars. The cars were positioned as if they all wanted to get inside at the same time.

What is this? I wondered.

I honked a few times, but when no one responded, I stepped out of my car.

My euphoria was soon about to change.

6

The cars were parked in a strange way, almost like the blades of a fan spread around the gate. When I stepped out of my car and walked up, it soon became clear that something was wrong. The Melika Fruits workers were standing around the site in large groups. I saw dozens of uniformed men walking and running around. Some of them had shotguns in their hands, others had smaller weapons. From the uniforms I could tell that they were customs officers. One of them nervously walked around with a handheld camera. I heard screaming everywhere and the workers looked terrified.

What's going on here?

I waved at the gateway to the officers and called to them several times, but they didn't see or hear me. Eventually, one of them came up to me. Meanwhile, several curious passing drivers had put their vehicles aside and dozens of people began to form around me.

"Who are you and what do you want?"

"Uh, my name is Joseph and I work for a Dutch company," I replied. I watched the officer looking at me with his eyes growing larger... "What's going on?" I asked.

"Follow me!" he snapped.

I squeezed myself between the cars and followed him.

I walked up to the site to watch the spectacle up close. The workers were looking ahead, confused, surprised and frightened. The women of the packaging department, the men who manufacture the pallets, the box makers, truck drivers; they were all there, like a flock of sheep under the guarding eye of the barking customs officers. The workers looked at me for answers, but I shrugged my shoulders having no response. I didn't understand any of this circus. The grumpy customs officer who accompanied me, had yet to answer my question. What was all of this about? He took me to the group of forklift drivers and told me that no one was allowed to talk.

A little later, I started talking because I wanted to know what was going on. But I was immediately snubbed by another officer holding a very large shotgun. I was shocked by his reaction and backed away. I have seen shotguns before in computer games, but in reality such a weapon looks much more threatening. I wisely kept my mouth shut.

Then I saw the owner of the packing station surrounded by a group of officers. He looked very serious. I waved to him, but he seemed to ignore me as they brought him into the site. There I stood, surrounded by hundreds of fellow sufferers, waiting for more than fifteen minutes. There was a tense silence. The situation began to annoy me.

Why is no one telling me anything? I have work to do, damn.

My whole schedule was falling apart.

My body language must have spoken volumes, because a really friendly customs officer called me over to him. He brought me to a white Mercedes van that was a little further on site. In front of this van, another identical white van was parked. The officer opened the back of the van and showed me the reason behind all of this commotion. The van was loaded to the brim with brown plastic packages. In front of the packets, I saw some wooden Sword fruits-mandarin boxes.

"What is it?" I asked.

The officer laughed and said: "Hashish, khoya[3], hashish."

"Oh?" I said surprised.

"And that other van is also full," he continued.

"Is that the problem?" I asked, totally unaware of the seriousness of the case. The officer laughed as he took a mandarin from one of the boxes. He pealed the mandarin and gave half of it to me. It tasted deliciously sweet.

About two hours after the customs officers completed their raid, the local police arrived.

---

3. Khoya is pronounced as "gòya" meaning "brother". In the Moroccan language, the word is often used as a stopgap.

Very late, I thought, but I wasn't really surprised. I was already quite used to the "relaxed" approach of the Moroccans.

In the packing station, the local police quickly rushed over to the owner, who was still guarded by the customs officers.

The friendly customs officer brought me inside with him too. A police officer noticed me and began to ask me questions about what I was doing here and where I came from.

"The Netherlands," I said.

"Ah, the Netherlands. Beautiful country," he said. "Could I see your passport please?"

I handed over my passport.

"Thank you. I have been there once," the police officer said with a smile. "Nice people there."

"Certainly! I like the country too," I answered.

"Only a bit cold," he added, as he thumbed through my passport.

"Yeah, but here it can also be cold."

He looked at me and asked if he could just keep my passport.

"Yes, if you have to. No problem."

The policemen allowed me to walk around, but, throughout the site, I could still see people being ordered to put their hands on their head, after which they were searched. Dogs were searching the packing station as well. All packed and numbered pallets destined for export were torn and searched. They were looking for drugs, but nothing was found.

An hour passed and I still hadn't gotten my passport back.

My phone rang. The name "Andre Laarhoven", the business controller of Sword fruits, lit up on my display.

"Hey Andre, it's Joseph," I answered.

On the other side of the line, Andre sounded a little worried. Sword fruits had apparently already heard the news.

"Joseph, I have the number of a lawyer, named Ahroumi.

Call him, just to be sure. There seems to be something seriously wrong."

Call a lawyer?

I thought it was a little exaggerated, but I did it anyway.

The lawyer spoke to me in a serious tone.

...

"Make sure you get away from that place!"

"Why?" I asked.

"Ask for your passport and leave as soon as possible!"

"But..."

"No further questions, listen to me! Ask for your passport and get out of there! NOW!"

...

The lawyer hung up.

What was going on? What should I do? I became slightly panicked.

Where is the policeman with my passport?

I went out looking for him.

... Away from this place...

It was all I could think of.

Why was that lawyer so worried? I haven't done anything...

I found the policeman and asked for my passport.

But he didn't give it back to me.

Instead, the police commander ordered me to accompany him to the police station

"Why?"

"For questioning"

He grabbed my arms and handcuffed me.

"What are you doing?" I asked indignantly.

"Get in the car! NOW!"

7

With ten other men, we were transferred to the police station. At the site, the commander had pointed to us randomly, one by one, to come along. Just as I asked for my passport, I saw his finger pointing at me and I was dragged by the collar into the van.

The owner of the packing station, the guards, truck drivers, an administrator, a few packers and I were sitting in the van, handcuffed. At the station we had to wait in a room for hours. It was cold and poorly lit. As we sat there waiting, I hadn't yet seen the owner of the packing station. I assumed that he was being kept apart. The workers were called one by one, until finally, it was my turn. It was already late in the evening,

"I don't know what's going on, but could we please handle this quickly?" I asked annoyed. "Because of this whole thing, my schedule is messed up and tomorrow I have to catch an early plane."

Two policemen were sitting in front of me, looking at me glassy-eyed. Later, they started asking me a few superficial questions and they asked me to empty my pockets. From my big Sword fruits coat, I took out my wallet, three telephones and a digital camera. Everything was carefully analyzed, as if they were looking at these things for the first time in their lives.

"The digital camera, what do you use it for?" one of them asked.

"To take pictures," I replied smartly, but truthfully.

"Of what?" the interrogator continued seriously. He had a stern look, short white hair, a white mustache and prying eyes. I estimated him to be around the age of fifty.

"I'll show you," I said and took the camera from him. "Here," I said, pointing to the screen of the camera, "these are pallets well fabricated... These pallets are not okay..." I leaned across the desk and flipped through, while the interrogator looked as if interested. "These are the pallets stored in Nador, these are mandarins of good quality in a box, these are bad mandarins, and here you see the trees which are harvested, this is me in the picture with some friends..."

The interrogator snatched the camera from my hands and flipped through it himself frantically.

"Why did you take those pictures?"

Another savvy question.

I was about to say "To make a holiday album," but I wisely said I took the pictures on behalf of my boss so I could display images of what went right and what went wrong during the job.

"Who is your boss?" the interrogator asked with flashing eyes.

"Wilko van der Zwaard."

"Is he here?"

"No, he is in the Netherlands."

"Could you ask him to come to Morocco?"

"Sure, if I may call him."

"You may, you've got three phones, so that shouldn't be a problem," the interrogator said smartly. "Why do you actually have three phones?"

He clearly was dying to ask this question for some time. I wanted to sigh very deeply, but remained polite.

"This one," I took my Samsung mobile in my hand, "is my own private phone. This, an Ericsson-mobile, is from Sword fruits with a Dutch number and this, a low-cost Nokia 3310, I bought here, because it's very expensive for the local people to call my Dutch number."

The interrogator looked at me stiff and flipped through the contacts of my Samsung and Nokia, while I was calling Wilko with my Ericsson phone.

"Hey, Joseph," Wilko answered, "what's going on there?"

I explained to him what happened the past few hours and asked him if he would come to Morocco.

"Tell him I have planned to come next Wednesday."

I had to keep the conversation brief and hung up.

"Wednesday," I told the interrogator, "Wilko van der Zwaard will come to Morocco."

I was allowed to go, back to the cold waiting loft. It was late and I started to get pretty tired. All I wanted to do was go to sleep, and catch my plane home.

A few minutes later, the commander entered the hallway. Most of the others had already left and I also expected to be allowed to go soon. However, I had to come along to the commander's office. Here I saw the owner of the packing station. I glanced at him and then looked around the room. It was a big office with little furniture. Very typical for Moroccan high officials: not too much fuss. A nice shiny desk, a few luxury leather armchairs and a large framed picture of the king on the wall. Nothing more, nothing less.

I greeted both men politely and sat down.

"You gave us a lot of work," the commander said. A short, mustached and stern-looking man with a typical leader's charisma.

"What do you mean, 'you'?" I asked irritated.

"Almost eighteen thousand pounds of hashish. That's quite something."

Wow, that's really quite something!

It was the first time I had heard about this amount and I frowned.

"Who's behind it?" I asked, without thinking about whether the owner of the packing station might have something to do with it, and whether they regarded me as a suspect. I got no answer. Instead, the eyes in the bare room were focused on the available TV. The late night news was being broadcasted. With wide eyes I looked at the images that were being shown. Images I had seen myself earlier today that were now being revealed throughout Morocco.

That man of the customs with the camera! So that's why he had it with him. The whole city of Berkane, and all of Morocco, was in an uproar.

There was a pause after the subject on the news ended. The commander broke the silence and told me that the owner of the packing station had stated that he wished to take all responsibility. I nodded and asked what would happen now.

"The station will be temporarily held by the State until there is more clarity," the commander replied.

The owner was looking glum. Suddenly, I realized that my workbag with my laptop in it was still at the packing station.

"Sir?" I asked, while I was sitting up straight. "My workbag is still at the station. Is it possible to pick it up?"

"Sure, no problem," the commander replied, while looking in my passport. "Would you mind waiting in the hall?"

I nodded, stood up and moved the chair back neatly in its place. Relieved that I could go, I stayed for a minute chatting with a police officer, who was lighting a cigarette and was about to go home with his jacket over his arm. He seemed like a nice guy to me, but he was looking tired. Tired I thought, of the hopeless existence as a police officer in this country. In my conversations with different policemen previously today, I heard them speaking ill of the governmental system. They all complained openly about the poor working conditions, low salaries and long working days.

A few minutes later, the commander entered the hall.

The police officer, with whom I was talking, abruptly stopped, threw his cigarette away and jumped to attention. The commander walked over to me and clapped with my passport in his hands, as if he wanted to spank me with it.

"Mr. Oubelkas, I'm afraid you'll have to stay here. I've just had contact with the public prosecutor and he instructed me to keep you here for a while."

"What?" I shouted. "Why?"

"The prosecutor thinks it's suspicious that you have many entry and exit stamps in your passport." The commander looked at me sternly. "And I actually think the same."

"What do you mean by many stamps? All of my colleagues have many stamps in their passports as well. We travel a lot for our work!"

"I'm sorry, but I have to ask you to remove your belt and shoelaces."

"You can't be serious! My flight is scheduled in a few hours. They expect me at home!"

"You may inform someone back home that you won't be coming tomorrow."

I became panicked and felt tears welling up.

I have to get home, it's Christmas! I can't stay!

Damn, what is this? Some kind of a joke?

The commander saw me hesitating.

"Your belt and shoelaces."

It wasn't a joke. I called my mom.

"Janny."

Boom. Lump in my throat.

"Mom, it's me," my voice was cracking.

"Hi, sweet boy, I heard it from Sword fruits," my mom said warm and calmly.

"Yeah, damn, what do they want from me? They say I have to stay here!"

"Don't worry. Sword fruits is working on it. They have a lawyer and they will arrange a new ticket for the next flight." My mom's voice sounded firm and that gave me courage again. Soon, this would be over. I knew that I had done nothing wrong and they would soon understand that too.

Right?

8

With my lace-less shoes and sagging pants, I was escorted to the cells. I was very upset. What would happen? I had never been in trouble with the law, let alone arrested. I didn't even know that I was arrested. Nobody told me *"You have the right to remain silent ..."* or something along those lines, as you see in the movies.

The police officer who accompanied me ordered me to stop walking. I saw three cells, side by side, and it reminded me of a zoo. Bars were from the ceiling to the floor and wall to wall. The left cell was inhabited by two heaps of human beings, deeply asleep. Meanwhile, it was already after midnight. The other two cells were empty. I was taken to the right cell and saw an empty loft, within its corner a trash bag, where a cat was reaching in. When the police officer opened the cell door, the cat was startled wildly and took to his heels. The trash bag fell to the ground as the cat left a trail of junk behind it.

"Where do I sleep?" I asked, while looking into the dark loft. The police officer said nothing, because he obviously was fed up with his night shift. He turned around with a sigh and walked to a closet, where he pulled out a dusty gray blanket. He threw the blanket in the cell and then pointed me to my bed with an exaggerated finger, like a waiter in a restaurant allocates his customer a table. I walked inside and heard the cell door slam with a bang.

"Whoa, wait a minute! The trash bag!" I cried.

"Later!" I heard the policeman say further down the hallway.

Later? I grabbed the bag and put it back into the corner. With my foot, I wiped the junk on the ground together. I took the musty blanket in both hands and folded it a couple of times to lie down. I could smell the sour contents of the bag. *Why is there a trash bag in here at all?*

It was cold and I still didn't realize what was happening. I was exhausted and starving. I looked at my watch. *In about 4 hours and 45 minutes, my plane would be leaving.*

The first hour I was lying there, I didn't sleep a wink. I had taken out my contact lenses and put them in the lens case I always carry with me. All the while, I was tossing and turning and very cold. My feet tingled from the cold, so I took off my shoes and folded the blanket twice around my feet. It barely helped, but I had no alternative. A bit later, I got company. The old 24-hour guard from Melika Fruits entered the cell.

Why is he here and why isn't he going home? What did he do?

He was pushed toward me with a blanket in his hand. I didn't know where the owner of Melika Fruits was. Would he be at home?

Time passed more slowly than ever. I surely thought I had slept for at least half an hour, but I used the dull light from the hallway lamp to see my watch discovering it was only a few minutes later. The 24-hour guard and I said nothing to each other. What should we say? He was musing a little. I knew this man was in his early seventies and had been living in a room on the site of Melika Fruits in order to complete his duties as a 24-hour guard. He probably knew that things were very wrong, while I still had high hopes of being free again the next day.

9

Friday, December 24, 2004.

I don't know how I fell asleep, but I managed to get a few hours before I woke up early in the morning. My watch indicated that it was about half past six. My plane was already in the air for forty-five minutes. *Damn.*

My stomach tightened with hunger and I needed to go to the

bathroom. I called a police officer and, after he made it clear to me several times that I had to wait, he finally took me to the restroom. My bladder almost burst. I was also allowed to take out the trash bag. The officer gestured me to put the bag in the hallway against the wall. He then stood outside the door, as if he was my bodyguard. The bathroom was dark and rancid. A penetrating smell of piss caught my breath, but I didn't care. The relief of emptying my bladder easily overcame my sense of smell.

Back in the cell, I sat on the blanket with my legs pulled up, staring in front of me. The 24-hour guard was snoring loudly. The whole time, I was thinking of home and the moment I would be allowed to leave. My stomach kept growling. Breakfast from the day before was the last meal I had.

I had been sitting there for several long hours, when a boy came to the bars. He was a nephew of the owner of Melika Fruits. He brought a bag with fruit, drinks, bread, cheese, chicken and yogurt. Surprised, but grateful, I took the food out of the bag through the bars. The boy told me he would bring me something to eat regularly. I thanked him for that, but as I greedily ate a chicken sandwich after he left, I got tears in my eyes. I felt humiliated, like a beast that was just fed.

Around noon, I was taken under the guidance of an army of policemen with dogs, to the rental house where I stayed during my work... Again, I was handcuffed.

"Is that really necessary?" I asked.

"Yeah, sorry, that's the procedure," the police officer apologized.

I was sitting in a car between five policemen. Two other cars filled with policemen were driving along. One in front of us, and one behind. I noticed that they were old rickety cars and not actual police cars. To my question why that was, they answered that they had a shortage of police cars and therefore had to drive in their own cars.

When we arrived at the house, the entire neighborhood was

there. I watched as it was turned inside out with the help of drug dogs. Earlier at the police station, I was asked if I objected to this search. "No, go ahead," I said. "I want to help with the investigation however I can."

During the search, I asked if I could take some things, like my glasses and toiletries. That was okay.

The policemen were kind and apologized every time, telling me they knew I had nothing to do with this significant amount of drugs. That reassured me and gave me hope for a quick release. These men were just doing their job of course. Nothing was found in the house, which I knew all along. I had nothing to hide.

10

Saturday, December 25, 2004.

It was Christmas Day and I was questioned at the police station a few more times. I got some tea and sometimes I could eat with the policemen. I even helped them fix their PC that was giving them problems while making my official report. I was assisted by an "interpreter", a man who was picked up on the streets because he happened to live in the Netherlands for a couple of years. He looked like a teddy bear and his Dutch was poor, even though I thought we understood each other pretty well. During the questioning, I thought carefully about what I had seen and experienced. I told them how I arrived at the gate of the packing station and how surprised I was seeing the road block and the customs officers with their guns. I explained how I walked over to the customs officers and called out to them to ask what was going on. I had no idea! I said I thought the two vans in question were already on the site when I arrived on Monday to come and get the company car. I thought I remembered that one of the vans, which was closest to the main entrance of the building, had a flat tire. I was thinking hard. They could obviously do more research as they would have more information.

After questioning, there were pictures made of my face; from the front and side. I asked why that was, but the policemen still told me not to worry: "Tomorrow you can go home."

I believed them and was glad to hear that tomorrow, it would all be over.

II

Sunday, December 26, 2004.

It was Boxing Day, and awfully quiet at the station. It wasn't until around three o'clock in the afternoon that police forces came upon us and said to hurry up.

What? Where are we going? Can I leave?

The police officer, who asked for my passport three days ago at the packing station, opened the cell door. He told me to his regret that I couldn't go home yet. I first had to stop by the public prosecutor's office. Apparently, it was standard procedure. And of course, I still didn't have to worry.

Hastily, he showed me a printed copy of the official report they typed on the PC asking if I would sign it. It was in Arabic and I couldn't read it. At first glance I refused to sign it, but the police officer ensured me that it was okay. "It was the official report as we had discussed with the interpreter." He pulled out a stamp box. "Come on, we have to hurry."

A lot of policemen, who were all eager to leave, looked at me.

"I really don't have to worry?" I asked to be sure.

The police officer smiled, shook his head slightly and shoved the report and stamp box toward me. I looked at the impatiently waiting policemen, looked at the report, with all the twists, jitters and points which represent the Arabic alphabet, dipped my right thumb in the stamp box and did what I was asked for.

12

That Sunday afternoon we arrived at a large, stately building: the courthouse. Red flags with a green star were waving proudly on the roof. The 24-hour guard, the owner of the packing station and I were guided to the office of the public prosecutor. The owner of the packing station turned out to be at the police station in a separate room the entire time and was looking as tired as we were. In the prosecutor's office was a man, dressed in a kind of black gown with jabot. It was my lawyer. He had white hair, was stout and about as tall as me. With an uninterested look, he told me that he would represent me. His double chin moved as he spoke. Sword fruits hired this lawyer on the recommendation of one of their business associates in Morocco.

The prosecutor looked at me, asking what my job was and whether I knew anything about the hashish. I told him I knew nothing about it.

"Are you sure you don't know anything about the drugs?" he asked accusingly.

"Very sure," I replied firmly. "I knew nothing. The customs officers had already invaded the packing station when I arrived there. I asked them what was going on and..." The prosecutor gestured with his hand indicating I had to stop talking and looked at me intently with his arrogant ruthless eyes. I knew this man only a few minutes, and I already thought he was a heartless guy. Without saying a word in response, he waved me away. The lawyer walked me out and wryly told me that I would be transported to the local prison of Berkane.

"What! To prison? Damn, I just had the most humiliating

period of my life! Everyone keeps telling me that I don't have to worry and I can go home soon, and now I have to go to prison?! What does this all mean?"

The lawyer remained calm and said it was a standard procedure.

"Yeah, right. Standard procedure. They have told me this every time!"

"Tomorrow you will be brought before the tribunal and then you may go home," the lawyer said, completely ignoring my frustration.

I could explode, but I decided to keep cool. One night in prison. Tomorrow it would be Monday. That one extra night just had to be...

13

The three of us were taken to the prison. I thought I knew everything there was to know about the town of Berkane, but I didn't know there was a prison.

Among the surrounding houses, the prison really didn't stand out. It was quite a normal looking building with a broad path that ran down to the main entrance. The policemen, who were guiding us, knocked on the gate. A flap opened, where someone was peeking through. The flap shut again, followed by a hard click of the lock. Creaking and squeaking, the rugged iron door opened. We entered slowly and in amazement.

Through the entrance, in a separate room, a man with a friendly round face took our information. He wore a dark blue uniform and gave me a prison number: "53548".

Weird. A number, when I would be leaving tomorrow again.

Anyway, "standard procedure", of course, so I stopped thinking about it.

I examined the prison's reception room and saw a dozen tables and benches, surrounded by plants in jars. The walls were painted with images of nature. It looked homely, almost cozy. Later, I realized that it was the visitors room. I really wasn't worried. It couldn't be that bad, I thought.

After all three of us had our turn, the policemen left the prison and we were assigned to the prison guards.

In the visitors room, there was a wall, apparently to block the entrance to the real prison area. Two guards walked us down the wall. Behind it was a thick steel door with a flap at eye level too. The guards knocked on the door and the eye flap quickly whizzed aside, as if it was the back entrance of a sleazy nightclub. I thought they would be asked for a password or something, but instead, the flap shut again.

Click, clack.

It was that sound again, of a lock opening. A disturbing sound. The heavy door opened.

It's happening. I'm actually entering prison.

Who would ever have thought that I would be locked up in prison?

I took a deep breath and continued my journey with the guards. I decided to try and think positive; head up, be strong. "This doesn't bother me," I repeatedly told myself. "This does not bother me." But once I got in, I got the fear of my life.

This does bother me!

We entered a dark low hallway. To the left, about fifty feet away from me, I saw a gang of inmates, hanging in the bars. Curious as they were, they pushed each other aside to get a glimpse of the new arrival. I heard them babbling, hissing and laughing. I looked at them briefly, but quickly turned my eyes back to the front. We continued to walk and arrived at an open courtyard. On the left, I saw a room with an old desk and a chair with a worn out seat. On the right, I saw a desolate, neglected recreation room with rickety benches, a TV and a bar. We walked straight into another hallway and I was surprised by the prisoners, who now were standing right next to me behind the bars. Their hissing and laughter was terrifying! The inmates were covered with scars on their faces and arms. It was so intimidating and frightening, that I backed away. The guards snapped at the prisoners and beat on the bars with their rubber bats, like they were zoo keepers trying to calm down a pair of hungry tigers. My heart was pounding in my throat.

We were then taken to the prison doctor. He had a small messy office reeking of disinfectant. Outdated instruments were displayed, as if they represented the latest technology. When I sat down at the doctor's desk, I became short of breath. The doctor looked weird with his winter hat, glasses and dirty white cotton coat. He had a big cold sore, plastered over with a thick white ointment. Next to him stood a tall burly man with a wide black and grey mustache. I thought he was the physician's assistant, but he was an inmate, who assisted the doctor.

The doctor began to ask whether I was allergic to anything, but I couldn't get a word out of my mouth. I was in shock seeing the inmates with their scars standing so close to me.

In a minute, they are going to throw me between them.

Images of movies about prisons, in which men rape and mutilate each other, raged through my mind.

Where the hell am I?

Suddenly, I couldn't hold it back anymore. In front of the men, I started to cry and laid my head in my folded arms on the table.

The doctor reassured me and said that I didn't have to be afraid.

"But I don't even know why I'm here," I said confused with my voice breaking.

"Me neither, Mr. Oubelkas. We are just doing our job here, you know?"

Mr. Oubelkas.

After some time, I realized the meaning of these words.

Mr. Oubelkas. That's right. I was twenty-four, a man, right? And certainly no wimp. I dried my tears and encouraged myself. If anyone would even dare to touch me...

With red eyes, but a firm look, I answered the doctor's questions. I was then escorted to the cell where I would spend the night, together with the tall burly man.

The courtyards were empty now and everyone was in their cell. The evening roll call had taken place. The courtyard we were walking through was surrounded by three large cell rooms. On top of the cell door where we stopped, was the number "3". The door was open and I walked in with the burly man behind me. With one stroke, the metal cell door closed behind us and what I saw then was incredible and incomprehensible at the same time.

14

Actually, I had no words to describe the feeling I had at that time. If one could see the images of what I was looking at, then the magnitude of the situation would become clear. I was looking into a small room, crammed with people. It was so crowded, that it seemed as if the people were intertwined or tangled with their limbs. They all looked at me while I continued to observe the room. The floor was covered with blankets, the walls were covered with all kinds of sacks and bags, and high up on a platform was a little TV. On my left were two toilets – two stalls with a hole in the ground – smelling sultry.

How can one live here?

Parakeets in a pet shop have more space in their cage than the people in this loft.

"Take off your shoes," the burly man behind me said quietly. Everyone was walking on their socks in the cell because of the blankets on the ground. "Don't worry; the people here were looking forward to meeting you. You were on the news." I glanced at him, but didn't answer. I took off my shoes and was handed a plastic bag to put them in. The plastic bag was taken by a boy who was sitting near the entrance. He told me to sit next to him. I looked at the burly man again and saw him nodding at me. I sat down, a little uncomfortable, while the Moroccan boy began talking to me. I didn't understand a word he was saying.

A few minutes later, someone else was sitting down with me. It was a skinny man, looking wisely. He had typical professor-like glasses, low on his nose, and a neatly shaved fringe of a beard. A wooly, warm looking djellaba protected him from the cold. I was still wearing the clothes from Thursday, my hair was messed up and I could smell myself. I had never felt so dirty and insignificant.

"My name is Karim," said the wise-looking man. I looked up. He was lighting a cigarette. Karim spoke Dutch. The rest of the evening I got to know the other inmates in the presence of Karim, until it was time to go to sleep. Sleeping seemed impossible in this cell, but I would soon come to realize that sleep was the least of my worries.

15

First night in prison.

The way the prisoners slept in this small room was called the sardine-system. Men were lying alternately, with their heads and feet in opposite directions like sardines in a can. This way, they were saving space.

We were lying down, stuck against each other, side by side, in a space less than fifteen inches wide! The cell was so crowded that some inmates simply couldn't lay down anywhere. It was up to the *Kabran* – prison jargon for "leader of the cell" – to come up with a solution. He was very innovative, because I never could have imagined what happened next.

The toilet doors in our cell were detached and then laid horizontally across the separation walls between the toilets. This way, extra "beds" were created on the doors above the toilets.

I was lying on the ground with the feet of the prisoners on either side of my head. Horrible.

It was so cold that I kept my Sword fruits coat on. I couldn't wash myself because the prison did not provide me with anything. Not even any blankets.

I was shivering with cold.

Well, here I am.

What a miserable Boxing Day. I should be lying in my own bed right now, after two days of eating as much as I could, not between a gang of snoring criminals.

I didn't sleep a moment. Every other minute, someone was using the toilet, so the cell was filled with a nasty smell. People were talking and shouting. From the other cells I heard faint sounds; I tried to trace them unsuccessfully.

As the night progressed it became more quiet, but I still couldn't sleep at all. The sleeping area was extremely narrow and I was constantly pushing feet out of my face.

I looked up into the emptiness of the dark and thought of home.

I quickly wiped a tear from my cheek. Soon it will be over, I told myself.

There I was, hoping for an early return. But it would be years before I would spend another Christmas at home.

16

Monday, December 27, 2004.

What is this noise?

I was already awake for a while and until now, all I could hear was the chirping of sparrows who were hopping around in the courtyard. From out of nowhere, I heard the sound of shrieking whistles and people shouting. Again and again the same words: *"Wokaf, wokaf! Ahteeram*[4]*!"*

The Kabran got up and began clapping his hands. Everyone had to get up. The inmates hoisted themselves up slowly, one by one, and lined up neatly in a row, shoulder to shoulder.

The Kabran was pacing nervously up and down the cell. He still had his pajama pants on and wore a thick cap. I was sitting on my knees and didn't know what to do or what was going to happen. I noticed a cellmate standing at the cell door. "Cell one! Roll call!" he shouted through the cell.

The Kabran began to clap harder and tapped the dormant inmates roughly to wake them. "Wake up, guys! It's not summer camp!" he shouted.

"Cell two! Roll call!" the inmate at the cell door shouted.

Everyone was prepared now, though half drowsy. I stood between them and waited for what was about to happen.

"Roll call, ROLL CALL!" the boy at the cell door shouted with all his strength. *"Wokaaaaf! AHTEERAM!"* he continued, and two incoming prison guards. The guards counted our heads, pointing their fingers at each of our faces. They counted thirty men. All of us were in a cell the size of about forty by ten feet... When roll call was over, all the blankets were removed from the ground and rolled up.

---

4. Wokaf means "get up" or "stand ready". Ahteeram means "respect".

The blanket rolls were called "rolos" in prison. Literally, these were rolls of blankets that were stacked together in the daytime to make room in the cell.

While everyone was getting ready for breakfast, I was called for departure to court. The owner of the packing station and the 24-hour guard, who slept in another cell, were also called. In the main hall, we were standing with some other prisoners in line. Besides the occasional "good morning" we said nothing to each other. A prison guard read our names from a list. When I heard my name, I walked to the visitors room where I was handcuffed. I heard a loud "krrt" sound and felt the cuffs closing tightly around my wrists. They felt cold, but I kept a straight face. A police officer directed me over to the police van.

After a quick ride with sirens blaring, our handcuffs were taken off at the tribunal. While rubbing my wrists, I noticed some red welts. We were escorted to a collective cell where the white walls were daubed with all kinds of texts, slogans and drawings. One of these especially caught my eye: *Only God Can Judge Me – 2Pac*. That thought made me smile a little. Not only because of the reassurance it assumed, but also because of the fact that apparently a Moroccan or a foreigner had been here, who, just like me, could appreciate 2Pac as an artist.

The cell had no windows, nothing. It was an empty loft, where people were pacing back and forth, hanging around or squatting on the ground nervously. Every time the collective loft door opened, a police officer shouted a name, the person would leave the room and the door would closed again with a smack. I noticed that most of them came back again within a few minutes.

We were the last to be called. We walked in through a side door of the courtroom. I looked around me in astonishment and saw a high shiny hall where the colors brown and yellow predominated. The room was intimidating to me. First, I looked to the right and saw dozens of wooden benches. In front of the benches, the lawyer I met yesterday was standing with someone next to him. He turned out to be Ahroumi, an attorney from Casablanca, and the one who told me on the phone at the packing station that I had to leave as soon as possible. They were standing at the pulpit where they were going to make their plea. I turned sideways to the left and was standing in front of a wooden fence, along with the owner and the 24-hour guard. We were looking up against a raised, dark brown stage. At the far left, that scary prosecutor was sitting in a black and green robe. His piercing accusatory eyes looked straight through me. I was disgusted by his appearance. Sitting right in front of us were three men, who also wore black and green robes. The judge sat in the middle and was bald-headed. He seemed nervous. I wasn't getting a good feeling about him either. Sitting far right was a man – also in a black green robe – with his head bowed constantly. He turned out to be the registrar. It felt as if the panel of men were towering over me like a mountain of judgment.

The words of the prosecutor, the judge and the lawyers were echoing high into the room. I couldn't understand anything being said. After some Arabic words from both sides, we could leave again.

What happened? I looked around me.

I didn't say a thing. Can I go home now? Can anyone tell me anything?

The owner and the two guards didn't understand much about it either, I thought. Back in jail, I realized that the hearing was postponed until January 12th.

"What? January twelfth?" I asked shockingly to the first lawyer who came to visit me right after the hearing – Ahroumi had to go straight to the airport. "Then what did they say?"

"We've asked for a postponement so we can examine the case more," the lawyer said quietly.

"Postponement? Case? Which case? But I would go home

today! Another two and a half weeks in that stuffy jail? No Christmas, and now no New Year celebration at home either?"

Damn! Surely this can't be true?

17

It felt like I had vanished from earth. I had nothing in jail. Things I would use daily, such as the internet, telephone, email and music had become unreachable.

I thought of my friends and business contacts, who would probably wonder why they couldn't reach me on my mobile, or why I didn't respond to their emails.

January 12th seemed infinitely far away. The days seemed endless. I was constantly thinking about home. How would my mom do? My girlfriend, Amber? I thought a lot about William, my best friend, and about my father and his family.

What would my business partners think? The IT company we set up together ran like clockwork, and I hoped of course that they would support me through all of this. Would my grandfather know? What about my family here in Morocco? Getting into contact with home through the prisoner's phone room was virtually impossible. To get in touch with someone I was required to provide them with a copy of the passport of the person I wanted to call.

The days crept by and as they passed, I felt less significant to the world and loneliness grew. It took almost a week for me to use the bathroom for the first time for a number two. I couldn't bring myself to do it sooner. I didn't dare because I was afraid of being ridiculed due to the smell. There was absolutely no privacy or space. Twenty-four hours a day I was surrounded in the cell by an average of thirty people.

I hardly washed myself because it was too cold. Once a week, there was hot water in the common shower, but by then it was so chockfull of prisoners that it was impossible to join them.

I had all of my hair cut off because of a lice infestation.

I slept terribly in the crowded cell. At night I often woke up terrified after which it took me a few seconds before I realized where I was. Sometimes I was soaked in sweat, and would lay awake for hours. Occasionally I wiped away a tear. I felt forgotten.

How quickly a life could turn upside down! A week ago, I was a successful young man, cheerfully singing under a hot shower in the rental house. Now I was a dirty pile of misery in a filthy cell.

Fortunately, I was accepted by the group of prisoners in the cell and by Karim, the Dutch-speaking Moroccan. However, regardless of the kindness they showed me, I couldn't turn my thoughts away from home. Why did this happen to me now? Especially when everything in my life was going so well.

18

Just like Christmas, New Year's Eve was also a sad happening. As I sat here in my cell, stuck listening to a music program filled with annoying singing, the people back home in the Netherlands were partying and eating doughnut balls with their families.

There was nothing that reminded me of traditional New Year celebrations. Fireworks were banned here; what a fly in the ointment. It seemed as if nothing happened, New Year's Day was just another day which started as always with that vexatious roll call. From the beginning I thought of this as the worst part of the day.

MAIL!

They told me I had mail!

Suddenly, there was a bright ray of sunshine into the dark life that I led, a sign of life beyond the walls. I jumped up and went to retrieve my mail with a boy who was dressed in a black and white striped jacket with matching pants. A real prison suit. They were called "plantos", also known as helpers or trustees. They were inmates – often disadvantaged – who worked as slaves for the guards. They also helped the other inmates with small jobs, like carrying bags of food and things from home. In exchange the plantos got cigarettes, food or money.

I was sure there would be mail from my mom. In the phone room, where the mail was collected, stood the chief prison guard with his big mustache and stern but endearing look. He was about as tall as me, wore a green military suit and black coarse military boots. His name was Nordin. As it would turn out, I became very good friends with him. Behind that stern look was a very sympathetic and sensitive man. I experienced this for the first time while I was translating the letter I received from my mom. At his command, I read him the letter, and he began to purse his lips together after he saw my eyes filling with tears.

"... When you're back home, you'll see how much everyone cares about you and how we've done our best for you as one big family. The greatest courage, however, must come from you. Hang on, sweetheart. You're innocent, we all know that."

Strong as my mom was, she gave me tips on how I mustn't ignore the small things in life. For example, the course changes of the sun, or how I could study a bird in every detail, and how I must stay very conscious about taking care of myself. She told me that I had to write everything down exactly as if in a diary. I was very proud of my mom and realized that when people would ask me who my biggest role models were, my mom would unconditionally remain number one.

I read my mom's first letter countless times and kept it with me constantly, in the pocket of my Sword fruits jacket. At that time, her letter was the most precious thing in my life.

"All our thoughts are coming to you in invisible threads. Be strong and hang in there, son."

19

Tuesday, January 11, 2005.

The date of the hearing, January 11th, came closer slowly but surely. My mom would visit me a day before the hearing, together with Fouza, my father's wife. When I was twelve, my dad and mom divorced, but my mom and Fouza could get along with each other well.

Strangely enough, I was quite nervous to see these two women who mean so much to me. That morning, just after roll call, the plantos made their first visit announcements and a black and white striped boy came toward me into the cell.

"ZIARA!" he told me.

I looked at him puzzled.

"Joseph?" he asked. I nodded at him. "Visitors," he said in French.

"MOM!" I yelled spontaneously. Automatically, I'm straightening my clothes in a desperate attempt to look as good as possible. I ran my hands over my head and hoped my mom wouldn't shy away from my short hair.

I followed the planto through the prison. After showing a crumpled piece of paper with my name on it, the heavy door that led to the visitors room opened. I walked past the guard wall and saw my mom sitting to the left, around the corner. Beside her sat Fouza and a Moroccan aunt of mine. I shivered. Finally, they were there. It felt like ages since we had seen each other. In my mind I was that little boy from daycare in Breda. Every time I was so excited to see my mom again that I would run as quickly as possible into her open arms. It didn't really matter where I was, for I was always excited whenever I saw her. She was my safe haven.

As I saw my mom, tears filled my eyes. I walked up to her and we hugged. Back in her arms, I was protected again from the evil outside world. We looked at each other. Her eyes were red and she looked tired. From under her glasses, a tear ran down her left cheek. I hugged Fouza and my aunt. Then they sat down again on the bench in front of me. The table kept us separated. My mom looked at me sympathetically. Here I was, her only child. I felt lost and weak.

"Oh, dear boy, are you okay?" my mom asked gently.

I couldn't say a word. The lump in my throat was too big. I was shaking my head.

"I don't know... I don't know what I'm doing here mom, why I'm here..." I began my story, full of sorrow and frustration. I felt large tears rolling down over my cheeks. They tasted saltier than normal.

"Jail sucks, it is rancid, we sleep on the floor in an overcrowded cell, it's cold, I can't have a shower, I feel dirty..." I looked down at the table. My vision was blurred by tears. "Mom, it's just not fair, I don't belong here!"

My mom leaned her elbows on the table and held my hands. Fouza and my aunt let their tears run silently and wiped them away one by one.

"I know, my son, it isn't fair."

It was quiet. I looked at my mom for a minute and then turned away from her with a feeling of shame.

How could this happen to me? How is this possible?

"Oh, come here," my mom continued lovingly as she stretched out her arms. I stood up, strolled over around the table to her and sat down, half on her lap. I buried my head in my mom's arms and felt her warm hand on my cropped head. I let my tears flow freely.

Normally, the inmates had to stay on the other side of the table, but Nordin, the chief, was in the visiting room and he allowed it. He allowed me to have a good cry with my mom. He had a hard time looking at us, and a little later, he walked away. After drying my tears, I went back to my side of the table.

"Are you feeling a little better?" my mom asked lovingly.

I nodded and wiped away my last tears.

"How was your trip?" I asked softly and shrugged my nose.

"Heavy." "Exhausting." My mom and Fouza answered at the same time and had to laugh a little. Their laughter sounded weak and tired. This morning, they left early by train from Rabat, the capital of Morocco, to Oujda, and from there they took a cab to the prison in Berkane. At the prison gate they had to wait for a while before they could enter. They checked and double checked if this European white woman really was the mother of this colored, non-European looking guy. I was upset that these bastards were now not only hurting me, but also the people around me who care about me and love me.

"How are dad and the little men?" I asked, realizing how much I missed those cheerful little monkeys. My dad and Fouza had two sons, Amir and Malik, who were seven and three years old. Officially, they're my half-brothers, but to me they are my true brothers and I often called them "my little men".

"Dad is having a hard time. Your brothers don't know anything, they think you're still here for your work," Fouza replied.

I nodded. "And grandpa, mom?"

"No, he also doesn't know anything. That man is too old to handle this injustice."

"How's Amber? How did she take it? And what does William think?"

"Everyone sympathizes a lot with you. They think it's terrible, but they all are convinced that it won't last long and that the people here will quickly see that you don't belong here."

My mother reassured me with her words. That's what I thought too.

We talked for an hour about how we had spent our past few weeks. I told them in detail exactly what happened and my mom spoke about everyone at home.

Soon the guards were clapping and shouting, the hour was over. The hour seemed to last only a minute. Why did it seem so short now? Damn!

It was time to say goodbye. The next day, my mom, Fouza and my aunt would be present at the hearing. This nightmare would only take one more night. So I thought...

20

Wednesday, January 12, 2005.

After another long, sleepless night, I was transported to the tribunal – handcuffed and with screaming sirens we made our way. There I was again, in the brown and yellow courtroom, standing in front of the nervous bald-headed judge and that scary prosecutor. When entering, I looked straight into the room looking for my mom. She was sitting on one of the benches, right behind the lawyers. I saw her sweet encouraging smile and she waved at me modestly. Fouza and my aunt, who were sitting next to her, both smiled at me too. The room was half full. Most of the faces were unknown to me.

I felt strong with the three women behind me.

Soon it will be over now.

Again, there was a lot of jabbering back and forth in Arabic, unrecognizable to me. It was all gobbledygook to me, but it didn't matter. I couldn't keep my thoughts anyway. As I daydreamed about my departure home, I occasionally looked around at my mother and Fouza. In my mind, I was sitting beside them on the plane, high in the sky flying toward the Netherlands, far away from this place.

When I saw the judge organizing his papers, my daydream suddenly popped, like a soap bubble. Confused, I looked around me.

What is it? Are we ready?

I turned around and saw that something was wrong. My mom shook her head sadly.

What? No? Fouza had already whispered in her ear.

Postponed until February 2nd.

Holy shit! They couldn't be serious! Postponed again? Three weeks?! That was as long as the time I had already spent here. It seemed like three years! And now I had to go through it all again?

I felt my legs go limp as the police escorted me out again through the side door. I looked back over my shoulder and saw my mom, becoming smaller and smaller in the dark, ominous courtroom.

21

Thursday, January 13, 2005.

The next morning, my mom, Fouza and my aunt came back to visit me in jail. They were sitting in the visiting room again at the same table as last time. They encouraged me. Fouza was convinced I would be released on February 2nd, but my mom warned me not to count on this date, as it might be postponed again. "That's perfectly normal in lawsuits," my mom said. She was realistic, and although I hoped Fouza was right, I kept it in the back of my mind unwillingly, that the legal proceedings might take longer than February 2nd.

In her first letter, my mom wrote that I had to write down what I had been through; what I had felt and thought every single day. And she told me again. I picked up the hint and after that day, January 13th, 2005, I would keep a diary for the rest of my confinement.

Our goodbye was emotional, but we agreed that we would stay strong. It was hard to see my mom walking through the door of freedom, while I had to go the other way. I had to go back through the protective wall, back through the prison door. I was back inside again.

Now what?

I stopped. Dazed, I looked around me. I had never felt so empty.

Another three weeks in this misery and again I'm isolated from the outside world.

That day I wrote a letter to my mom. A letter that I never had the strength to send, but always kept.

"Hi mom, I want to thank you for coming here and for your support and encouragement. I needed it. I miss you again already. I had hoped so badly to fly home with you...

I love you very much. I'm realizing this even more. I want my life back. I long for your attention, your voice, your touch.

I just think about the past, about my happy childhood and about the future, all the wonderful things that are still ahead of me. When I close my eyes, I know that you stand beside me..."

22

Over the next three weeks, it felt like time stood still. It tormented me. I missed the outside world, consciously and unconsciously. I felt dirty. Since my detention, I had only washed myself once, with a tub, at the tap in the toilet.

Everyone in the town of Berkane was talking about "el Hollandi" or "the Dutchman". The inmates told me that their visitors wanted to know how I looked and how I behaved. The prisoners were saying that being twenty-four years was way too young to be held responsible for such a large amount of drugs. They thought I was a decent and well-spoken guy, not at all what they expected. They expected some fat old man. Someone with money and status who smoked cigars and wore tailored design suits. Not some kind of rookie who couldn't speak a word of Moroccan and, inside the prison walls, seemed so insecure.

I dreamed intensely almost every night, and I was frequently startled awake. Each morning, when we were woken up for roll call by the annoying shrill of whistles, clapping and yelling, I felt tired.

Daily, there were fights and discussions about the most trivial of things. But what would you expect with so many people confined to such a small space.

Thankfully, I could now use the jail phone, because my mom provided the necessary documents. Chief Nordin turned a blind eye so that I could also call my dad, Fouza, Amber, William and Wilko from Sword fruits. Everyone let me know that they were fighting for me, which was really nice to hear.

Chief Nordin also gave me back my discman and CDs. These items were officially banned in prison, but he was happy to let me have them provided that I didn't show them to anyone. I hid the discman in the pocket of my Sword fruits jacket, like my mom's first letter. I was as happy as a kid on Christmas. Finally, I could listen to Lenny Kravitz again!

In the cell, I got a "fixed" place to sleep. That meant that I no longer had to lie down in the narrow aisle! While lying on my back, I could actually sleep normally again. But it was still a disaster with all those people around me. And it was cold! It had snowed and there was no heating in the cell. We drank lots of tea to warm ourselves.

I spent a lot of time writing. On many sheets of paper, I wrote down my thoughts about home, my feelings, and also about the future of my company. I philosophized about life and society as I saw them.

I realized that freedom is very easily taken for granted, whereas it is something so valuable.

An outlet for me was a nature program on TV, called *Les ailes de la nature* – The wings of nature. It beautifully showed the migration of birds and was broadcasted weekly on Saturday mornings. No one else in the cell was interested, but I was always enjoying the images with my mouth half-opened in a gaze. I could dream myself away completely. I flew along with the geese, from continent to continent. In the courtyard, my dreams continued as I watched the dark or blue skies and the white, or sometimes gray, passing clouds.

Back then, my only thought was: if I could just fly.

23

MAIL!

Awesome! I had mail again! It was an average day when out of nowhere, a planto tapped me on the shoulder to tell me that I had received mail. I was standing in the courtyard, looking up, and in my mind, I had never flown so high. Once arriving back on earth, I excitedly walked with the planto.

There were three letters.

I quickly opened the first one from my mom and started reading:

"... It's up to you now. Behave yourself well. You're such a lovable, intelligent boy and I would like everyone to say that about you. Also

in there. When I was there and hugged you during our visit, and felt your soft cheeks, I had to think back to the time when you were a baby. Your skin and your hair are still as soft. You are and will always be my handsome son. A boy to be proud of, and a man who works very hard to make a living. And you will surely succeed."

Then the tears came again. I couldn't help it. I wanted to go home so badly. From the very first moment, my mom had supported me with her letters.

Since my birth, she has always been there for me and taught me a lot. One of the first lessons of life I can remember is that all people are equal: "Never forget that you're no more than the beggar on the street." She taught me that you don't have to be rich to have a wealthy life. That was also one of the first lessons of life she inherited from her parents. My mom grew up in a typical Dutch rural family with a hardworking father, a diligent stay-at-home mom and three younger brothers. They used to be penniless, only earning enough to have meat and eggs once a week, but my mom didn't mind at all. "My parents had time for us," she said. "We had a rich life without loads of money."

I looked at the other two letters. One came from William:

"*... You can count on me. Our friendship is unbreakable. You already know, but I'll say it again: we are friends for life! This is straight from my heart. You're like a brother to me! When your mom told me you'd also said the same about me to her, tears were welling in my eyes..."*

I have known William since I was eight years old. He is very loyal and wryly at the same time; down-to-earth, sober-minded and straight-faced. I was playing marbles in the street, when William came up to me and asked if he could join. I said "sure", and from that moment on, we became and stayed best friends.

The final letter came from Amber. My mother told me she was very sympathetic with me.

"... You know, I think a lot about you. I have these moments when I want to give you hope and I want you to feel me thinking about you. As I concentrate with you in my mind, I tell you what I want to say to you...

If I had one wish, I would wish for an unexpected trip. A one-way ticket, for one person to the Netherlands.

On any given day, your voice plays in my mind a million times, but I try to stay as strong as possible, because I know you want me to do so..."

Amber unconditionally supported me through everything. A wonderful girl. And very pretty. It was the first thing I noticed, when I laid eyes on her at a nightclub, back in 1999. Slim, beautiful shape, wavy brown hair and bright blue eyes. Totally my type. That night, I was determined not to let her go, and it stayed that way for the following years.

24

Wednesday, February 2, 2005.

Finally... The three weeks were over and February 2nd had arrived.

It was the same circus during transport to the tribunal: the handcuffs, the sirens, the waiting, the courtroom with the intimidating judge and the scary prosecutor. As always, I couldn't understand what was being said. After the hearing, things became more clear. The lawyers told me that the prosecutor had demanded ten years imprisonment...

What! Come again?

The prosecutor has demanded ten years imprisonment.

I was completely upset.

25

Diary, Day 42 – February 3, 2005.

"How I miss a hug and the warmth of someone who really knows me. It's a day after the third hearing at the tribunal. I had never been so scared and so nervous. What a slap in the face it was, listening to their accusations as the suspect of exporting that junk and they want to sentence me to ten years. I feel trapped in a true nightmare, like in a movie, in which you are found guilty of something when you have done nothing. Truly a scary feeling. Just consider it, try to truly realize what it would be like to be trapped in the same room for ten years. The feeling of missing all the people whom you love, missing them grow up and develop in a world that is moving forward, while you remain standing still. Standing by, only to watch your body age as you grow older.

The hearing was postponed again until February 15th. Despite the positive news, I'm afraid the judge will decide otherwise. Of course I don't know what he's thinking, but he looked so strange and accusingly at me, even though they simply have no evidence. All they have are two vans with nearly eight tons of drugs. Other than that, they have invented an alluring story based solely on speculations. Without any research, without any evidence. That's how they put people away here and cases get 'resolved'.

Everyone was upset yesterday. Although I had no one to take care of me, while the owner of the packing station – against whom they demanded ten years too – had his whole family around him, it was me who comforted him and the 24-hour guard of the packing station. I told them to be brave. Today, I'm feeling the blow. I am alone again. Alone in this cell, awaiting my fate. It is all so unimaginable. So hard..."

By priority mail, I received the fourth letter from my mom with words I drew comfort from again.

"You know, Joe, that you, even in your loneliness, were able to comfort two grown men, that's a sign of a very strong spirit. That's why I'm proud of you, why I love you, why I think you are brave. It's a sign of something else too, it's a sign of your innocence. Hold that close and you'll get yourself through. For me it's also hell. When I am out somewhere, I think 'Joe', when I wake up at night, I think 'Joe'; at work, home, inside, outside, everywhere. My child, gather some courage. Even if it takes a bit longer than we've thought, everything will be okay, really. Make sure I can stay proud of you. The natural civilization that is within you and your natural ways of accomplishing things will prove to be invaluable..."

26

"The fifteenth will be the end of the tunnel," lawyer Ahroumi from Casablanca said. These words were constantly in my mind and helped me through the final five days until February 15th. I was really having a hard time. Maybe because deep down inside, somehow I knew it wouldn't work out the way it should be...

Diary, Day 49 – February 10, 2005.

"I'm in a deep slump. I can't remember ever being this unhappy. I was in the prime of my life and it felt so good. All was going well and my life was perfect. Maybe that's what was wrong? Was it wrong that I felt so good? Wasn't that right? Is that why I'm feeling so down now?

It is very exhausting, the constant uncertainty, the nerves and the fear. The stories of people around me aren't very promising. And then the cold eyes, focused on me in the courtroom, in which you can see that they truly believe I am guilty. What is happening to me?

I just got an icy cold feeling. Why is it that something inside me keeps telling me that this nightmare is far from over? I'm shivering, because I'm nervous. Why do I feel this way? The feeling that I am going to be found guilty. The feeling that I am going to receive a harsh sentence, one that I will probably serve part of. How is it possible that in this country, without any hard evidence, a foreigner can be put behind bars? This is a violation of human rights! I don't wanna be here! I wanna go home, back to my own life. Please don't let it be true that I have to stay here any longer. I feel so alone. I love you, mom. That's all I think about now. I do my best, mom, I'm trying to be strong, but it is so hard."

27

Wednesday, February 16, 2005.

Morning roll call had just taken place.

"Please freshen up. Chief Nordin is expecting you in his office," Karim, my cellmate says.

I can tell from Karim's face that something is wrong. It makes me nervous.

It can't be?

Yesterday had been a long, exhausting day at the tribunal and today I would get to hear the verdict.

I wash my hands and my face from the tap on the toilet, staring into the small space.

It can't be…?

I dry my face with trembling hands and walk slowly to the office of Chief Nordin. My heart is pounding ruthlessly.

Why am I so nervous?

In front of the office I see a few guards, surrounded by a group of inmates. They are staring at me and seem to be afraid, as if an all-out war has been declared by neighboring country Algeria, Morocco's number one enemy of the state for many years. Their eyes make me even more nervous.

In front of me is Chief Nordin. I look him straight in the eye. Eyes that already betray.

"I'm sorry..." I hear him saying. "They sentenced you to ten years in prison..."

They sentenced you to ten years in prison...

Ten years in prison...

Ten years...

The words still echo in my head many times after.

I'm still looking at Chief Nordin, but my sight is blurred. It becomes quiet around me. I'm losing my balance and lean over onto the chief's desk. He carefully hands me a pen and points to the paper on his desk. Stunned, I take the pen while bending over the paper. I'm looking around confused; I hear the murmuring of the people surrounding me. The voices seem to echo, as if they were approaching me from miles away. Faces and figures are shrinking to miniscule size, and the room I am in seems to be getting larger.

I look at the paper and only see Arabic characters that seem to laugh at me. The only thing I can read is the date: "2014/12/23".

December 2014? And then the lights go out.

I can feel the world around me disappear while an ever-growing tidal wave washes over me. An enormous feeling of rage and sadness enters into my mind.

"What...?" I say breathlessly.

I can only see that date. I hear nothing but the pounding of my heart in my head.

"What is this...? What is this!"

"Ten years... How can this be? TEN YEARS?! Why? WHY?"

I'm looking around and all I see are sad and pitying eyes.

"But I haven't done anything at all! NOTHING!"

Large tears begin to fall from my cheeks but no one seems to understand. It feels like life is being sucked out of me. It makes me dizzy and I start to scream.

"DO YOU KNOW WHAT THIS MEANS? TEN YEARS?! TEN YEARS?! HOW CAN THIS BE?! WHY? I WON'T SIGN ANYTHING! I WON'T SIGN ANYTHING AT ALL! DAMN IT, I HAVEN'T DONE ANYTHING AT ALL!"

Furiously, I throw the pen away, turn around and force my way through the guards and inmates. They have gathered with dozens and are blocking the entrance of the little room. My sight is still blurred, vague. I go back to the cell.

I can't remember the walk back to my cell from the chief's office any more. That part has become a black hole in my memory. The only thing I know, is that in that cell, I was sitting in a corner crying. Just crying, crying and crying...

Baa, baa, black sheep,
Have you any wool?
Yes sir, yes sir,
Three bags full.
One for the master,
One for the dame,
One for the little boy
Who lives down the lane.
Baa, baa, black sheep,
Have you any wool?
Yes sir, yes sir,
Three bags full.

"Do you remember this lullaby? When I would sing it for you, you would fall asleep, as a child, so sweet... "

28

Mom, where are you? Where are you?

I am convicted. I am sentenced to ten years in prison. For the time being, I can no longer see you. I'm sorry, mom.

Mama? Can you hear me? Where are you? I need you. They have convicted me. Did you hear that? I don't understand why, mom. I don't understand why I need to be in prison. Why they've convicted me? Mama…?

I am completely lost, all alone. Alone in my mind. Lost in pure grief. Voices from the past are echoing in my head. I am a little boy again.

"Mommy, I like you."

"Oh, baby, come here."

"Do you like me too, mommy?"

"But of course! You're not only sweet, but you're also such an adorable little guy!"

"I am?"

"Yes, you are. You're so funny, eager to learn and curious. Always going out to explore the world..."

In the distance, I hear laughter. Laughter from my mom, laughter from me as a child.

Then suddenly, I hear two other voices. They are the voices of Amber and William. Their words seem to overlap.

"Don't forget that we'll never forget you, sweetheart!"

"How can you be forgotten?"

"I think about you a lot."

"Don't be afraid of the big guys, Joseph."

"I miss you."

"I wanna tell you so much more."

"In my mind, I'm with you."

"I will protect you. Now and forever!"

Every now and then, I come back to my senses and realize how unbelievable this is, how unjust. Then I slip away again, into the distance, I hear my mom singing the lullaby that she used to sing to me. *Baa, baa, black sheep, have you any wool?*

My grief is deeply intense. My idea of a fair, righteous world has been replaced with despair. The safe world in which I grew up now ceases to exist. Everything that has happened goes against my principles about how people should treat one another. It goes against the values that my mother instilled in me as a child.

No matter how strong I try to keep myself, it is a nightmare. A nightmare that I relive every night in my dreams. One that turns out to be reality when I wake up. So unlikely, so unreal.

I really am in prison. I really have been sentenced to ten years. Again and again, it hits me and I get a terrible sick feeling inside and have to throw up. I feel enormously fragile and every thought of home ends up in a cry. I have never felt so many emotions. I am exhausted, but I just can't sleep because of the injustice, the frustration. I feel powerless.

Ten years. Ten years!

I am constantly worrying by the thought of spending ten years here.

In ten years I'll be thirty-four, my mom sixty-five, my brothers seventeen and thirteen, and my grandfather probably won't be alive anymore. Tears well in my eyes with these thoughts.

Ten years...

What would the world look like? How would I look? And my friends? And Amber? Will she wait for me? Will they believe me in the Netherlands? The thought of people not believing me terrifies me... I begin to ask myself hundreds, if not thousands of questions.

I look and feel like a zombie. I don't eat, drink less and sleep little. My body is walking around and I'm breathing, but my mind is gone, lost. I'm at the end of my rope.

29

The first few weeks after my sentencing are a blur in my life. I guess the sadness would be similar to the grief of losing a loved one. You are in a constant struggle of having to accept this fate, but not wanting to. You fight a battle that is already lost within yourself. In the end, you have to accept it... And then the trick is how to deal with it.

My mother once told me that a man, when deprived of all responsibility, is no different than an animal. And this was the way it was in prison.

"Focus, take responsibility, set your goals and reach them. You will succeed, if you want to!"

Until now, the letters I received were mainly from my mom, Amber and William. However, the story of my sentencing to ten years spread like wildfire throughout the Netherlands. I was flooded with letters from family, friends, colleagues and even strangers. Inside the prison, they were amazed at the amount of mail that was coming in. The words I read were incredible, inspiring and gave me strength. I could fill hundreds of pages of this book.

Of course I read my mom's letter first.

"Sweetheart, you're at the top of the list of my personal heroes. We sympathize with you tremendously and shed many tears for you. I've already written to you that you will be an example for everyone by taking responsibility. And many people already respect you a lot. All of your friends, the neighbors, and your relatives unanimously have said: 'This happened to Joseph? Impossible!'

So many people are thinking about you, and I think this collection of thoughts is constantly present. Please try to remain strong, for all of us and especially yourself. Remember that every time you feel a warm breeze around you, it's me, standing next to you. I love you, my son."

Amber wrote to me:

"Our phones are working overtime. Everyone is in disbelief and wants to help. I hope that the time we had together gives you strength. We've shared so much together. Some big things, but also small, like holding and hugging each other, or sitting in the garden, where you would look upon the beautiful red-colored skies. I miss you Joe, please hang in there, okay? We are fighting really hard for you. I love you, my beautiful and strong man, and that won't change, no matter how far you are away from me."

William's letter:

"You wouldn't believe how bad I felt when I heard the verdict. I was very worried about you. I couldn't stop thinking about what you must be feeling. Your mom called to say that you are having a very hard time, but remaining strong. That's really great! The past few days have been rough, but now that I know you are keeping up well, I sleep a little bit better. My dad asked me to say hello to you too. He also hopes that it will soon be over. He still can't understand it, and that goes for all of us. We sympathize with you tremendously and we love you. The moment when they realize their mistake is coming, we'll see you again soon!"

Fouza, my father's wife, wasn't really a writer, but she had tried:

"You're not alone. Everyone, the whole family here and in Morocco, is thinking about you. Your mother is a strong woman. She really does her best for you. Your father too, but in his own way. He loves you very much, you shouldn't forget that. We're really proud of you."

Amber's sister was very upset too:

"When I heard about it, I couldn't stop crying. Amber came and put her arm around me, and said that everything would be okay. That was sweet of her. I should have comforted her."

Amber's parents encouraged me by writing:

"Joseph, keep up your spirit. From all sides, we are working hard to get you back home quickly. We won't let your mom down, we'll take good care of her."

There were also many beautiful words from others:

"Every time, at night, when I wake up, I think of you and it makes me sad. I was afraid to speak to your mom, but what a wonderful woman she is. What a power she has." – Mieke

"All the people who know you, whether it's for a day or a lifetime, believe in you." – Margot

"This shouldn't be allowed to happen, especially to you. What I hate the most is the fact that it happened to someone I look up to. Someone who really succeeded and always kept caring about everyone else." – Emre

"I've thought a thousand times about how I would feel in your situation, but it's impossible. You wouldn't believe how often I think about you, but I'm confident!" – Bart

"When I heard the unbelievable news, it took me a week to actually comprehend what was going on. It's really too bizarre for words. I am angry and sad at the same time. I miss you, Joe." – Erik

"They have to face the real situation there! You're a real swell guy. We miss hanging out buddy, but justice will prevail." – Paul

"What a strange thought. I'm sitting here on the couch writing this letter to one of my best friends who's sitting innocently behind bars. Dude, you have all my support and I am always there for you!" – Hein

"I think about you every day and, if possible, I wouldn't mind changing places with you for a while." – John

"Whenever we look in our room, at the Moroccan chess board you gave Rob for his birthday, we think about you. The board is always there, sitting in front of us, so please know how often we think about you..." – Rob and Joyce

And the letters just kept on coming...

30

The steady stream of letters with the words and reactions of all those people made me stronger. Therefore, for the first time, I decided to read my verdict, which was translated into Dutch.

On what grounds could they possibly have convicted me?

That's what I wanted to know. I knew there couldn't be any evidence against me, simply because I had nothing to do with the whole thing.

The judge detailed the following four points – literally retyped directly from my verdict – which apparently showed that I deserved a sentence of ten years in prison:

- The accused has used several airports in Morocco, i.e. Oujda, Mohammed V (Casablanca), El Masira in Agadir, Laraoui in Nador and Boukhalef in Tangier. Additionally, the accused has twenty-two entry visas against seventeen exit visas in his passport.
- The accused arrived at the station on 12/23/2004 at a time when the station was surrounded by police and a large quantity of drugs were found in two Mercedes vans, Type 410 and 210, which were loaded with boxes bearing the

Sword fruits logo on them.

- The accused stated that one of the tires of the Mercedes was flat and that he was responsible for inspecting the products before they were packaged and exported.
- The accused had been observing things from afar. He exerted supervision regarding the packaging of the products, and was arrested at the time of the drug discovery at the station. Therefore, this is convincing evidence that he committed the allegations against him.

Apparently, I was also found guilty of forging license plates. Sure, why not, go ahead while you're at it and pin that against me too. I read the verdict over and over.

This was it? This was their evidence? I frantically turned the verdict papers over and looked to see whether something was written on the back. Or maybe I was reading it upside down.

Where was the evidence that showed that I was a kingpin, a smuggler, a criminal?

The first point said that I had used the Tangier airport. But that wasn't true. I've never set foot in that airport in my entire life! This point was the driving force behind my reason to put on my Sherlock Holmes-hat and begin to investigate the arguments.

I was dedicated to proving my innocence.

31

I started my research with the stamps in my passport. Apparently, at the tribunal, there was a lot of disagreement about them. I remembered that the judge was highly suspicious that every time I arrived in Morocco, I went to a different airport. The places Oujda, Casablanca, Agadir, Nador and Tangier were discussed. I explained to the judge, under oath, that I myself didn't choose the tickets and flights, but that it was done by my client. Their travel agent always chose an available seat for a flight on a certain day and it just so happened to be landing at different airports.

But Tangier? I had never been there!

According to the verdict, there were twenty-two entry stamps in my passport and seventeen exit stamps. The judge found this difference to be very suspicious. For him, it was proof that I did not always leave with the regular flights. Therefore, I was taking smuggling routes. After thinking about it, the number of stamps didn't make sense to me. I hadn't been back and forth that many times. To verify the number of stamps myself, I asked Chief Nordin if I could have access to my passport. Officially it wasn't allowed, because my passport had been confiscated, but the chief could see from my expression that I was serious. A bit later, he had my passport secretly taken from the administration. He handed it to me in his small office. Then he left me alone and shut the door.

"Just knock when you're done," he said before closing the door.

I looked at him and nodded firmly. A little tense, I opened my passport. I had no idea how many stamps I had. Who would keep that up? Sure, some people do, but I don't.

"One, two, three..." I began to count the stamps aloud. I counted several times just to be sure, and the total was twenty-one stamps: eleven entry stamps and ten exit stamps. That was exactly right! So there was no question of a "suspicious" difference of five stamps at all!

Didn't they even bother to take my passport and count the stamps? A simple job that would have only taken a few minutes!

They just wrote something down! Something that wasn't true at all! This was proof to me that the police and the court never really investigated the case. I was shocked, yet happy. My little investigation paid off! I informed Chief Nordin and he was also glad about it.

Relieved, I walked back to the cell and told Karim about my discovery.

The remaining evidence was so meaningless that I paid little attention to it.

It wasn't special to me that paragraph two indicated that in a number of Sword fruits boxes, blocks of hashish were packed. These boxes were everywhere, in all parts of the world where Sword fruits operated. Besides, the two vans in which the boxes were found were not destined for export, and therefore not checked by me. I only checked whole pallets which were loaded on authorized trucks. Those pallets were all opened and controlled by the customs officers and policemen with dogs at the packing station. In those boxes nothing was found!

Point three of the verdict: "The defendant stated that one of the tires of the Mercedes was flat."

What? I stated that to the police myself! And now they were using this as evidence against me? Because I had seen the flat tire and told them the truth in all honesty? Besides, everyone had seen that flat tire!

Point four of the verdict said that I was "observing". I didn't understand this point either and told the judge that, at the time of the invasion by the customs officers, I wasn't even there. After arriving at the station, I even went to the gate myself to ask what was going on. This was further confirmed by the police. So, the "fact" that I was arrested at the same time the drugs were found, wasn't true either.

If I really knew about those sixteen thousand pounds of drugs, would I just walk up to the armed customs officers to blatantly ask what was going on? And by the way, I wasn't "observing"; they let me onto the site after I waved to the customs officers. Then, they put me with hundreds of other workers who all were watching what was happening. I started to become despondent. Whatever I said and whatever I brought up to the tribunal was not being taken into consideration. I repeatedly offered to tell them everything about me and that I sincerely wanted to help. Accounts, background check, my history, my friends, my education, and so on. Then, at least they would get an impression of the person they were dealing with. Then, they would know who Joseph Oubelkas was. But nothing. They didn't investigate anything at all.

They even knew who the owner of the vans was where the hashish were found. Seems pretty relevant to me; name, address, telephone number. They knew everything about this man but never contacted him. Why?

And who were the drivers of the vans? They had their fingerprints.

Who called the customs with the tip about the hashish?

These were questions I never got answers to.

Apparently, they already had their offenders: the owner of the packing station, a seventy year old guard and a Dutchman. All three of them received ten years in prison

Case closed.

32

Many of the inmates in Berkane advised me to pay off the Court of Appeals, in exchange for a reduced sentence or perhaps even my freedom.

"Paying?" I asked angrily. "Never! I would rather sit innocently in prison for ten years, before I give a penny to some corrupt judge!"

The thought of paying was crazy to me. I knew I was falsely accused and I could even contradict the so-called evidence in the verdict!

My lawyers were excited about my findings, while at the same time amazed at my "detective work". They would certainly do something about this during my appeal that would start March 2nd.

In the cell, a man chuckled at my response and shook his head. It was the "pen man".

He always sat with a curved back in a corner of the cell, decorating pens. He did this by wrapping different colors of wire and beads around them. A beautiful piece of art, I thought.

The pen man had a thin face with eyes slanting downwards that reminded me of Droopy the dog. He wore a woolen hat that seemed a bit too big for his head.

"Do you wanna go home?" he asked.

"Of course!"

"Then you have to play the game and you have to pay, kid," he said, while concentrating on the decorated pen in his hands.

"No," I said, "I'll play it fair. I have confidence in the Appeal."

"Fair? Confidence?" the man laughed. "Shall I tell you something about our world here? A world that you as a Westerner obviously misunderstand."

"What do you mean?" I asked.

He looked at me and smiled. He pounded his hand a few times on the floor and motioned for me to come and sit down next to him. I did.

"Look, I've been in the hashish business for years. Never large quantities, but about twenty to hundred pounds a week. I earn a living at it, because I have no other choice. Well, that's not entirely true, I do have the choice to work from 7:00 a.m. to 7:00 p.m. for fifty dirham[5] per day, which is less than five dollars, but I don't want to do that. With this business, there is a chance that I'll occasionally go to jail, which I am willing to accept. At least I can afford to send my kids to school and support my wife and family."

5. The Moroccan dirham is the official currency of Morocco.

"So your wife and kids don't mind?" I asked.

"No, they understand that there is no other way and that I choose this to provide them a better life"

"Oh…"

"Let me tell you how it's done. You know what judges earn here?"

"No," I said. I really had no idea.

"Around ten thousand dirham a month. Say one thousand dollars a month. Not bad, considering the average salary here."

"What is the average?"

"Well, the prison guards here earn less than two hundred and fifty dollars a month."

"That's not much."

"Yeah, so a thousand dollars a month is pretty reasonable, you might think. However, the judges all drive expensive cars and possess one or more large villas. They buy expensive clothes, send their children to private schools and live as members of the bourgeoisie."

I listened intensively as the pen man continued.

"They can't afford all of these luxuries based on their salaries, so where does the extra money come from?" He paused.

"Drugs?" I asked. The man had to laugh.

"Yeah, there are judges who are definitely involved in the business. But the largest part comes from the inmates, from the suspects who are lined up in court day in and day out. Think of it as a machine, where people are thrown in and squeezed out. Whoever pays is released, those who refuse or have nothing, will eventually pay, whether the person is guilty or not. They don't care."

"Are you serious? That just can't be!"

The man laughed again. "I told you, as a Westerner, you don't understand our world. Just forget about Dutch law for a minute, okay? You people in Europe are looking at the situation from a moral perspective, but on this continent, it is purely about money. Judges even buy their way onto the court here; they aren't assigned their position just like that."

I noticed that the pen man was intelligent. Very articulate, clean and quiet. He radiated calmness as if he had fully accepted everything in his life as it was.

"And the lawyers play along just as well."

"The lawyers?" I asked surprised. "What's their part in this matter?"

He was clearly enjoying this, telling his story to an unknowing person like me.

"The lawyers often play in cahoots with the judges and ensure the agreement between the accused and the judge. The lawyer starts negotiations with a judge behind the scenes and discusses what will be possible in exchange for a certain amount. This way, for example, it can be agreed that for a thousand dollars, the accused will only be given a year in prison, or for two thousand dollars, acquittal. Once that is determined, there's a show in court. It's a big game, because everything is already determined in advance."

I was quiet. Stunned.

"But I have evidence," I said. "I have evidence that I'm innocent; that they made a lot of mistakes and there wasn't even an investigation. My lawyers told me that they've never been as positive as they are in my case."

The pen man burst out into laughter and I was shocked at his response. I asked resentfully what was so funny.

"Oh, kid! Of course they say they've never have been so positive! They don't want the judge to get any of your money. They'd rather put everything in their own pockets. They see you and the company you work for and their eyes are filled with dollar signs!"

Then I stood up. I didn't want to hear anymore. My case was different. I had confidence in my lawyers. They really wanted the best for me.

The pen man watched me as I walked away. At that moment, he probably thought to himself: "You don't know what you're caught up in, kid."

33

My cellmates speculated incessantly about the result of my appeal. Many were convinced that I would be released. The Judge for the Court of Appeals was a serious man. I had also heard people say that my sentence might be reduced by half. "You won't get ten years, but five years," they said with a smile. But I wasn't waiting around for five years. I didn't want to spend another day here.

"But," they said, "you won't stay in this prison. All foreigners are being relocated to Salé, a place with a large jail complex near the capital Rabat."

That prison apparently was the Valhalla. Salé would have a separate wing just for foreigners. "It really is a beautiful prison!" It almost seemed as if they were cheering me on when they said that.

"Beautiful? What do you mean, beautiful?" I said. "My mom's Norwegian wooden house is beautiful. The flowers in her garden are beautiful. Sunsets are beautiful... "

I discussed with Wilko from Sword fruits what the pen man had told me. How the judges were bribed and turned a blind eye. However, Wilko and I decided to appeal our case through the normal channels. Everything was so clear. The judge simply couldn't ignore what happened. I kept repeating to myself what my Dutch lawyer said: "We're standing strong."

The Dutch lawyer was hired by Sword fruits to assist the Moroccan lawyers. Foreign lawyers were not allowed to interfere with the legal proceedings in Morocco, so the Dutch lawyer was hired only to assist. As a lawyer, one of the things he criticized the most, was that the customs officers and policemen immediately initiated the raid, after the anonymous phone call with the tip about the hashish. "Normally, they should have waited and observed what was going to happen with the drugs. This way, they could catch the people red-handed. Now, they have two vans, filled with hashish and nobody knows where they came from and nor did anyone know where they were going. Because of this mistake, they decided to interview people at random and invent a story to back up their actions. Report these facts well!" the Dutch lawyer said to the Moroccan lawyers.

I trusted the army of people who were supporting me and were convinced of my innocence. I was hoping for more support from the Netherlands and decided that there had to be a website about my story. A website where people could respond with their comments. This way, an even wider audience could be informed about the injustice that was being done to me.

And that was how www.freesef.com started.

The website was launched on March 10th, 2005. That same day, it had more than four hundred unique visitors and over one hundred comments. My business partners were managing the site. They received more than thirty phone calls, numerous email responses and many letters by mail. From friends, acquaintances, customers, suppliers, former colleagues, former classmates and students, and even strangers. People were spreading the news on the internet by adding the website's name in their chat name. An article about my conviction was published in the newspaper. Amber told me about it in a letter: *"I saw the front page and almost fell over. It was you! Three-quarters of a full page! Joseph Oubelkas. A very good article."*

The article was titled "The worst case", and was published in "BN/De Stem" the largest newspaper in the Southern Netherlands. The article was a hit.

The responses kept coming, one even more beautiful than the other.

When I first got the responses, I was stunned and felt very happy and satisfied inside. Besides all of the tremendous positive energy that I was feeling from the Netherlands, I was hoping, of course, for a common sense of the judge. With this, I knew things had to be fine.

34

Would mom be there during the appeal? I suddenly asked myself.

It had almost been a week since I had spoken to her on the phone. I couldn't reach her at home and was getting a little worried. It was probably nothing, I thought.

I was wrong.

My mother was apparently hospitalized with diverticulitis. Diverti-what?

Names of diseases you can't easily pronounce are never good.

My mother had a tumor in her stomach and she was unknowingly walking around with it for a long time. Apparently she already had diverticulitis when she visited me in jail. The past few weeks, my mom started to sound weaker when speaking to her on the phone, but no one expected a tumor was the cause. The family doctor sent her home with some painkillers and thought they would revive her. They didn't.

After Amber brought her to the hospital, she was immediately admitted. Amber had found my mom in bed, completely dehydrated and emaciated. She was so weakened that she could barely move.

When I heard this story, I became furious. Furious because I was powerless to help. It made me feel frustrated. If Amber hadn't found my mom, then what? One of the worst things about prison life is that you're helpless. You can't go anywhere; you can't do anything except stand on the sidelines and watch how things happen to the people you deeply love.

There she was, lying in the hospital with wires and drips coming out of her. I wanted to be at her bedside, holding her hand and asking her how she was doing, whether she needed anything. I wanted to hear her voice and look into her eyes.

Now I felt like a hamster on a treadmill. No matter how hard or fast I ran, there was no one there to help me. It was an enormous blow to my confidence, right before the Court of Appeals.

Please, let these bastards release me quickly! I thought to myself.

For the umpteenth time...

35

Thursday, March 31, 2005.

It was the third time standing before the Judge of Appeals. Since March, the case had been postponed twice. It was an early spring in Morocco, and every time the lukewarm wind blew through the courtroom, I thought of my mom.

"Remember that every time you feel a warm breeze around you, it's me, standing next to you..."

I had prepared myself well and even felt pretty good about the judge this time. He had a relatively large head, big gray hair and bushy eyebrows. With his small owl glasses, he seemed to me an honest man. My lawyers criticized the judge and reported my Sherlock Holmes-results intensively. Good.

I felt pretty proud, despite my helpless situation behind bars, I did achieve something with my little investigation and the website freesef.com.

During the lawyers' attack, in which they quoted the obvious and shameless errors of the previous judge again and again, this judge began to look increasingly acidic.

It looked completely different in the courtroom than at the first hearing. The room was packed. The case attracted a great deal of interest from the media and there were many journalists there from the town of Berkane. I also saw a lot of Melika Fruits employees and family and friends of the co-defendants. Instead of having my mom and Fouza there, two women from the Dutch embassy (the Dutch embassy only attends court hearings in exceptional cases) were present along with Andre Laarhoven from Sword fruits who was flown in with the Dutch lawyer. They watched intently, and were constantly informed by an interpreter about what was being said in the courtroom.

The Arabic sounds filled the air of the room. Whatever they said, I didn't care. Everything was to my advantage.

Then suddenly, something happened.

There was a kind of wave that overtook the room, one of relief, together with applause and cheers. I didn't know what happened or what was said, but when I turned around, I saw my lawyers looking very happy. Andre and the Dutch lawyer made a victorious gesture with their fist, and the two ladies of the embassy were sitting with tears of joy in their eyes. In a flash, I looked at my interpreter and poked him in his side.

"What is it? What is it?" I asked hastily.

"I told you so, everything will be all right," the interpreter said with a strong Moroccan accent. It was the same interpreter from the previous session. He still reminded me of a teddy bear. I would like to hug him, but that would be silly in the courtroom, I thought to myself. Instead, I quickly looked back toward the audience and only then I realized that it was over.

I am acquitted! I am free!

Tears welled up in my eyes. My Sherlock Holmes-investigation worked!

I was completely at a loss for words when I walked into the room to see Andre. I wanted to hug him. He and the Dutch lawyer were standing up, smiling from ear to ear. The applause of the people in the room was loud. In the background, the judge pounded hard with his gavel to restore order. A police officer waved for me to take my seat again.

It became quiet again in the room. The trial resumed.

I dreamed away and visualized how I would announce the good news at home and to my cellmates. *How happy everyone will be.* My mom and I will finally be able to close this nightmare.

At the end of the trial, the judge asked each of us if we had any final words. I answered what was in my head the entire time: "I just want to go home. Home where I belong and where my mom is waiting for me."

36

I didn't go home right away. The court decision wouldn't be officially announced until the next morning, on April 1st. We were called up again and transported to the tribunal, but we didn't get to see the judge. We had to go back to prison because Mr. Judge was "too busy". This afternoon it would be our turn, we were told. But we would never go back.

At lunchtime, I was in the small room of Chief Nordin when I noticed the owner of the packing station sitting on one of the wooden chairs, crying. Surprised, I looked up at the chief. He shook his head and said with a deep sigh that they had left the first court decision unchanged.

"What are you saying? That's not true, right?" I said, still convinced of the idea that I was released. "Did they give us ten years again?"

Chief Nordin slowly nodded with a pout, while the owner of Melika Fruits was blowing his nose.

Okay, I thought, this had to be a bad April's fool joke. My brain was running at full speed and my thoughts were doing somersaults. What should I do? How should I respond? All kinds of words and images flashed through my mind: ten years, acquittal, cheering, crying, my sick mom, my little brothers, William, Amber, my father, Fouza, grandpa, my friends. My head was exploding. I felt my brain pressing against my skull and it was as if my eyes were about to pop. I grabbed my head.

Damn it. DAMN IT!

Dirty bastards. What cunning dirty bastards they are!

I was having a hard time. I almost lost my temper and wanted to cry. But I decided not to.

Fuck it! They won't get me again! It's not the same this time around! I've shed too many tears already and they are not worth it to me!

I took a deep breath and asked Chief Nordin as calmly as possible if I could call my mom. Self-controlled, but with tears in my eyes. Heavy tears, threatening to fall.

37

The moment before I had called my mom after just learning that I was again convicted to ten years in prison, would be a turning point, a defining moment in my life. I knew now that I would be staying in prison for a long time. I knew that prison life had become my life. And that I would most likely see the "beautiful" Salé prison. I had an unnamable pain in my heart, but I was determined: *"They can imprison my body, but my spirit will always be as free as a bird."*

From the beginning of this ordeal, when I was "arrested", the case had been settled within three months. It was clear to me; I was behind bars because someone wanted me there. Even after the mistakes in the first verdict and the so-called "evidence". Why, for what or whom, I didn't know.

"This is mom," my mother answered the phone. She knew it was me.

She was just released from the hospital after several major surgeries. The tumor in her stomach appeared to be benign. I always found that to be such a strange word, "benign". Because no matter how benign the tumor was, it had nearly taken my mom's life. Anyway, she now had a stoma – or "poop bag" as my mom used to joke about – and every day, a nurse came by to take care of her.

"Hi mom," I answered with a faint smile.

"Hello, dear brave son of mine. Don't worry, we'll keep standing behind you and keep on fighting till the last gasp." My mom already heard the news of the verdict late last night. She was very upset, but fortunately had the same spirit as I, and that made me stronger.

"Definitely, mom!" I answered firmly. "The truth will eventually prevail!"

My mom wasn't home alone. Amber, William, my father and Fouza were also there. We encouraged each other. I explained to everyone that they didn't need to worry about me. With great tears in my eyes, which I refused to let run, I told them that I would pretend my time here was like spending time at a military training camp. "Everything will be fine. One day everything will be fine again..."

Chief Nordin entered the phone room and told me that I had a visitor. It was Andre Laarhoven. I told my mom I had to go. It was hard to hang up the phone, but I had to. The voices in my ear allowed me to forget the prison around me for a while. We wished each other strength and hung up. The smash of putting the receiver down on the hook, slapped me back into reality.

A little later, I arrived in the visiting room and saw the owner of Melika Fruits crying. He was comforted by his family, who sat around him in a circle. On the other side was Andre, who stood up hastily after seeing me enter the room, as if he was afraid to be told off.

"Hey Joseph, how are you?" Andre asked clumsily.

"Well, what can I say..." I said with a nonchalant smile. I shook Andre's hand and sat down beside him. "Maybe you should ask him how he is," I said, nodding to the sniveling owner of the packing station. Andre just came back from a restaurant and told me that he couldn't eat anything because of the verdict.

"I didn't know how you would feel after the terrible news," Andre said. "I even brought you a ticket for crying out loud. We were so convinced that you could go home!"

"Yes, me too," I answered. We were quiet as we watched the crying people in front of us. Andre looked at me again and told me that I could also shed a few tears if I needed to. I answered almost stoically that I couldn't cry. The people who had locked me up here were not worth my tears!

"But why..." I suddenly asked Andre, "why did they say that I was acquitted? Why was everyone cheering in the courtroom? Could I go home? What did the judge exactly say?"

I heard a deep sigh. Andre opened his mouth, but there was no sound. He struggled to find his words.

"At some point, the judge said that *based on these facts, Mr. Oubelkas should be acquitted,* and then the cheering began. But that wasn't his verdict yet and later, he withdrew."

"Really? That's why the judge was yelling for order in the courtroom. Damn it. He knows. He knows that I have nothing to do with this case."

I leaned back on the bench, sliding down in my seat. I looked at the ceiling and saw how it was finished neatly by the plasterers, with typical round ornaments, detailed with star-forming limestone. A commonly used decoration in Morocco. Contradictory to how the prison looked on the inside, it all looked so beautiful in the visiting room.

Andre talked about the battle ahead of us regarding the cassation. With the Supreme Court there was still a chance for acquittal. I nodded, but was not in the mood for it. I didn't want to go through another court procedure. I just wanted to go home, along with Andre. His flight would be leaving in a few hours, so he had to go. We had a hard time saying goodbye. It was all so unfair.

I told Andre that I would focus on prison life. "I now know that I will be here for a while. I don't know for how long, six months, one year, two... But I have to let go of the life I used to know, and try to keep myself as strong as possible, however long it may take..."

Andre looked at me with tearful eyes.

We hugged, and I noticed how much he cared about me. That made me happy.

Andre went home and I returned to the cell.

Real prison life had begun.

"Prison locale de Berkane" was my home, "cell three" my room, "number 53548" my name.

38

"Hello, hero of mine. Disbelief, dismay and outrage about what has happened to you are the feelings that have taken over the Netherlands like a wave. Thanks to the media, everyone now knows how brave you are. Your words 'I think of it like a military training camp which I can learn from' and 'justice will ultimately prevail' have become headlines in the newspapers, on TV and the internet. It is sometimes hard to

understand the meaning of certain things, but you're a brave man, my own personal Nelson Mandela. Mama will love you unconditionally, no matter what happens. Try not to be bitter, I've never allowed myself to be. Despite all the misery, I have known many happy times and I enjoy every wonderful moment. I still do."

"You are a hero for your mom, but also for me. I admire you deeply for how you are dealing with the situation. Your mom and I agreed to go out one day soon, when she has recovered a little. We will sit down together to talk about what things lie within our power to help set you free. Everyone sympathizes with you. I miss you, sweetie. I miss your arms around me, your presence, your laughter, the bustle that you may cause. I miss looking into those beautiful eyes and spending time together. I just miss you. Hang in there. I'll write this in every letter. It is the only thing I'll ask from you."

"We were very happy to hear your voice when you called. Everyone here is thinking of you and they all want to help. We all know that you're innocent, so it'll be fine. Every beginning has an end. Your father would do anything to get you free. He told the lawyer that he wants to switch places with you, so that you will get out and he will stay there. He'll do anything. And those little brothers of yours, you know; every time I want them to eat something, I say: 'Look, if you eat all this, you'll be as strong as your big brother, Joseph.' Then they look up at me with their big eyes and say: 'Really mommy? Then I'll eat everything!' Nice, isn't it?"

"Besides being my best friend and brother, you're also the coolest, relaxed and most honest guy I know. I'll always be there for you, no matter how difficult the situation will be. If you feel lonely, think of all the people who care about you. Feel our love and they'll never break your spirit. My grandparents have seen you on TV and my grandmother literally said: 'Such a handsome hunk and innocent? They should release him

quickly! Ha-ha.' Even the people who read the whole story on your website are immediately convinced of your innocence. That says more than enough about the state of affairs over there. We think about you every day. Stay positive and strong; this injustice will be undone!"

The letters from my mom, Amber, Fouza and William, and also my friends and acquaintances continued to pour in again. They all unanimously expressed their respect and admiration. It made me blush and it gave me the support I needed.

My mom and Amber organized a petition. They got lots of help from almost everyone who knew me. They all went to ask their family, friends and acquaintances. Others went to the streets, armed with clipboards, and began talking to strangers asking for them to sign the petition. They went to markets, visited schools and companies, and even went so far as to walk through the buses and trains. Eventually, they collected nearly four thousand signatures!

The lists were copied and bundled with letters that were addressed to the King of Morocco. Also among the letters were testimonials from my former employers, former teachers and even the mayor of my hometown, Raamsdonksveer.

In total, there were ten neatly bundled packages of documented support that were officially stamped by the notary and mailed to the king and various other authorities in Morocco. They were also sent to the Human Rights headquarters in Vienna and the Dutch Ministry of Justice and Foreign Affairs.

"I knew how many signatures were collected, but when you see all of them laid out in front of you, it's a little more intense," William said about the operation.

Additionally, many comments were left on freesef.com, not only from my acquaintances but also from people who had seen me on TV, and heard my story on the radio, or read it in the newspaper or on the internet. Seeing these words of love and support made me happy, but their belief in my innocence and the blunders of the Moroccan justice system, gave me an even greater strength. My biggest fear was not being believed by the people who knew me, but after all of this, my fear had completely disappeared…

39

Life in prison was one of routine, roll calls and lock-ups.

Every morning, afternoon and evening, the heads were counted. From 9:30 till 11:00 a.m. and from 3:00 to 5:00 p.m., the cells were opened and we were allowed access to the courtyards. The rest of the time, we were locked in a loft and had to entertain ourselves.

Every day, on the dot at midnight, the electricity was turned off with a loud bang and the prison went quiet.

Daily, you could feel the tension between many of the prisoners. We were locked in a tiny room and the lack of space was getting to some of them. There always was a shouting match with the occasional fight. I never interfered, but the fighting always caused an unwelcomed stress within my stomach. Fights are never pleasant, especially in here because you never knew what was going to happen.

Our cell was quite narrow, but the other cells certainly were not any better. Thirty people packed into approximately four hundred square feet is small by any standards. Cell two, next to ours was a lot bigger, but it housed an average one hundred and twenty prisoners. Cell one, in front of our cell, had an average of forty men. Cells four, five and six were on the other side of the prison. Cells four and five were populated by about fifty men. Cell six was just like ours, with around thirty, but it was a cell for the elderly. The owner of Melika Fruits and the 24-hour guard were placed here.

Then there was the separate cell, the so-called arrival cell, with an average of one hundred men. It was a cell for the people who weren't convicted yet. It was by far the worst cell in the prison. People were crammed together, even closer than in our cell. The room smelled and there was no TV or electricity. I suddenly realized how fortunate I was that I wasn't sent to the arrival cell and instead, Chief Nordin had sent me directly to cell three.

In the middle of the prison there was a small, separate section for about a hundred juvenile inmates. All in all, there was a total of around five hundred men – not including the women's wing – in a prison that was built by the French to house ninety men!

In jail, I was keeping myself busy with reading, writing and philosophizing. I often listened to music on my discman and radio. Every five minutes I was fighting off a cockroach and there was still the problem of lice to consider. I was fortunate to receive lice shampoo from home to keep my head lice-free, but I would still find those nasty little creatures in the seams of my clothes. I could always give my clothes to the guys in the cell who provided the "anti-lice service". They would examine the clothing thoroughly and ensure that they were lice-free.

I found myself spending a lot of time with Karim. He was sentenced to two years in prison for a little over four pounds of hashish that was found in his car. He had loaned his car to a friend, who apparently had hidden the drugs inside without Karim ever knowing about it. "It is a trick often used in drug smuggling," Karim told me.

He showed me the ropes of prison life: "Jails in Morocco are nothing more than concrete buildings with lofts and iron bars that separate you from the outside world. Jail doesn't provide you with anything. Don't rely on the guards. You must arrange and buy everything yourself. The inmates offer services and products that you can buy with cigarettes."

There were two brands of cigarettes that were being traded: the private label Marquise, or the better known brand, Marlboro. A pack of Marquise costs seventeen dirham, for a pack of Marlboro it was thirty-four. Karim arranged, among other things, that I could get my own blankets for three packs of Marquise. These came from inmates who got their goods from home and sold it. This way, they had extra money or cigarettes for drugs.

Each cell had at least one drug baron who would arrange deals with the guards for the smuggling and selling of drugs.

Karim told me not to trust anyone, not even him. "Karim!" I said. "Of course I trust you. You mean a lot to me and you are always there for me. That's hard to come by in here." I saw Karim blushing a little.

Almost daily we sat together in the "recreation room", with the broken TV, empty benches and unused bar. We would sit in the window sill of the barred window overlooking one of the courtyards and discussed about anything and everything.

During our conversations I would watch the sky, the passing clouds and the birds flying overhead.

As time passed, I started to fit in well with the prisoners. I kept to myself and treated my cellmates with respect. In exchange, I too was respected. I started learning how to say a few words in Moroccan and my cellmates would sometimes laugh at the way I pronounced them.

In the cell, Karim and I would often eat in a group with a few of the other guys. There was always the prison food, but you wouldn't eat that, even if you were dying from hunger. Twice a day, the plantos, in their black and white striped outfits, would come out from the prison kitchen carrying huge iron pans in which floated a green, yellow or brown indefinable waste. Even pigs would turn up their noses to this. Only the inmates without visitors would eat it, unless there were leftovers from the visitor food. Prisoners receiving visitors were allowed to have them bring food from home. The prison management knew as well as anyone that we couldn't live more than a week on the prison diet.

Every morning during breakfast we would take turns standing in line for the little kitchen, to get some fried eggs or a cup of tea. We used the heating coils from the cooking sets as our own personal stove. In the afternoon, we got to enjoy a hot dinner thanks to the visitors. Afterwards, we would wrap our "hot" pans with towels, so that in the evening, the food would still be a little bit warm. While waiting in line, fights would often break out. Jumping your turn wasn't tolerated by the other prisoners.

Every week, we could write down on a piece of paper the things we needed from the shops in town. From food and cigarettes, to batteries, notebooks and pens. My mom sent me money every month, so I could buy what I needed.

One time, I bought twenty pens and two cartons of cigarettes and walked up to see the pen man. As usual, he was sitting bent over in the corner of the cell. The tip of his tongue was sticking out of his mouth as he was busy focusing on his meticulous work. I saluted him and he smiled up at me, again with his calm appearance.

"Could you perhaps make me some pens?" I asked, holding the pens and cartons of cigarettes.

"Of course."

I sat down beside him.

"Sorry I reacted that way the other day and walked away from you..."

"It's okay. I understand your situation all too well. What names would you like to have on them?"

The pens could be decorated with names. He did this by

wrapping them first in white plastic and then covering it with different colors of wire which would spell the letters. A very painstaking task. After thinking about it, I made him a list of names and handed it over along with the cartons and pens. One decorated pen would cost me a pack of Marquise. That's nothing compared to the six hours of work he put in on each pen.

"You were right. I'm starting to think all they care about is the money. I don't understand how this is possible and is allowed to go on..."

The pen man said nothing. He put the cartons of cigarettes under his blanket and the pens in a special plastic bag where he also kept his beads and wires. I saw that it was a plastic bag from the Netherlands from the Albert Heijn, a known supermarket. I said to the pen man that I had worked for four years at a supermarket in the fruit and vegetable department.

He smiled back and continued on about my appeal.

"I understand why you didn't pay them. You knew yourself that you didn't do anything wrong and therefore you stayed positive. You trusted justice, the system. Of course you don't want to pay. Especially because they have no evidence. But now do you realize that a lawyer can say whatever he wants, and you can say whatever you want, but ultimately the court holds all the power. If the judge knows that your lawyer is being paid well, but he isn't, he will respond maliciously to your case. The judge, of course, has to be able to maintain his lifestyle of fancy cars, houses and his family. When he saw you in court, he thought he could get you to pay well because you're from the Netherlands. If the judge doesn't get paid, the process is simple: he asks the lawyer if he's done talking, he asks whether you're done talking and then says: 'Yes? Yes? Ready? Okay, ten years for the suspect! Goodbye. Next suspect!' And there's nothing you can do about it."

I looked at him and thought I noticed frustration on his face. I kept finding this unbelievable, but I quickly remembered that

I was right in the middle of it. This is exactly what happened to me... I accepted the fact that this was the way it was, but I still found it unfair. How was this even possible or allowed? That I was just thrown behind bars?

At night, I often woke up terrified. I would sit up, confused for a minute, usually sweating as I looked around into the darkness of the cell. It was difficult to fall back to sleep. Sometimes I was dizzy or nauseous, but the next morning I was feeling a little better again.

I kept wondering how long this would all take. I thought about who had done this to me and I wanted to know who was really behind this large amount of drugs. What really happened? I never was convinced that the owner of the packing station and the old 24-hour guard were guilty. If they could so easily give me ten years in prison, they could have done the same to them.

I missed my life. I missed everyone around me. I missed spending time with my mom, my dad, Fouza and the little men. I missed William, and of course, Amber.

"Hey sweetie. Are you still hanging in there? What a stupid question. You have to get out of there! You are there and no matter how much I sympathize with you, think about you and worry about you, I can't imagine what you must be going through. That hurts me so much. I really hope that I can come and visit you soon, but of course my greatest hope is for you to come home. I know it's easier for me to say it than for you to go through it, but I know that you can do this. You're strong and courageous. You're the person I look up to and I couldn't be more proud of you. You are my beautiful man, my Joseph."

"Do you know what's amazingly beautiful right now?" my mom wrote in a letter. *"The sky. Those gigantic cloudscapes flying above the flat country. I refer to them as Joseph-skies. I always loved how much you enjoy watching the sky. I truly hope that you will be home this summer to watch the roses bloom in our garden. Every day I continue*

to burn three tea lights for you. When it's two o'clock your time and four o'clock here, I light them. Around nine o'clock, they are burned up and then I go to bed around ten. Try to calm your mind before going to sleep. Think, with your eyes closed, of the beautiful things you are going to do when you're with us again. I will do the same."

40

The two women from the Dutch embassy who were present at the appeal came to visit me in prison shortly afterwards. They sat in front of me quietly, as I told my story about how all of this was actually possible. Everyone clearly saw how I was thrown behind bars without any real evidence.

"How can this happen?" I asked. "How can anyone be falsely accused and imprisoned like this?"

The women were powerless and went on to defend their inaction by telling me that Morocco was a sovereign state and that they had signed the Convention of Human Rights.

"We cannot and may not interfere in the judicial process," they said.

Great. So basically no one could do anything about it.

"But I'm not a criminal! I'm not from that world! I'm not some sleazy guy that deals in these matters. I never have been! Everyone knows this! Ask my family, ask my friends and coworkers! Read the testimonials from my employers and teachers. How is this possible? How can they do this?"

I kept repeating myself.

The women from the embassy shrugged their shoulders. They didn't know either. Again, the tears of injustice and frustration began to well up in me, but I kept them inside.

In front of me laid the A4 sheet of paper containing the translated verdict from the appeal. It was plain to see that the mistakes from the first verdict – like the number of stamps in my passport – were simply wiped away. However, the other points of the judge's verdict, along with the ten year sentence were upheld. What a joke. Their decision was so clearly a set-up that out of sheer frustration, I crumpled the verdict into a ball and threw it over my shoulder.

41

Life outside the walls went on.

Holidays, such as Queen's Day and Liberation Day - how ironic! - went by, just like my mom's and William's birthday. I called them to wish them well.

"Liberation Day, nice words, people cheering, but little action," my mom said on the phone. "They pretend to stand up against injustice. Well, if that were true they may want to start with your case to prove their point. That would be a great mission for the Ministry of Justice."

On the evening of William's birthday, friends of ours came over to visit him.

"Damn it! You should be here!" William said.

"Yeah, damn it!" I answered.

"Don't worry, we'll make up for this next time!"

"Absolutely! Next year we'll celebrate it twice! What did you get for your birthday?" I asked.

"Oh, a few games and some things, but the best gift is talking to you right now!"

The calls were nice, but there was still a feeling of emptiness, a feeling that the situation wasn't going to get any better.

Later, Fouza gave me some surprising news: "You're going to have a little brother or sister!"

I laughed at her exuberance and the fact that she was pregnant made me happy.

And as the world kept turning, I walked my laps on the courtyards between the high walls. Prison life slowly became my life.

42

In the cell, the guys were able to get a monopoly board game through one of the guards, but they didn't exactly know how to play. After I explained it to them, we played the most famous board game in the world for weeks.

I found out that they also liked to play card games a lot. That gave me the idea to play Blackjack with the money from the Monopoly game. I'm not a big fan of card games, but I think Blackjack is amusing. My money-minded cellmates found it entertaining as well. At one time, instead of using the Monopoly money, they were putting up cigarettes. However, when someone lost, trouble would soon follow, so I left them to play the game without me. They figured it out themselves, even though it usually ended with a fight. Weird dudes.

Checkers was also very popular and much more pleasant. It touched me to see how some of the men had made homemade checkerboards. I couldn't really call them boards because they were white cloths, with squares drawn on them in blue pen. They used red and blue bottle caps as the checkers. You become more innovative when you have less.

On Friday afternoons I stayed outside as long as possible before the evening roll call began. Chief Nordin let me walk around until I was one of the last inmates in the yard. I enjoyed walking around in the empty main hall and on the empty courtyards. As I walked, I looked up at the colored sky. Admiring the ever-changing sky was a freedom that no one could take away from me. Although I missed watching the horizons and sunsets, the colors I would see were more than enough to make amends.

Even after the evening roll call, I often chatted with Chief Nordin in his room, enjoying a biscuit and some tea. Before leaving for home, he would personally walk me to the cell. Every time, he apologized for having to lock me up. If it had been up to Chief Nordin, I would have been released yesterday, but he was simply doing his job. Actually, I considered him a prisoner in many ways as well. A prisoner in his own country, because what kind of life did he have? He had no future. Chief Nordin had worked in this prison for nineteen years. So many years in such a depressing and dirty place. He thought prison life was horrible too, but he also said that if it was nice and clean, and the food was good, poor people from the outside would want to come to the prison. It was a philosophy I never considered: people would rather live as a bum on the streets than have to go to jail in this place...

"Have a nice weekend," the chief always said and every time I looked at him sheepishly. He looked back, feeling a little ashamed. Then we both chuckled and hugged each other before I walked into the cell. He meant well. From behind the bars of the cell door, I thanked him once again for his sympathy and assistance, and wished him a nice weekend too.

One day, Chief Nordin came to me and told me that they wanted the walls of the courtyards repainted.

"What color did you have in mind?" he asked me.

I was surprised that he would ask me to choose a color.

We were standing together on the courtyard, looking at the walls.

"Blue, heavenly blue," I replied, rubbing my chin. "Then the color of the walls will blend in with the sky and it will be like they're not even here."

Chief Nordin looked at me with his typical stern look I was accustomed to. I smiled. "Right? Isn't blue beautiful?"

His face thawed. "And blue it will be!" he laughed.

The next day I saw several plantos walking into the courtyard with large cans of paint in their hands, brushes in their mouth and ladders on their shoulders. The walls were painted blue, the exact shade of blue that I had pictured in my mind.

43

Chief Nordin typically led the so-called cell searches. A cell search occured weekly. Someone had snitched again and told the guards that there was hashish in the cell or something else that was forbidden. It never failed, when hearing the word "hashish", everyone in Morocco wearing a uniform became frantic. *Hashish has been found! Panic! Hell-fire!*

During the cell searches, everyone was forced outside as quickly as possible, with the guards shouting at us. In the courtyard, the prisoners were searched from head to toe, one by one, under the watchful eye of Chief Nordin. He almost always skipped me and even left my place untouched, while the rest of the cell was turned upside down. He gave specific instructions not to touch me. I felt blessed and was thankful for this gesture. Chief Nordin had taught me that, despite everything, despite this environment, there were always people who had their hearts in the right place and weren't afraid to show their feelings. People who weren't afraid to be true human beings.

Chief Nordin was highly respected by the prisoners and the guards, so I was treated well by everyone.

I couldn't believe it when my mom wrote in one of her letters that a French-speaking man had called and congratulated her on her birthday. It turned out to be Chief Nordin. He never even told me! The big softy.

"At that moment, we were very proud of you son, because we heard how much everyone there respected you."

44

During our daily "airtime", I would stand next to the entrance of our cell, watching a stork's nest which was built on top of a mosque that peeked out just above the prison walls. For months I followed the amorous stork couple. The inmates sometimes saw me looking up at the nest for ninety minutes. Every now and then, they would watch with me for a little while. I knew that once a pair of storks had found each other, they would never separate. Truly romantic. But even more romantic was how the couple greeted each other every time one of them would return from being away from home. They threw their heads back making a clattering sound while keeping motionless against each other. Beautiful.

At one point, two small little heads peeped above the top of the nest. Did I see that right? Did they have babies?

When I first saw them, I was so thrilled that I called my cellmates over to tell them that "my" storks had two babies. They all came to watch. So funny how they stood there: a gang of crooks watching two little baby storks. It was quite touching to see them gazing up at the nest.

After a while, the two babies were balancing on the edge of the nest, doing some flying exercises with their little wings.

Unfortunately, I wouldn't get to see them flying out. I was about to be transferred to another prison.

There was an entirely new bizarre adventure in store for me.

45

On the advice of my family and fellow inmates, I had personally submitted a transfer request to the prison of Salé. This prison was very close to the office of the Dutch embassy, which could provide the beneficial help I needed. And if the stories were true, then the prison of Salé should be better than Walt Disney World. The only thing missing would be Mickey Mouse. It was a Friday morning and I was called in to see Chief Nordin. I thought he was inviting me for our usual cup of tea, but the tea wasn't there.

"Take your seat," the chief said seriously.

"Quarrel with your wife this morning?" I asked jokingly. I saw a cautious smile appear on his face.

"No, not this time," he replied with the same offbeat humor. "No..." he continued seriously. "In a minute you'll go back to the cell and pack your things up quietly. You are going to be transferred today."

My smile disappeared faster than snow in the blazing Sahara sun. Although I knew of course that this day would come but still it was very hard to digest. I began to realize that I had built a life here and made friends after almost six months in captivity. Months that seemed to last for years since my "arrest", but still the announcement came unexpectedly. I would have to leave everyone behind and start all over again. I actually didn't want to go at all!

Still, I said to the chief in a calm tone of voice that I would start packing up my belongings.

The transfer news came hard to my cellmates, especially Karim. They stared at me noiseless as I looked at my place in the cell, fell down to my knees and started packing up slowly. Suddenly, from all sides, everyone rushed to help me. They wouldn't let me do a thing. The guys packed everything for me. My letters went in a red bag, my clothes and some food in a blue bag. They also packed my rolo. They rolled up my blankets and tied a sheet around them so they were easy to carry. While they were busy packing, I realized how fortunate I was, despite everything. Fortunate, that I wasn't alone and that I was lucky to experience unforgettable moments with these guys.

The entire prison seemed to come out to see me off. I walked behind the procession of people who carried my belongings and from all sides, I was greeted and embraced. I waved, shook hands and almost felt like the President of the United States, but different. I was pleasantly surprised by all of these warm gestures. I never expected this. From the many prisoners, I knew most of their names. I had chatted with almost all of them at one time or another. I noticed that they could appreciate that I took the time to listen to them and for me it was a great way to learn Moroccan. Karim was often there to translate. It was quite emotional saying goodbye to him.

"Thanks for everything," I said. He just smiled and looked at me from behind his glasses with his head bowed.

I looked over his shoulder for the pen man.

"Where is the pen man? Didn't he come with you?"

Karim looked at me. "You know him, he's at his place, decorating pens."

I nodded. We hugged each other for one last time, after which he turned around and disappeared into the crowd.

I was standing in the main hall, near the door with the sliding window that led to the visitors room. The owner of the packing station and the 24-hour guard were also there, along with several other prisoners who were being transferred. The plantos took our luggage to the transfer bus. For the other prisoners, the main hall was closed. I saw the guys and other inmates at the end of the hallway, packed together behind the bars. I remembered the first day I arrived, how the inmates at the end of the hall hissed at me. Now they were waving enthusiastically at me. They were mainly just human beings, with feelings and often small, sensitive hearts. They had lost their way on the path of life, which had now brought them to this place.

The owner of Melika Fruits was transferred to the prison of Oujda; the 24-hour guard and I to a place called Taza, a prison with a terrible bad reputation...

46

"TAZA?" I asked Chief Nordin startled. "But I thought I would go to Salé!"

"Yes, that's true," he answered, staring at the ground while a guard handcuffed me.

"Take it easy with those cuffs!" Chief Nordin commanded the guard who was being a little rough. "Taza is temporary... After that you'll go to Salé."

"Why Taza? And how long is temporary?"

I was upset, because I had heard lots of unpleasant stories about that prison. My stomach was turning. "Can't I go to Oujda first?" I asked, knowing its reputation wasn't nearly as bad.

"I'm sorry. These are orders from above," Chief Nordin said, clearly disappointed. He had just been told that I would be sent to Taza. "What I can do is contact the chief of the prison of Taza. I know this man well, and I will make sure that they treat you well there."

Chief Nordin found it hard to turn me over which made me emotional.

"Okay," I said softly with a lump in my throat. The chief gave me a hug. I immediately wanted to spread my arms, but I couldn't as I was handcuffed. I was standing a little off-balance as I felt a tear running down my cheek and, with both hands, I quickly wiped it away.

The guards of the transfer bus were running through the list of names and numbers, sternly calling us forward, one by one. The chief quickly put my discman in the pocket of my Sword fruits jacket. We agreed to do this, so that it would provide me with a little distraction on the way. Chief Nordin and I looked at each other. I knew for sure, that I would miss him. Just like Karim, the pen man and the other cellmates.

I heard my name and number.

"Thanks, Nordin. Thank you for teaching me that no matter how bad things are, there will always be good human beings, people who remain human…"

"It's okay, Joseph. It's okay. Stay strong, and behave yourself there like you did here. Then you will be fine for sure... Take care ..."

I nodded glumly, turned around without saying a word, and joined the row of inmates getting onto the bus.

47

With the other inmates, I step forward through the prison gate. I had hoped to walk through this door for the last time without handcuffs, without false accusations, without considering what would happen to me, but that wasn't meant to be.

I'm looking at the transfer bus with my eyes wide open. It is a black armored bus.

That roaring thing would look good in a Mad Max movie!

I hear the bus guards, dressed in army green, constantly shouting *Jallah! Jallah!*. We are hurried onto the bus like cattle. Apparently not fast enough, because the inmate behind me is pushed by a bus guard and hits me which made me stumble and trip. How humiliating.

I'm climbing into the Mad Max bus and looking around with wide eyes.

I have seen this before! Except that time I was at home, watching TV with snacks and drinks or in the cinema with sticky fingers from the sweet popcorn.

Just like in the movies, the bus has a barred cage. Inmates are sitting on hard plastic benches. They are observing us from head to toe. I glance back, but notice an open seat to the left of me and sit down quickly. I look around and see a couple of sleazy guys staring at me. I stare back for a moment, but then look out the window.

Don't pay any attention to those men. Chief Nordin told me.

The window view is hampered by wire mesh, but I'm content with being able to look into the distance after all that time. In the background, I can see light snow-capped mountains. These are the mountains I proudly showed to my mom, when she visited me during my work at Sword fruits last year. Nature is very beautiful there.

How is it possible that behind all the beauty of this country, lies so much injustice?

The last prisoner takes his seat and the cage is locked.

There I am: an ordinary boy, twenty-four years old, from a village somewhere in the Netherlands, branded as a drug criminal.

Too bizarre, too unreal and too incredible for words. It seems like a nightmare, a movie, but because my hands are cuffed, I know how real this is.

The armored bus begins to leave with a heavy shudder. I hear sirens and see a police car driving in front of us with flashing lights. A few moments later, there's a car behind us too. They're keeping it moving. They seem to be in a hurry.

Through the wire mesh I'm looking outside silently, and then realize that I have my discman in my pocket. After some fiddling, I hear *Calling All Angels* by Lenny Kravitz playing in my left ear. I'm only using one earpiece, because I don't want anyone to see. I would never have thought I would be listening to Lenny in a situation like this! Normally I sing loudly in my car or in my room. Not this time, I'm keeping quiet.

Later, with some effort, I pull a letter out of my pocket. A letter from my mom. I'm calmly reading her words and occasionally I see a big tear drop falling down onto the paper.

"Remember, my sweet son, that my thoughts and those of many, many others remain with you. None of your friends would ever think of letting you down. You needn't be afraid of that, my brave child. You are not forgotten. Instead, the circle of people who sympathize with you continues to grow. We have hundreds of helping hands. We are here for you and we'll help you get through this mentally. You have our unconditional love.

Don't worry about me. I know you wish me peace and happiness. The peace is a bit hard to find now, but throughout the years, I have entered a phase in which I find happiness everywhere. The greatest happiness is that I can be proud of you, because you are bravely pulling through this. You're just like me, so my parenting, which was aimed at making you an independent, brave, good and intelligent person has succeeded. That really makes me happy, even now. Happiness is also watching the blooming daffodils dancing in the wind during the spring. Happiness is hearing your voice, the conversations we have. Happiness is that I will get better. Happiness is that the world turns green again. Everything is fresh and new once again. Your life too will be as fresh as the budding spring, so you may give the gloomy, deep autumn time and dark days of winter a place in your life. Hopefully without bitterness. We're going to work on that. You won't forget this, but you don't have to, because if you can give it a place, you will be able to help others.

Don't give up my child. Lots of motherly love from mom."

48

Since I was born, I have always had a special bond with my mom. After my difficult birth, I was born by C-section, everything changed for her: "From the beginning, it was so nice and beautiful to watch you grow, inch by inch. It was so amusing to take you to places. Mommy knew everything! According to you."

My mom taught me to have responsibility and perseverance. She told me about the nonsense of violence and war, and how I should never be jealous about the neighbor's big expensive car or the palace of the Queen.

"There will always be people who will try to turn your goodness into bad," she once said. I found that hard to understand. "Why?" I always asked. "Why would people want to do that?" My mom never understood this either. "It's just the way it is. Maybe at their cradle stood a little devil instead of a little angel."

My mom loves flowers. Somehow, as a little boy, I could sense that already. As a toddler, I once saw a yellow flower in our backyard. I found this flower to be so beautiful that I picked it and gave it to my mom, who was cooking in the kitchen. It's funny that my mom remembered this as well: "You came to me holding the only blooming daffodil in the garden and said with shining eyes 'Nice huh, mommy?'. Then my mom lifted me up and gave me a kiss. "Thank you so much, little Joe. It's beautiful!"

From early on, I wanted to protect and help my mom. My mom once told me about a time when we were in a pasture, looking for grebes' nests and gnomes in hollow trees. "We had to climb over a fence. You had hopped over, but I couldn't make it. Then you were standing with your little five year old arms up and said: 'Jump mommy, I'll catch you!' So sweet."

My mom played a large role in my fascination for nature, the sky and the universe. "The elusiveness and brightness of those infinite little dots in the universe are part of the miracle of creation and named 'stars'. " She then continued by saying that there are even more great things between heaven and earth. "The guardian angels are always with you, don't you ever forget. Rely on their goodness."

My mom is also a very down-to-earth person. To questions like what she would do if she had one more day to live, she replies: "What a senseless question. What can you do? You wouldn't be able to make a journey around the world, so I think I would mow the grass and pluck the weed. If there was still time, I would polish the copper and clean the litter box. This way you wouldn't need to look after that for a while."

My mom would always tell me that I am spontaneous, social and honest. Although I find myself to be an average person, she would always say that somehow I attract attention: "Call it appearance or charisma, but people always seem to remember you..."

49

As we drove toward Taza, inmates were being transported in small groups to various prisons. We made a stop at the prison of Zaio, in a sandy mountain village, and stayed there for a few hours. Initially, we were sitting on the bus in the middle of the sun for half an hour, until the bus guards finally noticed that we were starting to shrivel up like prunes beneath the scorching heat. So they brought us into the prison. What a relief it was to be in a cool building and out of the sun.

The prison of Zaio was new and much more updated than the old jail in Berkane. It was systematically established, surrounded by high walls in a square with barbed wire and an observation tower at each corner. I was surprised to see that the walls were painted pink on this location deep in the mountains, far away from civilization.

My bladder was ready to burst so I asked a bus guard if I could go to the bathroom. He hesitated, but then saw that I was beginning to turn purple and walked with me. My handcuffs weren't taken off. Just imagine I would flee and run away into these mountains. Where would I go?! So I peed quite clumsily, but fortunately my bladder was empty...

Meanwhile, the stop was over. We were loaded back onto the bus and the cage was shut again with a bang. The bus roared to life and the sirens of the police escort turned on again.

Destination: Taza prison.

After a bumpy three-hour ride we arrived. Through the window, I noticed a lot of people standing at the prison gate. They were probably relatives, waiting to visit the inmates. When the bus came to a stop, we were ordered to get out. Rigid from the ride, we stood up, one by one, and shuffled out of the bus. The people outside were watching us carefully, staring at us like we came from planet Pluto. A little ashamed, I stared at the ground. They were probably wondering what I had done, what kind of a criminal I was. Or maybe they felt sorry for me, because after all, their relative was imprisoned too.

I turned around and asked the bus guards not to forget my luggage.

"Especially the red bag, please don't forget the red bag."

This bag contained all of the letters which I had received until now.

Before I turned back, I was forcibly grabbed by two prison guards who kept shouting at me to keep my mouth shut and hurry up.

"Hey, calm down!" I struggled, after which they squeezed me even tighter.

"I just don't want them to forget my luggage," I said outraged, trying to point toward the bus with my hands cuffed.

I had seen it happen before when they forgot the bags of a few other inmates. Everyone knows that if they are forgotten, they would be gone forever.

"Get inside!" they snarled, pushing me in my back. People were staring at me from all sides. I felt humiliated and small. Then, two other prison guards grabbed me on either side and walked me through the prison gate. I hesitantly walked inside and was placed on the bench in front of the administration area.

All of my mail, my clothes, I hoped they wouldn't forget my bags.

What would be waiting for me now?

Based on how I was treated so far, things didn't look good.

This prison was definitely living up to its reputation.

50

The administration area was a large open space. The floor and walls were painted in a white/cream color. I was sitting on the bench for almost half an hour when I heard my name called from a room. There they checked my records and pushed a yellow card into my hands which I had to carry with me at all times. There were three things on it: my name, my new number – 64113 – and the date of release – 12/23/2014.

Great, now I would be continually reminded of this.

My handcuffs were taken off and I was sent to the main hall where a pile of luggage and rolos were laying on the ground. Eagle-eyed, I searched through the stack. A guard who was standing next to it asked me what was mine and allowed me to search the stack.

My red bag with the letters, my red bag with the letters…

Yes! There it was! My letters! Luckily...

I also found the blue bag with my clothes and food. After getting my rolo a man came up to me. He had a surprising Eastern European look and was dressed in a green military uniform. He stopped right in front of me and asked if I was "Joseph Oubelkas". I knew then that the man wasn't European. He was the chief of staff of the prison of Taza. As I had expected, Chief Nordin had kept his word.

The chief looked at me and told the guard to put me in the cell with the "French boy". I wasn't searched and could go with the guard directly. I dragged my bags and rolo through the main hallway.

The main hall was about three hundred feet long, with steel cell doors on both sides that led to various departments. These doors were constantly monitored. No one was permitted to walk freely in the main hall. I walked through several gates to the end of the hall where I was handed over to another guard with a clean-shaved head. He opened the cell door and let me in. In front of me I saw a long, high cell room with bunk beds on either side. Some of the bunks were at least three beds high, and washing lines full of clothes were hanging everywhere. It was a busy cell. It reminded me of the old market streets in the medina – the old town – in the capital Rabat, but dirtier, much dirtier.

"Where is the French boy, sir?" I asked the bald guard.

"He has visitors. He'll be right back," he replied.

I was sitting on my rolo next to the cell door with my bags beside me. I looked at the cell again. It was called "La Croie" – I didn't know why – but it was packed with people, just like the cell I had gotten used to in the prison of Berkane. People sat on the beds, hanging out their laundry and singing along with the radio. They walked together along the narrow pathway between the bunks, talking and shouting incessantly. Just like the prisoners in Berkane, this group could argue with the best of them.

The floor was sticky, with brown stains all over. Walls were covered with posters and dusty flags showing pictures from the local pop heroes, but also Eminem, 2Pac, and Michael Jackson. The walls were also covered with dirty smears and the beds were largely rusted. There really wasn't a clean spot to be found. It was swarming with cockroaches and there was a musty, suffocating odor. It was overwhelmingly hot in the cell and my skin was sticky with sweat. I felt filthy...

It seemed to take a long time, but fifteen minutes later, Soufian introduced himself. The French boy. He was tall and thin with pale skin. He looked about my age. With his round eyes and checkered cap, he looked a bit cartoonish, but that could also have been caused by the heatstroke I probably had.

Soufian and I got along with each other from the start.

But what a tragedy would await us later on.

51

In the prison of Taza total anarchy ruled. Rogue gangs of murderers, rapists and drug dealers were rampant. It seemed the guards allowed the inmates to do anything. In the prison of Berkane they followed a strict regime that forbade everything from electronics to cutlery. In Taza, the prisoners had everything available to them: cell phones, TVs, DVD players, CDs, money, drugs, alcohol, knives, screwdrivers, soldering tools, you name it. The only thing they didn't have was machine guns… yet.

Between the different departments there was a lot of drug dealing. Inmates walked around with cell phones to their ears. The guards saw them, but did nothing about it! Several times a day, inmates were involved in fights and would be taken away, covered in blood. What a madhouse! Imagine having to live in this jungle for years!

There were quite a few prisoners who had to stay here for a while. In Berkane I was one of the few with a longer sentence, but here, many men got ten, fifteen, thirty years or life imprisonment.

Soufian wasn't surprised by anything anymore. He had been here for almost two years. He got sentenced to three years for seventy pounds of hashish. That first day, Soufian took me around for a short tour.

Opposite of our cell were the isolation cells, followed by the common shower which had been turned to a sleeping area with all the rolos laid out on the ground. As a result, showering was no longer possible here. It was a strange sight, seeing those blankets lying beneath the shower heads. To the left of our cell, you could walk down, toward the kitchen, or straight through to the classrooms, the youth section and a triangular courtyard. To the right of our cell was the main hall. The prison housed about fifteen hundred people which was three times as much as the prison of Berkane.

During the tour I noticed how widely respected Soufian was in prison. That was good. I thought.

I was exhausted from everything I had seen that day. Soufian made sure I had a bed to sleep in that night. Nice, my own bed. But I couldn't sleep a wink. I kept hearing a constant rustling and squeaking. What was that? I heard it next to my face and peered into the darkness around me, but I couldn't see anything. Were they cockroaches? Then I saw them. Well, I could see the outline of what was making those noises: they were rats!

What were these animals doing here?! I wasn't afraid of rats, but I certainly didn't want them in my bed. Every time I fell asleep of tiredness, I was startled awake when I heard them or felt them. Those squeaking beasts were running all over my legs and stomach!

How on earth could I sleep? It drove me crazy!

Soufian had a good laugh about it the next morning.

"Yeah, you laugh," I said with giant bags under my eyes. "I'm exhausted. How do these animals get in here, anyway?" I asked, dizzy from no sleep.

"From the kitchen downstairs," Soufian answered. "It's swarming with rats, and at night they come to visit us. Sometimes, they can be this big!" Soufian was holding his hands wide apart excessively, like a fisherman who boasted about the biggest fish he ever caught.

I looked at Soufian with disgust, annoyed by my lack of sleep.

"Sleep at my place whenever you would like. During the daytime the rats take shelter," he continued with a smile.

"Yeah, okay," I replied yawning. *"Merci!"*

I could get used to the cockroaches, but the rats were a different story. The rats didn't exactly look clean either. They were often wet and some had some open sores on their backs.

Sigh… I just had to accept them. After all, they lived here before me.

52

The day would start in typical fashion with a morning roll call. In the main hall, everyone had to line up in rows of two. It was the only type of discipline enforced in this prison. The afternoon and evening roll calls went much smoother.

In the evening, it was almost always dark in the cell because the light given off by the two ceiling light bulbs was barely noticeable. Only from the light of the eight TVs, which were attached in several of the bunks, we were able to see.

Some inmates decorated their bunks like a mini-bedroom. Soufian had hidden the iron frame of his bed with some sheets, and with a rope, he assembled a shelf above his feet. On the shelf were a TV and PlayStation 2. I was very surprised to see a PlayStation just like the one I had in my bedroom at home. Soufian also had a mobile phone, which opened up a whole new world for me.

"I thought that only the drug dealers had a phone. Can anyone have one?" I asked like a rookie, even greener than green.

Soufian looked at me sarcastically, as if it was perfectly normal to have a phone in your pocket. "Okay, okay! Stupid question," I said quickly, taking the attitude of "tough prisoner" again. Soufian would arrange a phone for me too, so I could have direct contact with my mom and everyone at home. This gave me a tremendous feeling of relief and it was the biggest – and actually the only – advantage to being in this rat's nest. Soufian told me that I constantly had to be on my guard in this prison and if someone asked me something, I should just play dumb. "Don't answer. Just act as if you don't understand them." I should never forget that every minute of every day I was locked up with people who were convicted of murder or assault. "For some guys here, a human life is worth less than a pack of cigarettes," Soufian stated.

The thought of this made me feel paranoid sometimes. Every time I looked over my shoulder I thought someone was staring at me suspiciously. Soufian's story didn't help me sleep any better either. I started to notice a constant tension in the cell, which held more than eighty men, almost all of whom had committed a brutal crime.

The cell was so crowded that some bunks were shared by three men. People even slept on the ground beneath the bunks.

We shared two toilets, but you couldn't call them toilets. They were holes in the ground, plugged with bottles to keep out the stench as much as possible. The bottles were always pissed on. Before I took them out, I first rinsed them with water. With the tip of my thumb and forefinger I took the bottle at its cap, as if I was fishing for the dirty underwear of a stranger.

Even worse, was that at certain times water wasn't available, making the holes clog which made the poop pile up. Something too filthy to describe. The most embarrassing thing was that the toilets had no door! Over the half wall, everyone could enjoy the show and count your falling droppings. When I first arrived in this jail, it took me five days before I went to the toilet.

Soufian and I were constantly together. He introduced me to his cousin, a guy with a round face, fringe of beard and small glasses. He knew a lot about IT so we had plenty to talk about.

Besides them, I spoke to no one else in the cell. "It's better just to ignore these guys," said Soufian repeatedly. He had arranged a bed for me that was next to his, and covered the cost of this space as well.

During the day, Soufian and I would walk around to the various departments and talk with the inmates who he knew well. Soon we became known in prison as the duo of "the Frenchman and the Dutchman". Late afternoon, the guards would let Soufian and I walk around outside the cell until after the evening roll call.

In the evening we stayed away from the criminals in jail and watched movies, called home or were quietly playing games on the PlayStation. I tried to adapt to my new surroundings as much as possible, but the idea of being locked up with people who didn't care about life, made me feel continuously restless. And I had good reason.

53

It was another noisy night in the cell. Music, TV sounds, shouting, fighting, smacking, burping, talking and other background noises.

Soufian and I were talking on the phone and texting. We had just eaten a pizza that Soufian had ordered. He was known at the local pizzeria, and almost every evening he ordered a pizza by phone from the cell. The pizza deliveryman came to the prison gate, and the guard, of course for a small fee – twenty dirham or a packet of cigarettes –, personally delivered us the pizza in the cell. Absolutely anything was possible here.

It was late and I got tired, so I told Soufian I was going to lie down. He nodded and wished me a good night's sleep, as he kept playing games on the PlayStation. He would often play into the wee hours of the morning.

It seemed I was asleep for only a few minutes, when I woke up startled by Soufian's voice. He shouted at the Kabran of the cell. I didn't exactly understand what it was about, but noticed that the electricity in the cell was turned off. I heard Soufian screaming in the dark that he still wanted to play on his PlayStation. He was furious that the power had been shut off.

"Just so we all go to sleep and you can rape those kids!" Soufian shouted. My eyes flew open.

What did he say? Raping kids? What was he talking about?

Not long after, the lights came on again and I began to hear the familiar background noises. I was so tired that I fell asleep again a little later.

The next morning, I asked Soufian what was going on.

He told me that the Kabran and a few cellmates brought a boy from the youth wing to stay with them.

"They agreed on this with the night guard," Soufian said. "A seventeen year old kid they use as a whore, the bastards!"

"What?" I couldn't believe my ears. "Are you serious?"

"Yes, it happens quite often," he said in a neutral way.

"And that's possible, just like that?" I asked disgustedly.

"With money, everything is possible! You know that now, right?"

"Yes, but this?!"

"But the lovemaking wasn't gonna happen," Soufian said with a sarcastic smile.

"Yeah right, you were raging pretty hard," I said. We both must have thought the same thing, because we burst out laughing at the same time, joking a little after. But I quickly stopped laughing, as I began to think about the bizarre world in which I was living at the moment. A world I had never thought about and never, absolutely never ever thought I would end up in.

54

One of the most unsavory characters in the cell was "Crackhead Charif". He was constantly under the influence of drugs and had already served thirteen of his fifteen year sentence. Back then, Charif was convicted of rape and abuse. He had a sunken face, and his cheekbones protruded unnaturally. His flaxen beard and skin looked like he hadn't showered in months.

Crackhead Charif was good friends with the Kabran. They agreed to shut off the power to try and create a peaceful night, as Charif was going to have a "visitor". But because of all the fuss with Soufian, this "party" was canceled. This frustrated Charif, who now wanted revenge.

55

Two days after the electricity incident, I am sitting on Soufian's bed and texting. Soufian is sitting on his cousin's bed in front of me and calling his girlfriend. Nothing is really going on, it is a rare quiet evening. Probably too quiet.

Suddenly, to my left, I see Crackhead Charif swaying. I'm thinking to myself what a scary guy he is. All of a sudden, he makes a weird drunk-like move, as if he's falling toward the unsuspecting, calling Soufian.

What happens next is in a flash.

Charif takes a swing at Soufian.

I hear a dull thud.

Soufian starts screaming like a madman and is kicking Charif away, who is struggling on top of him. Startled, I jump up to see Soufian's cousin and another cellmate pounce on Charif. They are beating on him with a drinking glass. Charif falls to the ground. I run over to Soufian and see blood gushing from his chest.

"Shit! You've been stabbed!" I call out.

Soufian is looking at his chest and sees the blood. He becomes furious and screams: "I'LL KILL HIM!" He shouts to his cousin who is beating on Charif ruthlessly. "Kill him! KILL HIM!"

I'm keeping Soufian under control as best as I can, while covering his wound with my hand.

"Take it easy, Soufian! Take it easy!!" I'm screaming.

Soufian's eyes look like those of a raging bull.

"Listen to me, man! Take it easy!"

The blood is seeping through my fingers. It feels warm. Soufian looks into my eyes and sees how serious this is. He is getting paler and weaker every second.

In the background, I hear the deafening abuse, shouting and trampling. It's as if the earth is moving.

I'm dragging the weakening Soufian over my shoulder with the help of a few cellmates. We are walking to the cell door.

Jesus, what is happening here! What is this? This isn't good.

"Hold on, Soufian! Hold on!" I keep calling.

I'm still pressing my hand on the wound, but the blood keeps coming. We are beating and kicking against the cell door, screaming to the night guards as loud as we can.

Soufian drops to his knees.

"Hey! Come on, Soufian! Come on! Hold on!" I'm calling again.

Soufian is coughing and I see blood slipping from the corners of his mouth. I'm thinking that he's going to die right in my arms here.

Look at all the blood. He's dying. He's dying right in front of me.

Soufian looks apathetically ahead, as if he has already given up. We are holding him up, but it's difficult. We keep on screaming.

"CHIEF! CHIEEEEF!"

We are kicking the cell door with all our strength. It seems like an eternity before someone responds.

Finally, two guards arrive, who at first are uninterested with what we have to say, but once they see the bloody scene they immediately open the cell.

Soufian is urgently taken away.

A little later, some other guards come to carry away Crackhead Charif. He looks miserable after all the beatings he took.

I stay behind in the cell, where it has never been so quiet.

56

I'm completely upset. I look down at my bloody hands. They're shaking heavily.

Frightened and bewildered, I sit there in my spot.

Did this really happen?

The scene of the incident is being played over and over in my mind.

Did all this really just happen?

It was so unexpected, so fast.

That dull thud, the screaming and kicking from Soufian, all the blood. It makes me nauseous.

I'm looking around, afraid that someone will come up and stab me next. Maybe a friend of Charif's or the Kabran.

Soufian's cousin comes up to me and tries to reassure me, but I can't hear him. I'm still in shock.

They're going to stab me next. They're after me too.

"Come. You need to freshen up and change clothes," Soufian's cousin says. His hands are shaking too. I look at my clothes and hands and see that Soufian's blood has now turned more of a brownish color.

I wash myself in the toilet and because of the shock I feel like I'm moving in slow motion. I can hear myself breathing loudly, as if my ears are clogged.

I have to tell William.

It's midnight, but I still call him. Hearing his voice reassures me and calms me down. I urge him not to tell my mom or Amber. They can't do anything anyway, so I don't want to worry them.

The embassy has to know what a dangerous prison this is. I call them, but when they don't answer the phone, I send a text message. I also informed my lawyers.

The next morning, the representative of the Dutch embassy and the lawyer from Berkane arrive. I am very grateful for their gesture of concern.

We are invited to a meeting by the director, who clearly isn't amused by my supporters at his door. The director is a short, dark, gray haired man. He assures us that nothing will happen to me and that I will be transferred to Salé as soon as possible.

This makes me feel slightly better, because I have to get out of here. Actually, I don't want to spend another minute in this place. This is no way to live.

However, I have to be patient a little longer.

The representative of the embassy and the lawyer head for home again.

I'm heading back to my cage.

57

I was disoriented and didn't know what to do.

The whole time I had been with Soufian, and now he was lying in the hospital.

Could he be rescued? How was he doing now? At night, sleeping was hard. I kept thinking that I would be stabbed too. Under my pillow, I hid a knife as a precaution, which I would hold onto for the entire night. The next few weeks, I had to cope with the situation on my own. Soufian's cousin had his own problems, so I couldn't count on him.

I walked through the prison alone. Thanks to Soufian, the guards knew me now, and some showed their sympathy by allowing me to walk freely. The visit from my supporters and meeting with the director probably contributed to that as well.

Lost in my thoughts, I wandered down through the kitchen, past the triangular courtyard, into the main hall and to the school department.

The school department had separate classrooms, some of which were used as cells. One of them was filled with only men who had beards, Orthodox Muslims. One day, I was invited to drink tea with them, and immediately I noticed a sense of peace and harmony about the room. Throughout the jail, there was a horrible noise, but in the room of these bearded friends, it was like an oasis of tranquility. I got to know a very gentle man, Abdellah, someone I would have nice conversations with in the coming days. Abdellah also got ten years in prison, but for killing a robber who threatened him with a knife in his shop. He didn't intend to kill this man, but unfortunately it happened.

We talked about everything, life, our cases, jail, Islam. He often quoted things from the Quran which I could hardly understand, but sounded very beautiful in Arabic. I decided for myself that one day I was going to read the Holy Book of Islam in Dutch.

Besides my talks with Abdellah, I chatted with a few of the other inmates as well. They told me how sorry they were about Soufian, and that I could come to them if something ever happened. A conversation that impressed me tremendously was with a young boy, not even twenty yet, who had lost a leg and had to walk on crutches. We were sitting on a piece of newspaper on the floor of the triangular courtyard with the sun shining on our faces. I asked what had happened to his leg and with a deep sigh he began to tell me his story. The boy said that when he was twelve, he was playing soccer with his friends on the street. The ball was kicked and he ran after it, but didn't see a car coming. He was hit and broke his leg. In the hospital, a complex bone fracture was detected. The boy came from an impoverished family and they didn't have the money for an operation. Instead of adequately treating his broken leg, they just cut it off! Fast, cheap and efficient: "Next patient!"

The boy held his hand curled around his mouth in an O-shape when speaking these words. I was looking for the right words to comfort him, but I didn't know what else to do other than look at him in silence.

"You're Soufian's friend, right?" he asked, as he looked at the ground.

"Yes," I answered, staring at the ground too. The sun had already disappeared behind the prison walls, but it was still very hot. I wiped my forehead with the palm of my hand, and from the corner of my eye, I could see the boy rubbing his stump.

"You know what the problem is?" he asked suddenly. I looked up at him.

"What is it?" I asked.

"This country is so beautiful. It has the outer beauty of a Bengal tiger. But once that tiger is hungry, there's nothing more dangerous..."

58

Because of my transfer from Berkane to Taza, my mail was delayed. The mail was first sent to the prison of Berkane. I was sure that it was Chief Nordin who was kind enough to forward it. We had talked a few times on the phone since I left. I told him I had it much better with him there, and he said that he was sorry he couldn't keep watching over me any longer. "Drinking tea in the morning was a lot more fun when you were still here," Chief Nordin told me.

My mother and I called each other frequently. Because of the charges our conversations were always short, but still very nice. My mom wrote to me that when we talked, she always had a "celebratory" feeling: *"It's so nice, even for those few minutes."*

I also spoke often with William and Amber. We talked about everything, life here, life there, friends, girlfriends, about what we would do in future, the weather, love, sex, our fantasies, anger, injustice, happiness and sorrow.

But however pleasant and fun, and sometimes painful too, the conversations were, spoken words perish, evaporate, dissolve into nothingness. Written words are forever.

My mom's letters kept coming. In a later letter that she wrote on Queen's day[6], I read something that touched me.

"Also on this April the 30th, I would have liked to make your life less difficult. I feel powerless. I would love to be able to take away some of the huge burden on your shoulders. I can only say that you must hold on, son. Remember, you're surrounded by our constant thoughts.

There was a program on TV today about Queen Beatrix's twenty-five years reign. They showed images of her crowning in 1980 and my heart began to hurt.

---

6. Queen's day in the Netherlands was celebrated on the 30th of April.

When I watched this happening twenty-five years ago, I felt you moving in my womb for the very first time. That's why you are a king's child to me. And that will never change."

59

Soufian was back! He had been away for two long weeks. I was so relieved and happy! When he returned, many inmates welcomed him as if he was the first man to land on the moon. Later, he told me what they had done with him after the guards had taken him away.

He was brought to the local hospital in Taza by ambulance, but they didn't have the proper means there to treat him. The knife had pierced his lung, less than half an inch below his heart. Slightly higher and it would have been fatal. He was then rushed to the hospital in Fez, a city approximately seventy miles to the west of Taza.

"It was a long, bumpy and painful journey," Soufian remembered. "I could feel the pain, but at the same time, I was in a state of ecstasy by which the pain did not seem real to me. I felt lightheaded, like I was floating."

They reached the hospital at the last minute. Soufian had lost a lot of blood, but they helped him immediately. He was lucky to have come from a wealthy family.

"They made an extra hole on the side of my lung," he said with his shirt pulled up. He pointed to the bandage over the wound. "My lung was filled with blood and had to be drained." The bandage was also around the wound below his heart. It really was a close call.

Soufian asked me what happened with Crackhead Charif.

"They brought him to isolation and the next day, the chief gave him a good beating," I answered. "We saw him being transported to the infirmary, all black and blue. He was covered with blood."

Soufian said that he would press charges against Crackhead Charif for attempted murder.

That Charif, he only had two years left on his sentence.

60

Soufian didn't want to stay in the same cell. Understandable. The director approved that we – Soufian, his cousin and I – could move to one of the classrooms in the school department. We were the only ones in this room and laid our rolos next to each other on the ground. We had a long table where we could put the TV, the PlayStation and other trinkets. We even had a blackboard at our disposal! Not that we used it for anything, but still, it was nice to have. It was if I was reliving one of the many sleepovers from my past at home with my mom. Despite her poor income, almost every weekend, William and my other friends would stay over and we always had lots of fun.

Soufian and I were just fine in our "private suite"! And the best part of this room was the view... The view!

There were two unused tables in the room that we had put on top of each other. We climbed up and now in the top of the room we could easily look outside through the bars.

I immediately fell in love with the view. Finally, I could see the horizon again. Mountains draped the background and in the valley a part of the city Taza was visible. So this prison had to be on a mountain.

I could see people as tiny as ants and cars as tiny as Dinky Toys, each with their own purpose. I saw life. For hours, I would sit up in the window sill of the room. Soufian frequently asked me whether I was tired of it yet, but no, I could never be tired of this. I thought the sunsets were especially breathtaking.

During the day, the mountains in the distance were a brownish-green color, the sky a clear blue. On the streets were mainly cars, but here and there you would see some pedestrians and carts with horses or donkeys. As the day went by and the sun sank, the mountains became darker and the sky turned orange and yellow. Once the street lights came on, the night fell fast. The mountains would blend in with the darkness and quickly become invisible. The sky turned from orange to purple, then blue and black. The stars came into sight, one by one. The lights in the houses came on shortly afterwards and the headlights from the cars became visible. By the dozens, people appeared from their houses as if they couldn't bear the sunlight. Soon the valley was swarming with people leaving it to be the only illuminated spot left in the dark environment.

I'll never grow tired of the phenomenon named sunset.

I was sitting up there, in the prison classroom when words came into my mind that I just had to share in a text message:

> I'm sitting here behind bars, watching the sun disappear behind the mountains. Looking at the people walking in the distance, I think to myself, who is actually the one behind bars? All who I see will eventually die and be forgotten. Did they ever really live? I don't want to be forgotten...
> [Send message?]
> [Yes]

I sent the text message to my mom, William and Amber. All three answered immediately that they would never forget me. Later, my mom put the words of my text message on the website freesef.com to share it with the rest of the world.

Soufian, his cousin and I would enjoy this private suite with a view for only one week. No longer.

61

Soufian and I were relaxing and watching a DVD about the life of 2Pac – I didn't know that this deceased rapper was so popular here, Soufian was also a big fan – when suddenly the prison director rushed in with some guards. The sudden invasion scared me to death.

"Pack up!" the director said abruptly. We jumped up at the same time.

"Uh, why?" Soufian asked, while I stood there awkwardly.

"This room has to be empty! Pack up!" the director ordered, as he turned around.

"But we like it here," Soufian said to the director's back.

"Yeah, we do," I agreed.

The director stopped, turned around, gave me a withering glance and then looked at Soufian.

"You know this is a classroom. There will be classes here."

"When?" Soufian asked. He was obviously disappointed, but I think I was more.

"As of now. So, pack up!"

The director looked at his watch. Apparently he was a busy man. His time might be better spent sorting out the enormous mess that was his prison. I had already heard that the director let things run their course, and earned a nice bit of pocket money by doing so from the drug dealers, among other things. Of course, I thought, that little, brown, gray-haired fool doesn't care what happens within his prison walls. It was surprising that he took the time to tell us, or Soufian I mean, the unpleasant news personally.

In the background 2Pac could be heard ranting about letting all the homeless people in America live in the White House, as we turned down the TV. With sagging shoulders and long faces, we started to pack up our things like we were so "kindly" asked.

We had to move to the room opposite the private suite. This room was slightly larger and populated by mostly older men. We created our own little corner and looked around. We had never seen such a filthy cell. Trash bins were bulging and surrounded by piles of garbage, in which cockroaches and rats were crawling. The toilet, that must have been white at one time, was stained brown and there were dozens of thick black flies flying above. Appallingly dirty. And the floor, so terribly rancid that my feet were literally sticking to it. Soufian and I looked at each other blankly. How did it come to this, in this cell? The move had already put a huge dent into our morale, but with the sight of our new home, it bottomed out.

I struggled to find the courage to clean the cell, when suddenly I thought of something my mom wrote to me in a letter: *"I don't want you to be in a dirty environment. I want you to look clean and proper there too."*

So buckle down!

"Come on, guys! We're going to clean this place up!" I said as enthusiastically as possible.

After some resistance and some deep, very deep sighs, I got Soufian and his cousin to help.

I could see the old men were simply too weak to do anything strenuous. Even lining up in rows for roll call was hard for them. That became clear when one morning a bald man with a gray beard collapsed and fell backwards during head count. His head made such a heavy thump, that it seemed as if a bowling ball had fallen to the ground. I was shocked by sound. The man was taken away unconscious with blood covering the back of his head. I never saw him again. What could these men have done to end up in jail in the first place? I wondered.

We had arranged for some cleaning supplies, a broom, scrubbing brush, wiper, mop, chlorine, soap, Moroccan Tide and two buckets. We were ready to get started. To complete the look, all we needed were yellow cleaning gloves and a towel around our heads.

It was stiflingly hot – the temperature on the inland of Morocco could easily reach 104 or 122 degrees Fahrenheit. We were almost melting, but the cell was visibly improving. Even the elderly, who were clearly tired of life, seemed revived. The guards appreciated it too and let us finish the cleaning until after evening roll call. Soufian occasionally grabbed his wounds and winced. Even though I told him to take it easy, he wanted to get the job done.

Afterwards, as a sort of thank you, the night guards, one of which was good friends with Soufian, let us outside on the patio till late at night. That was an impressive feat. My first night outside the cell! We inhaled the warm summer air and enjoyed the gentle breeze. Soufian and I were lying on some blankets, watching the clear sky. We saw millions of stars. We said nothing. We were tired, but enjoyed those elusive, bright little white miracles to the fullest extent.

62

A few days later, I would be transferred. I didn't have a lot of time to pack. After being called up by a guard late in the morning, everything had to be faster than fast. Soufian and his cousin helped me get my things together.

Although I felt sorry that I had to leave Soufian behind me, I felt a sense of relief. I was finally getting away from this dump and on to Salé, the oh so arcadian jail. Soufian and I hugged each other for at least one minute and promised, that one day, we would meet again at my place in Breda or his home in Strasbourg.

Soufian still wasn't able to lift heavy materials, so he sent a few plantos with me who he would pay. He gave me his 2Pac CD that I often listened to on my discman over the past few weeks. *Dear Mama* and *Unconditional Love* helped me to fall asleep many nights in the always noisy environment full of murderers and rapists. I felt happy by this gesture and even happier to close this short, tumultuous period in Taza prison.

Everything had to be better than this. At least, that's what I assumed.

63

The transfer bus eagerly roared to life again in front of the prison gate.

That thing was still a monster! It was surely quite different than bus 126 from my home town to the city of Breda.

The handcuffs were tightened firmly again and my luggage was thrown into the baggage cage. The sense of stress had returned. I shuffled into the bus and saw the barred cage. There was a bench available at the window again, at about the same place as the previous transfer. From the color of the benches I could see that it wasn't the same bus.

Again, it was too bizarre for words that I was here. I just couldn't believe it and tried to pretend it was a normal bus ride.

And what a ride it had been.

Accompanied by the screaming sirens from a number of police cars, we tore through the mountains and streets. Compared to this, the roller coaster Kingda Ka at Six Flags was dreary.

Everywhere we passed I saw hordes of people staring at the "Prison Break" bus. What a sight it had to be, watching this black armored bus come thundering past. Those people would certainly think that some very serious criminals were being transported. Unreal.

I was staring silently out the window, when the man next to me offered me some water. I turned it down. No pee problems for me, like with the previous transfer.

He was a quiet, friendly man who I estimated to be in his mid-forties. He had straight, medium hair and looked a little glassy. We started talking. I was stunned, because he had been in prison for seventeen years. I had seen him a few times, walking through the hallways in the prison of Taza and I heard his story through some of the others. Now, he was telling me personally.

He was sentenced to life in prison for murdering a police officer. It happened one evening when the man was playing cards with his friends in the street for money.

He was nineteen years old at the time – oops, I realized I estimated him to be ten years older – and that night he was having no luck. He had already lost a lot and things were about to get worse. Just then, two policemen showed up and ordered the boys to stop playing cards.

"It went pretty rough," the man said. He was staring straight ahead, as if he was envisioning the whole scene again. "I got angry by the way they were treating us, and of course because of the money I had lost playing cards..."

His voice sounded regretful. He paused.

"I grabbed one of the police officers by his throat and, in a haze of anger, strangled him to death. The other officer was beaten by the other boys, but he got away with some scratches and bruises."

I looked down at the cuffed hands of the man who had constricted the policeman's throat. He had big forearms and was solidly built. He was truly sorry, but couldn't turn back time. For the past six years, he was imprisoned in Taza and now wanted to spend some time in another jail.

"I needed a change," he said with a joyless laugh. His "stop" was the prison in the city of Meknes. We wished each other strength as I watched him leaving the bus, trudging.

"A lot of strength to you in your life," I said softly. I knew I would never see him again.

I looked aside and saw a boy staring at me. I nodded to him and looked out the window again.

"Are you from the Netherlands?" he asked in perfect Dutch.

Huh? What was going on? Was this bus number 126 heading toward Breda after all and was all of this no more than a delusion?

"Uh, yeah," I replied in amazement. "How did you know?"

"I heard you speaking Moroccan to that man, but with a clear Dutch accent," the boy smiled. "I'm Jeremy."

"Joseph."

The usual hand shaking was disregarded because of our limited "freedom of hands". When I saw Jeremy, I thought he was Moroccan, but he was of Brazilian origin. That explained his tinted look. He was athletic, with small twinkling eyes and a shaved head, except for a little tuft on his forehead. Jeremy was twenty-eight years old. He was caught with fifty-five pounds of hashish – surprisingly – and was sentenced to two years in prison. He came from the prison of Nador and was also on his way to Salé.

Cool guy, this Jeremy, I thought along the way. Not very clever, but that didn't bother me. I even found it funny how he would respond to certain things. Jeremy was astounded when I told him about "my" eight tons of hashish.

"Wow, were you trying to get the entire population of the Netherlands high? Eight tons!"

Before I could defend myself, he continued. "If you'd succeeded, you would have been set up for life! How much would you have gotten for the job?"

"Five million," I said dryly. I decided to play along with the game.

Jeremy was astounded even more as I watched him counting.

"Five million," he sighed, imagining himself as a famous rapper in a pimped out limo with twenty hot, champagne-drinking ladies around him.

"Jerem... Jeremy!" I pulled him out of his daydream. "Those drugs weren't mine."

"What?"

"Honestly, I knew nothing about those eight tons."

Jeremy looked at me in disbelief. It was a look I had seen quite often.

I started to tell my story...

"And they gave you ten years?" he asked in disbelief. "That's insane, man!"

"Yes, you could say that 'insane' is an understatement..."

We talked the rest of the trip, while the bus was getting empty and the sky outside turned dark.

We almost forgot we were prisoners being transported.

64

It was Friday night around nine o'clock as we arrived at the prison of Salé, our final destination.

Jeremy and I sat with our nose pressed against the window so we could see our new home as best as possible. The walls, perhaps forty feet high, came slowly toward us as the bus drove gradually through an immense looking passage. High at the prison corner, I could see an illuminated tower, with the black silhouette giving away the presence of an armed guard.

The bus stopped. It hissed loudly when the driver turned off the engine. The fierce roaring suddenly disappeared into a deep silence. Jeremy and I looked at each other motionless.

There we were.

There were only six of us left on the bus. The barred cage was opened and we were ordered to stand up and walk out calmly.

We obediently complied.

I walked ahead and got out of the bus first. While feeling the sultry summer heat on my face, I looked around, puzzled. I blinked a few times with my eyes, because the air was really dry. It was perfect weather to sit on a terrace at the Market Place back home in Breda, drinking a cold Red Bull.

We were surrounded by high walls and long paths lined with plants and palm trees. I saw barbed wire, lots of barbed wire. It was attached on top of the walls, on the sides of the walls, on the roofs. Everywhere I looked these spiky irons hatefully welcomed us. The local construction store must have had a sale: "Barbed Wire. Buy One. Get Four Free."

The prison complex was established very systematically. It reminded me of the pink building of the Zaio prison, with a similar structure. But compared to this, Zaio looked more like a little Barbie prison.

With my mouth still hanging half-open, observing the environment, my handcuffs were taken off. Jeremy too was amazed by the immensity of this storage depot for criminals. It was fascinating and frightening all at the same time.

Where of all places am I now? I wondered. I didn't know yet, but this weekend would become one of the worst weekends of my life.

65

The two bus guards assigned our group to three prison guards. They turned and got back in the bus. The driver started the engine and drove backwards through the prison gate. These men had done their work for today.

The prison guards then brought us inside the building.

I dragged my bags and rolo with difficulty, just like Jeremy and the other guys. We were exhausted after one hell of a trip without any food or water. After being guided through two barred doors, we arrived in the "reception hallway". This hallway alone was as large as the two courtyards in the prison of Berkane.

The prison guards ordered us to take off our shoes and socks and hand them over. They were searched thoroughly. The soles were removed and our socks were turned inside out. Our coats were taken and inspected rigorously as well. Then, they frisked our bodies from top to bottom.

I gritted my teeth and tightened my jaw muscles when I felt their searching hands between my legs. One of the guys had hidden some money in his underpants and was caught. I saw the four hundred dirham quickly disappear in the guard's back pocket.

"Please..." I heard the boy begging. "It's all I have."

"It's either this or isolation!" the guard shouted at him, brandishing his hand.

The boy cringed and kept quiet.

Then they searched our bags. I told the guard, who was searching my bag quite roughly, that I had nothing that wasn't allowed.

"We decide what is allowed and what is not!" he snapped.

All the bags were completely emptied. The guard ostentatiously held my discman and CDs in his hands. He didn't say anything, but it was clear to me that he would forbid them unless I gave him the two packs of Marlboro cigarettes I had in my bag. He looked at them eagerly. Soufian gave me those packs. "You'll probably need those to pay off some jerk of a guard," he told me just before I left. He was right.

I nodded to the guard that he could take the packs. He looked around nervously. I followed his eyes into the room and saw how the other two guards were greedily rummaging through the bags of Jeremy and the others. "Coast clear" the guard must have thought, as he rapidly took the cigarettes from my bag and put them in the pocket of his uniform. Then the guard grabbed my mail bag and quickly went through it. He grabbed one of the notebooks in which I kept my diary and I automatically tried to take it from him. The guard looked at me with a mean grin and, while flipping through it, he asked what kind of notebook this was. Somewhat embarrassed, I looked down and told him that it was my diary. The guard laughed mockingly.

What are you laughing at, man? I thought.

"Hmpf," the guard snorted, as he disrespectfully threw my diary on the ground. At that time, I would have loved to give this guy a good kick between his legs. Bastard.

He paid no further attention to it. Apparently he was satisfied with his loot of the two packs of cigarettes.

My belongings were everywhere on the ground and I had to pack everything again myself. I really hated this.

When everything was packed again, we were ordered to wait in front of a barred door that led to a courtyard. A courtyard, surrounded by dimly lit cells.

Our new home...

66

For half an hour we waited at the barred door. Our legs were tired. Finally, two guards on the other side opened the door. We walked over to the courtyard and I looked around. I could see seven different cells, and behind the barred doors I saw numerous bunks and people. Here too, the roof was lined with barbed wire. The prison boss was apparently afraid of people attempting to escape.

We were guided to a dark cell. The cell door opened with the familiar click-clack sound. One of the guards switched on the light next to the door. We were looking into a musty room with an open toilet in its corner. The room was empty, except for some trash, papers, banana peels and apple cores. The only residents were a few big cockroaches.

We had to stay here until we were called. Our question as to when that would be, was answered with a shrug.

The cell door was shut with a loud metal bang. Another sound that didn't surprise me anymore. It just seemed to become normal.

There we stood in our cell, awkward and uncomfortable, looking around. It turned out to be the gathering, or distribution cell, also known as the "rookie space". In this cell, the rookies were placed to await their registration with the prison administration and subsequent placement in a particular department. Few rookies in here, I thought, looking at our group of six, not knowing we were the first ones that weekend.

We swept the dirty concrete floor with a few newspapers from one of the guys, cleaning up the place where we would lay down our rolos.

As Jeremy and I were starving and very thirsty, we took out our ration. We sat down, cross-legged on our rolos, and laid everything out in front of us. I had mineral water, cheese, bread and yogurt drinks. Jeremy had lemonade, cookies, chocolate and crisps.

"Is that all you live on?" I teased Jeremy.

"No, your baguette will do, right?" Jeremy said laughing, as he swung my flabby baguette around like a sword.

"Alright, Zorro, at least it's healthier than what you have."

I snatched my baguette back and tore it into unequal parts – not on purpose. I looked at the two pieces and I gave the shortest one to Jeremy – on purpose. Jeremy first looked at my longer piece of bread and then he looked at me.

"Hey, my piece is smaller!" he almost cried.

I gave him the widest smile I could give. I didn't say anything.

"Okay, okay, no problem," Jeremy said. "But less chocolate for y–"

"No problem!" I said, even before he could finish his sentence. I attacked the cheese and opened a yogurt drink at the same time while grabbing one of Jeremy's cookies.

We ate greedily.

Jeremy and I shared our experiences about the body searches by those bastard guards. We talked with our mouths full as he grinned about the fact that they hadn't found his money.

"Where did you hide it then?" I mumbled with my mouth stuffed.

"In my butt crack," he said. He laughed while chocolate chips flew from his mouth.

I almost choked. "Ugh man, gross! I am eating!"

"You asked me where it was hidden."

"Yeah right, just spare me the details."

We stopped chewing for a second and looked at each other. Then we both started laughing again and continued eating.

Afterwards, I burped loudly. A bad habit that I couldn't get rid of. Jeremy looked at me with his eyes wide-open.

"What?" I asked while stretching my arms.

"Nothing," Jeremy laughed and shook his head.

We were preparing for bed.

We were exhausted.

67

The next morning, I heard the cell door being opened with a lot of fuss and shouting. A boy was brought in by a group of guards. He was handcuffed and covered in blood. Around his head was a bandage, hanging half off. He struggled and screamed like a pig that was about to have its throat cut. The guards ripped him over and pushed him into a corner of the cell, commanding him to shut his mouth.

What a nice way to wake up on a Saturday morning.

Jeremy was half awake and I wished him good morning. He moaned, half asleep. I looked around the cell and I saw four more people to my surprise.

Huh?

I rubbed my eyes. They weren't here last night. They must have been brought in while we were sleeping.

The wounded boy cried and muttered for a little longer. Later, a guard and a man in a long white coat took him away.

Instead of the injured boy, we got four new ones. I nudged Jeremy, who had fallen asleep again, and told him about the extra visitors. He mumbled something, rubbed his nose with his knuckles like toddlers do, and leaned on his elbows to see what was happening in our little territory.

"Wow, you look like crap," I said.

With one eye half open and the other still closed, he gazed up at me, let out a deep sigh and fell back onto his back.

"Ha-ha, you look like you haven't slept in three years!" I joked.

"No, you are looking handsome," he answered. He had buried his head in his blankets, so his voice was muffled.

"I'm going to ask the guards when we can leave this cell."

Jeremy stayed quiet.

I put my glasses on, which I had worn since the day of my "arrest", fixed my grown hair a little and stepped up to the guards. I was quickly sent back with a short "not yet" answer. Great.

I felt my stomach growling again, wondering when and what we would eat. Yesterday we had eaten almost everything, because we assumed that the next morning we would be put in a normal cell. I had digested the cheese baguette and later, after I had used the toilet, it was as if it never existed. I shook Jeremy awake.

"Do you have anything left over from yesterday?"

Jeremy groaned deeply again. "What?"

"Do you have anything left to eat from yesterday? I'm hungry."

I felt like my oldest little brother, Amir, who during our sleepovers, very early in the morning, would stand by my bedside begging for food and games.

"I think maybe some cookies and lemonade," Jeremy mumbled vaguely.

I searched his bag and ate the remaining cookies.

"Want some too?" I asked, with crumbs flying out of my mouth.

No answer.

Okay, have it your way, and I ate everything myself.

Just like Jeremy, I tried to go back to sleep, but I couldn't. Instead, I grabbed my bag with my mail and started marking post cards and letters. On each card, I marked phrases and words that made me feel good.

"If I could give the world to someone, it would be you, my friend. This letter will leave its mark on me too. Joseph, know that I have tears in my eyes while writing this." – Edward

"You understand now, better than we ever will, that there's nothing like freedom. Together with you, we keep on looking forward to that moment. Be patient and rely on yourself." – Frans and Henny

"Keep on hoping and believing. We know it's not easy after all of these setbacks, but cheer up. We sympathize with you every day and keep you in our daily prayers." – Danny and Barbara

"I'm so sorry that you can't be at my birthday. I miss you terribly. Amber came home today and said she'd spoken to you. She was so happy." – Molly

"I'm proud of you and the fact that you are able to manage this nightmare and those living conditions. You are strong, keep believing in that. Hang in there, strong man. You have my admiration. I love you and in our minds, we will always be together." – Amber

68

The cell was starting to get crowded, eight more people had already come in making things less than favorable, and they kept coming. The growling from my stomach was becoming louder. Jeremy was still snoring. Apparently, it didn't bother him. I kept myself busy with my letters, but I began to wonder what might happen as the cell continued to fill up. The first fight had already broken out after a few arguments. The guards kept telling us that it wasn't our turn yet to be assigned. Through the bars, I asked one of them if we could have some food. He nodded gruffly but a little later, two plantos appeared with a large iron pan and a basket full of bread. Like vultures, the inmates were hanging around the pan, pushing each other. I tapped Jeremy quickly and asked him if he had anything to put some food in.

"Hurry, hurry, before they leave!" I said hastily.

Jeremy, still groggy from sleeping, was moving slower than a sluggard toward his luggage, and pulled out a plastic Tupperware tray where we kept the chocolate.

How stupid of me; the cookie container was sitting right next to my rolo! Jumping up, I snatched the Tupperware tray out of Jeremy's hands, grabbed the empty cookie container, and quickly ran toward the hungry mob. I squeezed myself between them with a tray in each hand. My trays were unrecognizable among the others. The plantos generously slammed the gunk onto the various trays with a large wooden spoon. I could feel how my trays were filled up. I also felt that the food was overflowing onto my hands. I took my trays and walked back to the other planto who handed me two loaves of bread, which I clutched under my right arm.

Carefully balancing the overflowing trays with my messy hands, I moved over to Jeremy who now was sitting upright. He took the trays and the bread from me. I wanted to wash my hands at the toilet sink, but found myself waiting endlessly for a dirty, smelly man. From a distance, I saw Jeremy's face as he was examining the contents of the trays. The yellow filth, they referred to as food, looked like some sort mixture of white beans with pieces of carrot and potato. Then I saw Jeremy, testing the bread like a caveman, hitting it on his head and then biting into it.

"Do we really have to eat this?" he asked blankly, as I walked up with my hands dripping.

"Uh, I guess so," I said.

It didn't matter what I had to eat, as long as I could eat it. But that was easier said than done. We dipped the hard crust into the mash of "white beans-with-carrot-with potato-with something else" and chewed the food excessively slow, swallowing it with difficulty. We filled our empty bottles with tap water to try and rinse the taste out of our mouths. But the water tasted like chlorine, which didn't make things any better.

I was in a bad mood because of the food we had just consumed. It hadn't satisfied my hunger at all. Not a pleasant start in this great prison of Salé.

I could no longer hide in the sounds of my discman either – the batteries were dead – and the people just kept coming. By evening, we were crammed together with at least forty men. There's no more room for more, I thought, but the guards thought otherwise. The people who came in now, were standing at the cell door for a while because there was simply no place to put their things down. No one moved because everyone wanted to defend his own spot as much as possible. Many anthropologists could draw interesting conclusions about human behavior in these types of situations. I noticed that, at times like this, people aren't so different from animals. Jeremy and I were no different. We already had to give up a good part of our spot and there wasn't much room left. Regardless, the guards were still giving us orders on how we had to organize our spots.

The cell became so filled that Jeremy and I struggled to get around the people just to get to the toilet. Every time the plantos returned with more food, things would get a little crazy. Jeremy and I got our mash in turn, and every time, we bravely started to eat as if it was the first time, but it was just too disgusting. It smelled and tasted so sour that we occasionally gagged. We ate it, just to fill our stomachs.

That Saturday night, Jeremy and I slept back to back, surrounded by strangers who were packed against each other just as closely. But very little sleep was found. There was constant noise, shouting, and quarreling. At some point, the guards stopped organizing the spots and left us to our fate. Just when I thought things couldn't get any worse the inevitable happened.

69

Just like the people at the front of the audience at a concert, we are standing and sitting pressed together. Every time the guards come in with new inmates, the men in the cell begin shouting that there is no more room.

"How can you do this!"

"If there's more, we're coming after you!"

"Fuck those people!"

"We'll kill them!"

The threats do nothing, the guards keep coming.

Jeremy and I can do little, other than sitting and sometimes standing to stretch our legs. We have no choice! We have nothing to do and nowhere to go.

Time passes slower than ever.

Saturday is obviously the night to go out, because in the night from Saturday to Sunday morning, the guards mostly bring in people that are half drunk.

On Sundays I'm half awake, half asleep, and slightly delirious.

In a kind of delirium, I begin to hear more people in the cell speaking Dutch and I immediately think of home. But I'm not home. I am very far away from home. Far away from the safe world that I once knew.

I feel weak, dirty, skinny and sick. Jeremy is also exhausted. It baffles me, how fast a human body deteriorates without sleep and healthy food.

In the cell, there is constant pushing and pulling. The arguments continue with verbal abuse and every now and then a slap, as the tension increases...

And then it happens.

I'm not sure how it started, but a massive brawl breaks out. The screaming I hear is demonic!

I look around the room to find people that seem to be possessed. What we see is terrible. Inmates are pulling out razors and other sharp objects to attack each other. Jeremy and I are scared to the bone and back away.

People are stabbed and ripped apart, in the face, neck, arms, legs and stomach. Whatever the mad inmates can reach, they stab. Blood was everywhere!

Dozens of people are standing at the cell door screaming at the guards, but they won't come. Jeremy and I are terrified and press ourselves flat against the wall of the cell. I don't think I've ever been so scared until now, and I'm afraid that Jeremy and I will be stabbed next.

Just then, a guard unit with batons and shotguns rushes inside.

They smash into the rioters and handcuff them. Anyone who dares to say anything gets a beating.

Jeremy and I don't move, we stand side by side glued to the wall, wishing we could disappear through to the other side. We don't budge until calm has returned to the cell.

The seriously injured are immediately taken away and won't come back. Those with lighter injuries are taken later and return after treatment.

On Sunday night, everyone looks confused. Even with the rioters gone, the cell is still crowded. No one is bothering to remove the dried blood on the floor or walls. Some are still covered in blood, their clothing and bodies stained red, but look ahead indifferently.

Jeremy and I use our bags and belongings to sit on as we lean against the wall, with our knees bent. More and more, we fall over from exhaustion into the weirdest sleeping positions, only to wake up scared when we hear someone scream. We are constantly afraid that another huge fight is about to break out.

How we all sit and stand here could earn a World Press Photo award.

But then, on Monday morning, the cell door suddenly opens up and we are called for one by one. A sigh of relief and excitement passes through the cell. Finally!

I tap Jeremy, who is lying again in one of his impossible monkey-like positions.

Does that dude have any bones? I wonder, looking at him with my head sideways. Drool is running out of his folded mouth. He looks ahead, dazed as I wake him up. His eyeballs searching incessantly for the right direction as they finally focus on me.

"We are getting out, we are getting out!" I say and grab Jeremy's shoulders.

Jeremy puts his hands on mine.

"Really?"

"Yes, we can finally get out of here!"
I can't remember ever being so happy to leave a place.

70

Arranged in rows of two, we walked slowly across the courtyard, through the large reception and into another courtyard. It was a large area with a basketball court and a beautifully landscaped garden with palm trees, lemon trees and a remarkable number of red flowers. It was surrounded by wide covered pathways, leading to the different building departments.

The sunlight stung my eyes. Although I was overwhelmed by tiredness, the beauty of nature in the middle of this concrete complex gave me a nice, calm feeling.

"It's going to be okay," I said to Jeremy. "In a moment we will have a place of our own. We'll be able to sleep and eat normally with our cellmates."

Jeremy and I were directed to two guards sitting behind a table in the middle of the path. Over the weekend, the guys from our cell suggested to us several times to ask for Section A. Apparently this was the department for European prisoners, where the conditions were much better than in "Colombian Morocco" as the other departments were called. That name was probably conceived because of the reputation of those sections. They were as bad as the prisons in Colombia.

We begged the guards to send us to Section A, but when they heard we were Dutch, they looked at us sarcastically. First, they assigned us our jail number – Jeremy 12358, me 12359 – and then we heard which section we were assigned to; Jeremy to Section B and I to Section D.

Move! To *Colombian Morocco!*

We pleaded with the guards one last time to send us to Section

A, but they were already busy with two other inmates and ignored us. They had probably already forgotten that we even existed.

Plantos escorted us to our assigned sections. Jeremy walked in front of me, and before we could even say goodbye to each other, he was dragged into the stream of people entering his section. That was the last time I would see Jeremy.

I was alone again.

Inmates started to bump into me. I felt uncertain as I looked around with my luggage in my hands. The planto walked through the barred gate of Section D and waved at me, but what I saw there made me start worrying all over again.

71

Slowly, I entered the section, dragging my luggage with me. There I stood, staring down a long dark hallway with cell blocks on one side and a wall on the other. There was a hallway in front of me and to my left that formed the section's L-shape, and also provided access to the patio and a staircase to the first floor. The section reminded me of a school, one that was totally impoverished or forgotten.

Like the streets of a busy market, countless people were walking past each other. They were laughing, shouting, smoking, belching, spitting and glancing defyingly at each other as they walked by. Against the walls, people were sitting, playing cards, checkers or just hanging around. There was a deep penetrating smell. It was a tepid, indescribable mix of old sweat, waste bins, piss, cat feces, hashish and cigarettes. No one seemed to mind.

This can't be it? This can't be the prison they were talking about?

"Paradise among the Moroccan prisons."

Talk about euphemisms! Fuck.

The section leader sent me to cell sixteen on the first floor, after thoroughly examining me from head to toe and waving me away. I zigzagged up the crowded stairs. People were literally everywhere, somehow, I noticed that there was something different about them. They had a kind of look about them that was almost inhuman, as if they had no souls, as if they weren't people at all, just a carcass that seemed to be moving. They looked like zombies! But why? I couldn't understand what made me take notice all of a sudden. Maybe it was because I hadn't slept in days and my mind was playing tricks on me?

The planto walked ahead of me, wearing my backpack and holding one of my bags in his right hand. This was all normal to him, but I couldn't stop staring. I had never experienced anything like this before, those hollow and empty gazes that stared back at me from the cells as I passed them by. With every step I took, my heart sank further into my boots. All I could hear were the voices of those people who told me how wonderful it was to be here. But it was just a lie, this place was a pigsty!

All the cells were square and of equal size, about twenty-three by twenty-three feet. The cells had a toilet at the entrance, and small barred windows at the top of one of the walls. Each cell was filled with bunk beds standing close to each other. Just as in the other prisons, the walls were a collage of dirty spots, smudges, words and hanging bags. The floors were soggy, and cockroaches as big as mice were crawling around. The cells were overcrowded, but this was nothing new. It was perfectly normal here.

When I entered cell sixteen, the planto and I laid my things in the aisle between the bunks. He then looked at me, begging, and asking for cigarettes or something to eat.

"Sorry, but I have nothing," I said arduously. I was mad that I couldn't give the boy anything. He had helped me. I promised to make it up to him later, but he was obviously offended. He probably had heard countless empty promises from other prisoners. I truly meant to make it up, but convincing a senior citizen that Santa Claus really exists would have been easier. The boy angrily turned around and left me, alone. I said nothing. I sat down on my rolo with my hands in my hair. It was rather quiet in the cell compared to what I had experienced.

"Where you from?" someone suddenly asked after a few minutes of silence.

I turned to see a man with a mustache and a tired look, sitting at ease, rolling a large joint. With steady hands, he moistened the edge of the double paper with his tongue and gave the hash pipe a finishing touch by sealing the end of the paper with a twist. I was surprised when he didn't light the "cigarette". He pulled out a tin tray and gently placed the object inside, next to many other prepared, sizeable joints. They were for sale. The man then lit an ordinary Marlboro cigarette.

"Where you from?" he repeated his question calmly as he blew out the smoke from his first puff. Through the pungent cigarette smoke, he narrowed his eyes slightly.

I was startled, still half-awake in my never ending state of exhaustion.

"The rookie space… Uh, I mean, from Taza jail," I corrected myself quickly to let him know that I was anything but a rookie.

"Taza?" sounded from a bunk. A thin man with a mustache and a remarkable angular nose turned sideways on his bed to sit up.

In all the cells the bunks were placed parallel to each other, but in here, they had created a kind of nook, with a low table in the middle.

"Yeah, that's right," I said. "Taza. And before that, I was in Berkane."

"How is Taza these days? Is that bald guard Said still there?" the thin man asked.

"Uh, well, I didn't like it. And yes, I think Said still works there."

The man looked ahead, nodding.

"Why?" I asked.

"Oh nothing, I was there for four years. From 1999 to 2003." For a moment, it was quiet. "Why did you go to jail? You're not from Morocco, right?"

"No. The Netherlands."

People were giggling.

"Then you're in jail for hash?"

I sighed in annoyance, the stereotypical image of the Netherlands as a soft drugs filled country was confirmed for the umpteenth time.

"Yes, that's right," I said. "For eight tons," I said normally, completely accustomed to talking about this huge amount.

The joint maker suddenly looked up from his newly rolled leisure cigarette that seemed even bigger than the last one.

"Eight tons?!" The narrow man with the angled nose laughed. "Did you hear that, Kabran?"

The joint broker smiled for a moment. I now understood, he was the leader of the cell.

"My name is Khalid," the thin man introduced himself. "But forget that name, everyone calls me Satan."

Satan? What kind of nickname was that?

But now that he mentioned it, he looked a little like the stereotypical image of the red creature, armed with trident. His nickname had become as normal to him as the eight tons of hashish to me, so I understood. I never found out the name of the leader of the cell. Everyone called him "Kabran", even the guards. He had a certain kind of authority or charisma about him, which explained the respect he got from the prisoners and guards.

Kabran was a man of little words, but he had a lot of business with drugs. Through the prison guards, among others, he had hashish slices delivered daily to the cell, which were then cut into small triangles and sold like hot cakes for an average of fifty dirham a piece. Part of it was also used in the pre-rolled joints.

Satan handed me a small stool and invited me to come closer and sit at the table.

"Tea?"

"Yes, please."

I wanted to tell my story, but didn't get the chance. Nor did I have to mention that I was sentenced to ten years. They already knew from experience. Satan and Kabran were old hands at the section. They both came from the city of Ketema.

"Where's that? Ketema?" I asked.

For a moment, it was quiet. Very quiet. Satan and Kabran looked at each other in surprise.

"Wait a minute, you were caught with eight tons of chocolate[7] and you don't know where Ketema is?" Satan asked. He looked at me in disbelief.

I looked up from my cup of tea I had just sipped. The tea was far too sweet again. Why did they have so much sugar in it?

I looked at Satan and Kabran and didn't know how to answer them.

I looked at Satan and Kabran and didn't know how to answer them. In the two hashish experts' eyes, I could tell that asking where Ketema was, was a stupid question. Here I made a clean breast of it.

They could tell by the unsullied clown expression on my face that I really didn't know. They explained it to me and told me what the place was known for. From their story, I could tell that Ketema was the center of the hashish world.

There, they were given hashish from the proverbial "mother's milk". Toddlers were able to identify the quality of it based on the smell alone, and instead of a lollipop as a reward for good behavior, they got a piece of "space cake".

---

7. Chocolate, as the hashish dealers often called their "product".

"Oh," I said, wondering why I had never heard of it, when apparently it was a world famous city.

After that, they let me tell my story, since they were obviously dealing with an ignorant kid instead of a drug lord. The big drawback to this was that my respect plummeted tremendously. This was no Godfather standing in front of them, but an ordinary, average guy, called Joseph, IT engineer, who got an offer to work in Morocco and was thrown in the pen because of false accusations.

Despite my reduced status, Satan and Kabran still seemed to respect me. They knew all too well how the justice system did "business" here and could tell by my attitude and mannerisms that I didn't belong here. As the conversation progressed, they could tell I was about to collapse from a lack of sleep. Kabran said that I could rest a bit on top of his bunk. I gratefully accepted his offer and I think it took less than five seconds before I was in the Land of Nod.

72

I awoke. The world looked blurry through my eyes.

My glasses! I panicked slightly.

I knew that I had forgotten to take them off before I went to sleep. I looked down and saw Satan and Kabran with a couple of the other guys eating from a large plate. It was dark outside and the cell was filled with people. I noticed that they were being rather quiet. They talked, walked, said their prayers, played and cooked with composure. Apparently, Kabran didn't tolerate noise and that was respected by the others.

"Kabran? Kabran?" I asked in a low voice leaning down. Without taking his eyes from the plate of food, he grabbed my glasses from his bed with his left hand, and in one smooth motion, handed them over to me. Relieved, I put my glasses on. Everything was in focus again. Blind mole that I am.

Satan had a guy bringing me a plate of food and a piece of bread to the bunk. Real food! On the plate was a piece of beef, some potatoes, and vegetables that were dipped in an oily sauce. "Mrka" they called it in Moroccan cuisine. It was the best thing I had eaten in weeks. Satan smiled at me and said: "Bon appétit."

After dinner, everyone had to return to their bunks, because it was time for the daily cleaning and the floor had to be mopped.

Satan and Kabran arranged everything quietly. They were assisted by some drudges, who, like a well-oiled machine, made dinner, washed the dishes – in the toilet for that matter – and ordered the cellmates to make room for the clean-up operation.

After cleaning, the sleeping spots on the ground were arranged. Quite an undertaking, twenty-one people sleeping on the floor in the typical sardine-style manner. All in all, there were fifty-one men sleeping in the cell!

The Kabran told the helpers to save a special place on the floor for me. My rolo was now placed at the bedside of Kabran and his group. Finally, I was lying without someone else's body against me. It could have been a great deal worse.

73

At night, I would still wake up often. In Taza, the rats kept me company, here, the cockroaches marched around in quantities that seemed greater than the entire Chinese population. Killing them wasn't an option, because that would be too much of a mess. The most annoying thing was that they were constantly climbing from my feet into my pant legs. But I quickly found a solution: socks. I put the socks on and stuffed each end of the pant legs inside them so that my legs were sealed. I had rather have my legs and feet drenched in sweat, then endure the tickling and biting of those creatures – yes, those creatures bite, and they left spots that were itchier than mosquito bites!

People would watch TV well into the morning hours, talking and smoking, and smoking. And smoking. Thick fogs from the cigarettes and joints were clouding around me. Entire hashish slices were consumed like gingerbread.

In the morning, the roll call was carried out loudly. Just as in the other prisons, the guards would shout and demand respect and we had to be present. The helpers of the guards were beating on the walls, cell doors and aluminum safes. Now I understood why the safes in the hallway, which were out of use, were extremely dented. The first time during roll call, I stood up, assuming that it was required, but I quickly noticed that I was the only one standing. While they were lying, they just raised their hand, still stoned on the drugs of the previous night. It was tolerated and I quickly sat down again. After roll call, me and the other guys who were sleeping on the ground had to clean up our rolos. The rolos were usually put it in the hallway, but Kabran allowed me to leave mine in the cell.

After roll call, I was usually still tired, but during the daytime I was allowed to sleep near Kabran's bunk, as long as the owner of that spot would approve.

Apart from the hashish, there was little to do compared to Taza. From an early age, I really hated cigarettes, not to mention drugs. So there was really nothing for me to do. Much to my frustration, I wasn't allowed to use the phone to call. There were no pay-phones in our section. "These are only in Section A," I was told.

"Section A, how do I get to Section A?" I asked several times, but no one had an answer. It seemed an impossible place to reach. They talked about it as if it was the mythical, legendary island of Avalon.

They had special "jammer" stations scattered around the prison roof that were blocking the GSM signal, making it difficult for the prisoners to make cell phone calls. The jammers were elongated masts about six feet high and ten inches wide.

How do I call home now?

The section leader had a brilliant plan. I had to give him my home phone number, so he would call and notify my mom from his own phone.

"Does she speak French?" he asked.

"Yes," I said proudly. My mom was never called.

During my days at Section D, I somehow turned out to be lost to the outside world. Later, I found out that everyone at home was worried sick. In the prison of Taza, my mom was told that I was gone, and in Salé, they claimed to have never heard of anyone named "Joseph Oubelkas"!

So technically, I was "missing".

Meanwhile, here I was, wandering around in the dark smelly hallways and the crowded courtyard of Section D, in the finest prison of Morocco.

I was so distraught about not being able to call, that I even longed to return to Taza. Back there, at least I had contact with home regularly. I thought of my friends Soufian, Karim and Chief Nordin. Here, I had no one. Well okay, I had Satan. And Kabran. But they were completely lost in their world of hashish. A kind of "Hassan and the Hash Factory" as a take on "Charlie and the Chocolate Factory" came to mind. All these guys really did was talk about hashish.

Kabran relentlessly rolled his joints undisturbed, and Satan just couldn't say enough about how "crazy cool" it was to live in Ketema.

I didn't give a damn. All I could think about was my home.

The heat was really bad. Heat waves to people in prison are about as horrible as to polar bears on the North Pole. I thought of the people at the beach, who were jumping across the TV in the news, happier than school children on summer vacation. I began to imagine the beach at home during summer time, and therefore immediately picturing Amber in a bikini. I envisioned a scene of her as she walked up to me with two melting ice cream cones in her hands. My life seemed without worries. So normal. Things were quite different now. Thankfully, Amber couldn't see me now. I was skin and bones, pale, smelly, unshaven, had medium length tangled hair, glasses.

During airtime, hundreds of people would walk around the courtyard in large circles. I walked there between them, absentmindedly, as if I was part of a thoughtless herd.

My body was moving, but my spirit was somewhere else. Far, far away from here. I was no more than a shadow of my former self, and now I understood why there were so many people here with hollow eyes.

74

MAIL!

For two long weeks, I felt lonely and forgotten. Apparently, the prison administration had "found" me again. I experienced déjà vu. It was as if I received mail for the very first time back in Berkane prison. I was picked out by a planto who had a note that apparently had my name on it. He showed me, but the Arabic lettering was meaningless to me.

"Yes, that's me!" I told the planto, making him believe that I could obviously read it.

"Okay, follow me," the little guy said.

I walked behind him and wondered if it was a requirement to be short in order to register as a planto. Every one of them that escorted me was small and "Smurf" like. The only things they were missing were a white hat and a hopping gait. "Come then, we'll *smurf* your mail!" I expected them to say at any time.

It was a refreshing walk. Finally outside of the section, I walked through the large landscaped garden and into the reception hallway, where I was then guided upstairs to the administration office. In the office area, I noticed a huge mess of paperwork in the closets behind the officials' empty desks. It's no wonder data was lost here. I saw yellow folders, books and messy stacked files everywhere. Life on Mars would be easier to find than a simple name in this mess of papers.

But no one seemed to care.

Neither did I at that moment.

My mail! That's what this was about. It was an envelope containing the car magazine *Top Gear* and a game magazine. There was also a letter from William, a letter from Amber, a number of other friends, and from my mom! I was ecstatic. Super happy! The entire day, I was walking around the section with a smile from ear to ear. Satan and Kabran must have thought I discovered some new kind of drugs with the joker smile I had on my face.

I read the magazines immediately and kept the letters sealed until later that night, like a special dessert, something to look forward to. They contained the very welcome words of "hold on", "many greetings from" and "we think of you" again. Amber wrote about how much she missed and loved me and how she hoped that I would be home this Christmas. William said that he was working, gaming, chilling and eating take-out food, "but it wasn't the same" without me there. Fouza wrote that my brothers thought it had been long enough with my job here, and that it was time to stop and come home. And my mom wrote about her love for her only child:

"It's a full moon now, and all the silver streams of that same moon that shines there too, will carry my love for my brave child, and will

spin a beautiful dream of what is to come later, the time when you will be with us again."

75

The mail got me through the next couple of days.

I was peeing, when suddenly, out of nowhere, another planto Smurf jumped up from behind me and yelled my name. Cautiously, I turned around, afraid to dribble on my shoes. Normally I pulled the dirty green sheet curtain- which served as a door - to close behind me, but someone behind me was doing the dishes at the tap. The planto was looking straight at me, my pants half down, when I told him I was coming down. I buttoned up, turned around, stepped over the crouching boy who was doing the dishes, and thanked him. "No problem!" he said, as if it was the most natural thing in the world to urinate and wash dishes in the same small space. I wasn't surprised at anything anymore and quickly got used to the mess I was now living in. The cockroaches, the smell, the filth, the expressionless people with their hollow eyes... I refused to succumb to my surroundings. I kept my head up with all the support and love coming from home. I wasn't alone and would never be alone again. I knew that I had to represent myself and all those who did their utmost to get me out of here. All those people who were convinced of my innocence. All those people who really knew me. I refused to walk around here like a miserable man!

I thought the planto came to get me for my mail, but the burly Smurf – he was small and wide – said I had visitors.

Visitors?

Who? What? Where?

The planto didn't know.

I quickly changed T-shirts and put some water through my

hair as I ran my tongue over my teeth. They felt clean. I looked down and tugged on my clothes trying to smooth them out.

Who will it be?

My mom?

No, impossible.

The lawyer?

No, certainly not, because I was escorted to the visitors hallway. The hallway was so large that Lenny Kravitz himself would be able to hold a concert.

After a quick pat-down by the visitors area guards, the planto left me. It felt like I had walked into the arrivals section of an airport. Groups of people stood or sat behind a fence about ten yards away. I walked without knowing who to look for and waited for a sign or a wave from someone who might recognize me. I honestly didn't expect someone to be standing there with a banner or a sign with my name on it. Sure would have been easier though.

I scanned the faces of all the visitors.

Who would have come here for me?

And then I saw an outstretched arm that was attached to a familiar silhouette, one that looked a lot like an uncle of mine. Uncle Samir! It was him! My favorite uncle!

When I was a kid, during summer holidays in Morocco, he always took me to the beach – not even six miles away from this prison – where we played soccer until the sun went down. Before we went home, we always bought a Fanta lemonade and a fried sausage sandwich from a street stall. Uncle Samir always put me on his shoulders. I even slept in his room and we got up together every morning. I had wonderful memories of him that I cherished.

"Joseph!" uncle Samir waved with a smile. It was still the same smile I remembered.

"Uncle Samir!" I waved back and walked up to him.

We hugged each other, exchanged four kisses on the cheek, as is common in a greeting between men in Morocco, and looked at each other. By now, I was half a head taller than my uncle. Little boys grow up. I wouldn't dare jump on Samir's neck now. It would also look a little weird, two adult men in the visitors hallway playing like children riding a horse.

We were talking, half in French, half in Moroccan, about how everything was, what we had done lately and about the family. Then suddenly, my uncle said something important. He made a face like he was just about to tell me one of his biggest secrets, and leaned over the table. His nose almost touched mine.

"When you go back after this visit, you should try to talk to Bin Abdi."

"Bin Abdi? You mean Chief Bin Abdi?" I asked surprised.

"Yes, him. Tell him about me, he knows me very well. We used to play a lot of soccer together."

"Oh? Are you serious? Cool, okay, I'll pass it on."

Uncle Samir nodded satisfied and went right back to talking. I looked at him proudly knowing he was friends with the second most important person in this prison. This would certainly help my cause. I knew now that everything in Morocco was about money and connections.

Uncle Samir and I talked for the entire visiting hour, until a siren went off loudly. It shocked me. It was as if a bomb was activated, so loud. I almost hid under the table. I often heard this sound screaming from a distance from my section, and now I knew where it came from.

We said goodbye to each other and just before he got out of sight, he mouthed once more in an exaggerated way: "Bin Abdi." I read his lips, nodded and gave him the thumbs up.

76

At the exit of the visitors hallway, I joined the row of inmates heading back toward the units. I asked the guard who searched me where I could find Chief Bin Abdi. As he knelt down to search my legs, he answered that Bin Abdi was in his office. The guard looked at me, then looked in the direction of Bin Abdi's office and pointed to indicate the way, diagonally across the basketball court. I began to walk in the direction when in the distance, I saw two uniformed guards accompanied by a man in civil clothes. My guess was that this was Bin Abdi.

"Mr. Bin Abdi?" I asked as kindly – read "humbly" – as possible, to express my position as a prisoner – read "as a man less than a dog".

Three pairs of eyes were staring at me. They must have thought where the hell this piece of scum got the nerve to come up to them so directly.

Silence.

"What do you want?" the uniformed guard to the left of the man in civil clothes asked.

"Could I perhaps speak to Mr. Bin Abdi?"

"Why? What's your problem?" the same guard asked shortly while taking a step forward, as if he was about to push me away. Then the man in civil clothes put his arm in front of the guard. Like a pit bull being put back in place by his boss.

"What is it boy?" asked the man in civil clothes amicably.

"Are you Mr. Bin Abdi? The prison's chief of staff?" I asked. I added the last sentence deliberately to indicate that I recognized his status.

"Yes, that's me," Bin Abdi said, proud as a peacock. He was as tall as me with a dark tan skin, and wore spectacles with golden frames and a neat, beige suit. He had a charismatic and authoritative appearance. I have come to realize that all of these

Moroccan leaders seem to look so charismatic. "I've just come from the visitors room and wanted to say 'hi' from Samir."

"Samir?" Bin Abdi asked as he looked at the guards beside him and me alternately.

Oh, oh, I thought, he doesn't know him. But my uncle wouldn't just make it up?

"Yes, Samir, that's my uncle. He just came to visit me and he asked me specifically to say hi to you."

Bin Abdi frowned for a minute. I looked at him with a questioning look and felt a drop of sweat running down my temple. I was standing in the burning sun, facing the three men who were standing in the shade of the covered pathway.

"Come along," Bin Abdi said and then nodded to the two guards.

Following the chief to his office, I walked past the guard dogs. It was a neat, cool room with a big shiny desk, a TV, fridge and a conference table. In the corner of the office, there was a huge picture of the king displayed in a sparkling golden frame. It was always the same picture. Same protocol.

Bin Abdi took out two glasses and a bottle of cold water from the fridge. He poured one for me, one for himself and then sank back into his big leather armchair. He pointed for me to sit down in a chair at his desk and I thanked him properly.

"So Samir's your uncle?" Bin Abdi suddenly asked informally.

"Yes," I smiled gently.

"Damn good goalkeeper that uncle of yours, did you know that?"

I smiled fully. "Yeah, I know, I used to play soccer with him on the beach."

"Soccer is in his blood," Bin Abdi said, as if he hadn't heard my answer. "We told him he could play at the professional level, but Samir didn't believe enough in himself."

I looked at Bin Abdi with wide eyes, as if I was a grandchild, listening attentively to the stories of his grandfather. He went on for at least ten more minutes about the "Bin Abdi and Samir" soccer adventures. I remained silent.

"Where do you sleep now?" he asked.

My response was delayed as I switched from standby mode to active mode.

"Uh, D, Section D," I said quickly.

"Hmm, Section D." Pause. "You like it there?" Bin Abdi continued, asking the question clearly rhetorically.

"No, not really," I answered shyly, smiling a bit.

"Hmm. Where would you like to go?" he asked rhetorically again, at least it seemed that way to me.

This could be my chance to escape from the dark cave. "I heard that Section A was better," I said, still shy.

"Would you like to go there?"

"Yes, very much, if that's possible."

Bin Abdi swallowed the remaining water in his glass with a single gulp.

"Well, grab your things then, you can go there."

I was so glad that in my mind I was doing somersaults and performing the most complex break-dance moves.

"Thank you very much, Mr. Bin Abdi," I said calmly, but with a smile.

"No problem."

He walked past me out of the office. I quickly finished my glass and ran after him. I saw him talking to one of his guards, who then walked with me to inform the section leader of D that I could grab my stuff and would be moving to A.

As if I had just won a huge victory, my cellmates greeted me and wished me lots of strength in Section A. I said goodbye to Satan, the "joint rolling" Kabran and thanked them extensively for the space, the food and the time together. Satan laughed and congratulated me. Kabran looked at me, smiled and went back to his job.

My belongings were quickly packed and I nearly ran down the stairs.

Away from D and on to A!

This would mark the end of the most difficult and bizarre eight months of my life up until that point. I still held out hope, that one way or another, I would return home soon. But weeks had already become months, and months would eventually become years.

PART II

2005, 2006, 2007, 2008

Be brave and never become resentful. You will only harm yourself then, and others will eventually turn away from you. Of course you can talk about it, but never with great self-pity. Once again, follow the example of the greats, like Mandela, Gandhi and Martin Luther King, who also endured their guiltless captivity. Then Joseph Oubelkas will manage too.

Don't be nervous about the kind of task you will have in life, whatever that may be. Experience your life as a strong man, just like I experience it as a strong woman.

We think of you often, and never forget that a mother's love is everlasting.

Let life come to you, like waves running ashore.

I

"It is very pleasant in the early twilight. A breeze is blowing into the room. There is a beautiful evening sky with delicate colors that promise another beautiful summer day tomorrow. Through the window, it is quite green outside and on the front, you can see the flower-filled terrace. It is so heavenly."

This was the way my mom's letter started, the first one I had received since being moved to cell six of Section A. Her letters often began with a lively description of the weather, so I could envision the seasons slowly passing by.

During my transfer from the Taza prison to the prison of Salé, I had been officially "missing" for two weeks. My mother was worried sick at that time, but afterwards, she resumed writing quickly. *"At this point, I miss you so much!" she wrote. "I'm very curious to see how you look. Skinny I'm sure, but your look, your eyes and your hands will have the same strength."*

My eyes. When my mother speaks about them, I think of her eyes. Her bright eyes, shining into the world from behind her glasses. She always gives off a warm, wise impression. You can see that clearly in her photo, where she is shaking the hands of a woman in the audience after one of her lectures. Yes, my mother gives lectures. She gives lectures on subjects like myths and legends, and historical topics, like the 1953 flood[8]. I think it's wonderful to see how enthusiastic the audience is afterwards. The applause, all the happy faces of the people. My mom is shining the entire time.

My beacon of light.

---

8. The 1953 North Sea flood was a major flood caused by a heavy storm that occurred on the night of Saturday, January 31st 1953 and morning of Sunday, February 1st 1953. The floods struck the Netherlands, Belgium, England and Scotland.

2

It was a totally different world where I now was. Section A was nothing compared to Berkane, Taza or Section D. Here, it was open, lighter and cleaner. It was still not a hotel but it was better than what I was used to. Out of the nine sections, Section A proved to be the best – or rather, the least terrible. The other sections were like Section D, a horror.

The first thing I noticed after I was placed in cell six, was that there were tables and chairs. Chairs where you could just sit on. Tables where you could simply eat at.

There was a small, white tiled kitchen counter with a sink and two small cookers. The cell was just as big as in Section D, but instead of twenty bunk beds, here there were only ten – and instead of forty to fifty men, there were twenty to thirty. So there was a maximum of only ten people sleeping on the floor.

Some beds were positioned long-ways, the others on the short side against the wall, creating sitting areas. It was almost domestic. And the people I met were normal. Of course that depends on what you define by "normal", but most of the people here were neat, spoke quietly and acted civilized.

The cell's Kabran was a journalist, a man with smooth dark brown skin and a mouse-like appearance. He presented himself to me and then introduced me to the rest of the inmates.

After the handshake tour, I asked the journalist whether it was possible to call home. He told me that it was, but I needed to be patient. You could only call from certain places in the section's hallways. Places where the GSM signal wasn't blocked. The guards knew about this, so you could only make calls when the coast was clear. I got a place on one of the bunks and a German boy helped me arrange my things under the bed. The boy was my age, white, had blue eyes and cropped blonde hair. A true German, I thought to myself.

"Hai, mein Name ist Thomas," he introduced himself with a smile.

I shook his hand smiling and answered him in German that I already got that from the introduction. And from that moment on, Thomas and I would be spending a lot of time together over the next six months.

3

On the first floor of Section A was a small library. It was an L-shaped room with two tables and six chairs in the middle. Against the walls were eight bookcases with books in German, French, Spanish, Italian, English and Dutch. I visited the library with Thomas and walked down the rows containing Dutch books. I noticed a visibly often read book on the life of Nelson Mandela. What a coincidence. The very first book I wanted to read. I opened the book and the first line I read was: *"The habit of paying attention to small things and to appreciate small favors, is one of the most important characteristics of a good man."*

I quickly closed the book and realized happily that I would enjoy this book a lot.

Thomas had a German Quran under his arm and a German book with a strange title: *Feuchtgebiete.* A book of someone named Charlotte Roche.

"What are you going to do with that?" I asked mockingly.

"Oh, I just grabbed something," Thomas said dryly. "It's about humid regions."

"Yeah, what regions are you talking about?" I looked at Thomas crookedly. He had a twinkle in his eyes.

"Here, take this one," I said, as I picked up a book with an unpronounceable title. "Meine ehe… ehebrehe… rischehe…"

"Meine ehebrecherische Frau," Thomas said at once.

I looked at Thomas, laughing and gave him the book with the cover photo of a beautiful woman in lingerie. It turned out to be about an adulterous woman.

"No, I'm not taking that one!" he laughed. He took the book from me, threw it on the table and walked away from me.

"Okay, okay, then don't!" I picked up the book of the adulterous woman and put it neatly back into the bookcase. I walked over to Thomas, who was standing at the desk of the "librarian" where we noted our name, prison number, cell number and book titles.

On the way back to our cell we talked about our homes. Thomas was from a wealthy family. His parents owned a big hotel in Germany.

"But why are you here?" I asked surprised.

"Chose to go astray," Thomas answered.

"Oh?"

"Hanging with the wrong people, wanting to make lots of money, real fast, you know," Thomas said, referring to the fact that I was probably here for the same reason.

"Yeah I know, from the stories of others and from movies," I said laconically.

"How much did you get caught with?" Thomas asked.

The common question.

"Eight tons!"

The common answer.

Thomas abruptly stopped on the stairs, while I continued down a few steps further. I turned around and saw Thomas with a look in his eyes as if he had just heard from his parents that he was adopted as a baby.

"Come on, man," I said, as if the eight tons were eight grams.

"*Scheiße!*[9] And here I thought I had a lot!"

---

9. Scheiße is German for "Shit".

Thomas almost dropped his books, but just caught them, and quickly walked a few steps down until he was standing beside me.

"How much did you get caught with?" I asked, realizing that I wasn't really interested.

"Five hundred fifty pounds of hashish and one hundred pounds of coke."

"Coke? Like cocaine?"

"Yeah, not like Coca-Cola," Thomas laughed.

"Well, that's not bad!"

Thomas looked almost proud, but stopped laughing. He knew perfectly well that he had made a big mistake and was now in jail. In Germany, Thomas was arrested on the road when they found the drugs in his car. During the arrest, he escaped and ended up in Morocco. Through Interpol, Germany issued an international arrest warrant, and Thomas was finally tracked down and arrested in Morocco. Now, he was waiting to be extradited to his homeland.

A little later, back in the cell I told my story. We were sitting together on his bed. Thomas sympathized with me. He thought it was bad that he was imprisoned, but at least he knew he had done something wrong. The fact that I was a prisoner, was awful to him.

"Not having done anything and being trapped in here," Thomas sighed. "Harsh!"

Thomas had some pictures from home and asked if I wanted to see them. That was fine with me. He showed me pictures of his parents and brothers, of the hotel and the house where he lived. He also showed me a picture of his girlfriend, which I held a little longer.

"Pretty girl," I said and pushed my shoulder against Thomas'. I could've guessed that he had a beautiful girlfriend.

With Thomas' charming smile, naughty eyes and well-built body, he certainly wouldn't have had a lack of attention from women. He smiled at me and tried to get the picture back out of my hands, but I held it tightly. Thomas grabbed me around my neck and pulled the picture firmly out of my hands. We both laughed.

"Okay, okay, you can have your woman back. I understand that you're afraid to lose her to me."

"Yeah, sure you do, buddy, I don't think so!" Thomas smiled.

It was my turn to show my pictures from home now. Thomas fell in love with my mom's Norwegian wooden house and the garden full of flowers.

"Wow, wunderschön!"

I showed pictures of friends and Amber. I just got the ones of Amber. She had professional pictures taken for me and they looked great.

"WOW! *Noch schöner!*" Thomas said with my girl in his hands.

"Ja, *schöööön,* don't you think so?" I answered in exaggerated German. I was totally proud of my Amber, and just when I thought his drooling was getting out of hand I snatched the picture back at once.

"Hey!" Thomas shouted and grabbed for it. I kept the picture out of his reach.

"Yeah, what?" I answered smiling.

"And you think that she will be waiting for you at home?" Thomas asked.

I stopped laughing.

"Yes, of course, what do you think? Your girlfriend is waiting for you too, right?"

"Yes, but I'm going to Germany soon and then I can see her every week. You'll be here for ten years."

I got anxious. Thomas was right of course. Ten years.

"We call each other every week," I said in an attempt to reassure myself and convince Thomas that she really would wait for me. "I get many letters from her and she writes that she loves me."

"I hope so for you."

"What?"

"That she's waiting for you."

"I don't doubt that. Amber is my girl, my woman. She is the first woman who I would want to marry."

We were having a deep conversation, when the journalist came to us.

"You wanted to call?" he asked seriously.

"Yes," I answered.

"Then come with me." The journalist turned around and strode out of the cell.

I looked at Thomas.

"Go with him!" he said quickly.

With tension as if we were planning to escape, I walked out of the cell, following the journalist.

4

Throughout the prison, which housed about five thousand prisoners, there were only three phone booths. Two didn't work half the time. Just like the other prisons, I needed a file with a copy of the passport of the person I wanted to call.

The alternative was calling from a cell phone, but the jammers on the roof were making that difficult. And cell phones were in short supply. The journalist was one of the lucky ones who had one. A guard had probably arranged it.

The journalist snapped his fingers at a guy in the hallway who kept watch. We walked through a dead-end hallway toward a massive iron gate. It turned out to be the entrance of the isolation ward. The journalist put his cell phone carefully on the protruding gate lock. He put the handsfree set in the phone and asked me in a hurry which number had to be dialed. I gave him Amber's number. The phone rang twice and then he hung up. I knew Amber would immediately call back if she saw the Moroccan number – starting with +212 – illuminating on her phone screen. We both looked at the phone intently. Less than thirty seconds later, she called. I put in the earplugs quickly.

"Amber?" I heard noises. "Amber?"

"Joe?"

"Amber! Yes, it's me!" I said, excited to finally hear her sweet voice again.

"Joseph! Sweetie, how are you?"

"Good, good. I've had some crazy weeks, but I'm fine."

"How is it going there in your new setting? Gosh, it can't be easy trying to conquer a new place every time you're moved."

"It's okay at this unit. I got my own place and already made some new friends," I said.

I heard Amber giggling.

"People always tend to accept you, right? Just because you're you. I'm awfully proud of you!"

"Ha-ha, thanks."

"Really, I have great respect for you."

I became shy by Amber's words. I felt butterflies in my stomach.

"Hey, Joe...," Amber continued.

"Yeah?"

"I GOT MY FIRST-year!" Amber screamed happily.

I laughed.

"Are you serious? Way to go, girl! That's awesome!"

"Don't you think it's great?"

"Yes, pumpkin, I told you that you would make it in one year!"

"Yeah, I know," Amber said shyly. "But you know me! I'm always a little unsure."

"When is the ceremony?" I asked.

"In September."

"Hmm, I hope I'll be there, but I probably won't..."

"Always keep hoping, Joe."

"Yeah... Yes, of course," I sighed.

"Oh, and, my dad, your dad and I are coming to visit you next month!"

"Yeah? Is it really going to happen?" I asked happily.

"Sure! We planned to come from the eighth to the twelfth of August."

"That's more than great!"

"I think it's going to be awfully strange to see you in that situation. And for you to see me, of course."

"Yeah, you can say that again."

"I'm afraid, that when I have to go back, I won't be able to leave you there," Amber said sadly.

"That will be really hard indeed."

We both sighed.

"And Fouza is very pregnant, you know," Amber said, to change the subject in a pleasant way. "She's expecting the baby any day now."

"That's very exciting. It will probably be another little guy," I laughed. "My father can only make baby boys."

I heard Amber laughing and saw the journalist looking around impatiently. I almost forgot that I was in jail. Amber sounded so close. I looked back at the guy who was standing watch. Nothing to worry about. But the journalist motioned me to hurry up.

"Amber? I can't talk very long."

"Oh, okay, um, can I call you on this number next time too?"

"Well, that's a bit difficult, for the time being I'll ring you, okay?"

"Okay," Amber said sweet and softly. "But I don't want to hang up yet."

"Me neither, but it's just the way it is right now. Please tell everyone that I'm doing fine here, all things considered, okay?

And please tell my mom that I'll call her soon."

"Okay, sweetie. I love you so much."

"I love you too!"

"Remember what I always say, right? Every man pales in significance when standing next to you."

I laughed. "Yes! That's what I like to hear!"

Amber giggled.

"I'll try to call you back as soon as possible! I really have to go now! Bye, bye! Kiss!"

"Okay, kiss, my sweet man."

I hung up and handed the phone back to the journalist, who quickly hid it in his pants near his crotch. That's fresh I thought. Thankfully, the phone was connected to a handsfree set, and I didn't have to hold it myself.

The guy watching came toward us quickly. Guards were on their way, he gestured. I ended my call just in time. Pretty stressful, but I couldn't care less now. I was walking on air.

5

Before Amber, her dad and my dad would arrive on August 8th, it would be a turbulent summer at home. Fouza was in the hospital with her big belly. My dad was often with her and my mom was babysitting my little brothers. That was never a problem. It was very hot in the Netherlands that summer, so my mom hooked up the garden hose, and my brothers would play with it for a few hours. *"They were soaked and boy did they laugh!"* my mom wrote later on.

And then suddenly, along came brother number three: Kian. Much easier for me to write about then what Fouza went through. Although the birth went well, I'm sure it wasn't fun squeezing out that little baby boy. For this reason alone I thank our Lord that I'm a man. Women have my endless respect for the pain they have to endure during childbirth!

"Your brother is a little bear," my mom wrote. *"Just like you, back then. He weighs over eight pounds and his nails are already growing very long."*

I had to laugh about William, who later on, wrote me something funny. He came to visit my dad and Fouza and to see Kian. Kian's diaper was just being changed by his mom. *"So as he was lying there on his pink, naked, three-day old baby buttocks, Fouza took away the diaper: Splash! He pooped all over her and the table! I couldn't stop laughing!"*

When I read this, I couldn't help but laugh, but at the same time I realized again how much I wanted to be there with them.

My grandfather was also admitted to the hospital. He had to go to the ICU after the cardiologist found some serious heart arrhythmias. A few times a day, he would lose consciousness. He could have a heart attack at any time. Sometimes, his heart would even stop for six seconds! He had surgery and the doctors installed a pacemaker that revived him.

Staying on the hospital subject – ugh, prisons and hospitals, I hate them both! – my mom had to go back because her colostomy had to be removed.

"If they put me under anesthesia, I will think of you and when I wake up, I'll think of you then too."

The doctor who was about to operate on her, saw my mom writing a letter just before surgery. She explained to him that the letter was for her son: "At this moment, he's unjustly imprisoned in Morocco." The doctor replied that he knew the story.

"The doctor really likes how I build up my letters to you. Here, everyone keeps their fingers crossed for you too. Do you remember when I said that I'm a gentle breeze that is blowing across your face? Try to catch my whisper. It's a song of freedom that I will always sing for you. That day will come, my boy."

6

Monday, August 8, 2005, day 228.

Early in the morning, I woke up and got ready for my visit. Everything had to be perfect. I put some gel in my hair, brushed my teeth twice and dressed as nice as possible. The clothes I wore were from Thomas. The night before, we had tried on several T-shirts and pants, and finally, I chose a dark blue T-shirt with light blue jeans. Thomas thought I had to look top-notch.

Finally, I sprinkled some drops of cologne on my face, and Joseph was ready.

I'm going to see my girl, I'm going to see my girl!

I was really nervous. Finally, I was going to look into Amber's beautiful blue eyes and feel her soft skin.

Once the morning roll call was finished and the cell doors were opened, I walked to the section's main entrance to wait for my 'visitors card'. An hour crawled by. The whole time I wondered whether I looked good enough. I hoped Amber wouldn't be scared after seeing how much weight I had lost. I had to appear in good spirits, healthy and as strong as possible, that's what I wanted.

Suddenly, a planto walked through the section gate. A wave of excitement tingled through my body. I walked up to the guy and asked if my card was there. He asked for my name and flipped through the stack of papers. I moved my head eagerly along with his motions. "Here!" he suddenly said. He handed me the paper without looking at me and continued walking quickly. I held the paper in my hands tightly, as if it was more important than my Bachelor's degree. I stared at it for a little while and smiled.

Yes! On to the visitors hallway!

Tensely, I scanned the room. It shouldn't be hard to locate a white, European – and exceptionally beautiful – woman, especially between all of the other women wrapped in cloths and rags.

But I didn't see her. Harder to find her than I thought I guess.

I walked through the hallway, between the tables and chairs where people were waiting and chatting. Nothing. Or wait a minute... Maybe? Yes! I saw my dad! Alone... Alone?!

The smile that I had on my face until now disappeared immediately. I walked quickly over to my dad. He smiled, got up clumsily and reached out to welcome me. I held out hope that Amber and her dad would be there soon, and that they were running late because of security.

"Hey, dad," I said. "You're alone."

I hugged him. He was no longer my big strong father from the past. I stood taller than him and even had to bend slightly while hugging. My father wiped away a few tears. I kept it dry and asked where Amber and her father were.

"They're still outside," he said softly.

"Are they still coming?"

My dad shook his head.

"Are you serious? Why? Didn't they get their papers stamped by the embassy, stating that she is my fiancé, my future wife," I said angrily.

My dad looked at me worrisome as I went on.

"She even came along with her dad! You would think they would recognize that she's not just some girl?"

Apparently that didn't matter. Only people with the same family name or related family were allowed to visit me.

Fuck this, they can't be serious! Amber and her dad had come all this way, for nothing!

I plopped into a chair and dropped myself against the backrest. I slumped down, obviously upset by this news.

My dad asked me if I was okay.

"Yeah, fine, fine," I said, fed up and sighing. "How can they do this? I mean, what difference does it make? I really can't stand this anymore! Didn't you try to bribe the guards to let them in?" I asked my dad, as if he was the one to blame.

He had tried, he said, but without any luck.

My dad wanted to start a conversation. Speaking as best he could in Dutch, he tried to explain that we couldn't reject my appeal to the Supreme Court. I had actually thought about doing that, because if I did reject the appeal, any legal recourse I had here would be exhausted and I would then be allowed to be transferred to the Netherlands. But according to the lawyers, rejecting the appeal wouldn't be wise. It would basically be the same as admitting that I was guilty.

"Therefore, we have to wait for the Supreme Court," my father told me.

I get it. I get it. But what the heck does the appeal matter right now. At this moment.

Damn it. Why don't they just let Amber in?

My dad looked at me and kept quiet. This whole situation really bothered me. My father was feeling helpless and thought maybe I wasn't happy to see him at all. He probably felt bad that he was the one who had to disappoint his son. I started to feel guilty and tried to forget that Amber was less than fifty yards away from me.

My dad was still quiet. So was I.

To break the silence, my dad began to unpack the goods he brought from home with a cautious smile. He was obviously trying to make the best of it. I forced a smile on my face. I imagined this moment happening much differently. How would Amber be doing now? I pictured her outside, crying in her dad's arms.

Meanwhile, my dad laid out the things he brought one by one, every time, explaining what each item was, as if I couldn't make that up myself. Quasi-interested I looked at the items. I interrupted him by saying that he could just leave the things in the bags if he wanted. I didn't mind.

Silence.

It looked as though my dad felt ashamed, he couldn't look at me. It was painful to watch him doing his utmost to make the best of things.

"How are my brothers?" I asked. I was genuinely interested in hearing about them, even though it didn't seem that way to my dad. Everything was fine, he said. I continued on asking about them, but every time, my dad turned the conversation back to me. Then he told me with tears in his eyes, how much he missed me, how much it hurt him to see his first born son sitting in jail knowing that I deserved to be home with him. I got irritated a bit. I wanted to hear stories about my brothers, not about me or him.

"Dad, we're not crying," I said sternly.

He couldn't help it, the tears were coming, but he did his best to hold them back. With a brown checkered, cotton handkerchief, he quickly wiped away the few tears he already had. The hanky was the one he always carried with him in his pocket.

The conversation went over my head.

I couldn't get over what these suckers did to me. As if the guards ever followed the rules! Almost all of my cellmates were visited by friends and acquaintances who didn't have the same last name and were certainly not related! The guards only did this to prove to Amber and her father how "strict" they were in following the rules, and that they could not be bribed. They were probably afraid of the other guards narking them out if these two notable persons would be allowed in after all.

The piercing alarm went off, indicating the end of our visit. My father and I looked at each other. Again the silence.

"Well, I have to go back to the cell," I said. My father gave a disheartened nod. I got up first and grabbed the bags. He got up too and followed me to the gate where we would part ways. I put the bags down.

"I'm sorry," my dad said. I glanced down for a moment and felt the lump in my throat.

"No, no, it doesn't matter." I squeezed the words out of my mouth as I felt the tears coming.

The guards shrieked deafeningly with their loud whistles. How I wanted to jam those things down their throats. Sigh. I kept calm, said goodbye to my dad, hugging him hastily. I turned around and walked out of the hallway without looking back.

In the cell I was greeted by my happy cellmates, but I did not say anything, I threw down my unopened bags and lied on my stomach on the bed, out of sight from everyone. I began to cry in silence. I cried for Amber. I cried for the way I treated my dad. I couldn't help treating him so badly, when he came all this way for me. I was frustrated by everything around me, the injustice, the powerlessness, the prison. I stayed in my bed for the rest of the day and fell asleep early. I wished this day had never existed and would soon be over.

7

"Did you know that every night, before I go to sleep, I wish you goodnight?"

I began to think strongly about my mom, while my dad, Amber and her father were less than twelve miles away from me. They were staying at a farm owned by an aunt of Fouza, just outside Rabat. The next morning, Thomas and the journalist asked me what happened, but I told them it was nothing special and I just missed home. Apparently that was convincing enough, because they never asked me about it again.

Thomas and I unpacked the bags my dad brought with him.

In the biggest bag there was a duvet, some sheets and clothing. I found an mp3 player from William and I turned it on immediately. I never grew tired of Lenny Kravitz, whose music I still listened to every day on my discman, but the new music was very welcome. Thomas took a world receiver out of the bag and asked if he could use it.

"Natürlich."

Although I didn't show it, deep down inside, I was very happy with the items that were picked and packed carefully by my loved ones.

Amber made me a photo album in which she illustrated the way from her parents' home to her dorm in the city of Nijmegen, so that in my mind I could travel along with her.

I couldn't stop thinking about my dad and Amber, and the dirty trick the prison guards pulled earlier. If I could only have had five minutes to hold Amber in my arms.

My dad, Amber and her father planned to come visit me twice during their week-long stay. For foreigners, visiting twice a week was the maximum allowed. The journalist, who was able to cope with the prison director reasonably well, even put in a good word for me, but the director wouldn't budge.

Amber and her father would not be allowed in.

8

On Thursday, my dad came back for the second time. I decided not to act like an asshole this time and put on my "happy face". I saw my father sitting alone again. I got a lump in my throat as I realized how sorry I felt for him. He meant so well.

We greeted each other, hugged briefly and tried to smile. My dad handed me a letter from Amber that I started to read immediately:

"Here I am in the home of Fouza's aunt, crying and cursing at that fucking jail. Jesus, why are they being so difficult? Why won't they just let me visit you? I know it has to be worse for you. We are no more than one hundred yards apart, but can't hold each other. I can hardly bear it. You would think it's the least they could do… Fortunately you've seen your dad and have some new items...

This country is like another world. I often think of the text message you sent me from the prison of Taza about the future of these people. We should be glad that we live in the Netherlands.

Oh, and by the way, after we were turned away, I couldn't resist giving the prison the middle finger from the car window :).

Sweetie, you will hang in there! And God help you if I hear otherwise! Let those people get to know the beautiful person that you are. Love you. Kiss. Amber. "

I smiled.

"Thanks, dad," I said. My father smiled back at me and handed me a little box.

Huh? I know that box.

It was the box with the golden necklace and Our Lady of Fatima talisman I bought for Amber at a Moroccan market about a year ago. I gave her the necklace while sitting on a bench in the park of Breda. Embracing each other, we were enjoying the sunshine when I told her I had a surprise for her. Ever since then, she wore the necklace almost every day. Now it was a keepsake for me. There was a little note inside it: *"Honey, I may not be here now, but with my necklace in your hands, I will always be close to you. We have to make a deal, promise me that you'll give it back to me one day in person."*

I was going to keep this promise, no matter what it would take.

My dad and I continued talking, the way we used to.

Every time he took a Camel cigarette to his mouth he would lite it with a match. He always did that, lighting them with matches. He made a bowl with his hands so the flame would be protected. I wished I could be that flame, I thought.

My father pursed his lips a few times until the tip of the cigarette was glowing a bright orange. Then he blew out the matchstick and took the first puff. To this day, the typical pungent smell of a cigarette after the first puff reminds me of my dad.

After hearing the shrill of the alarm again, we said goodbye, but this time with a big hug. I noticed my dad started to let go, but I held him a moment longer. I felt his hand gently tapping on my shoulder. I let him go and smiled at him.

"I love you, dad."

My dad had tears in his eyes as he looked down. I turned around and walked to the entrance for the prisoners. Before I disappeared into the jail, I turned around one more time to wave goodbye to my dad. But he was already gone, lost in the crowd of people. I stopped and gazed at the spot where my father just stood. As I stared into the visitors hallway, I began to be pushed by inmates on either side, who, like me, had to return to their cells. Back to their cages, locked securely behind bars.

My dad was really gone. Gone from this wretched place and on his way home, where I too belonged. Outside, living in freedom, in the Netherlands, along with Amber. I turned around and walked with the flow of inmates, toward my cell to finish my day yet again.

This, apparently, was where I belonged now.

"*Did you know that I not only wish you good night before I go to sleep, but also good morning when I wake up? In the meantime, I do as many useful and fun things as possible, constantly hoping that your days are at least bearable for you. Every day, I have the same big wish: set my innocent child free. It would be one of the happiest days of my life.*

So far, the happiest day of my life was the day you were born.

And I can remember the moment when you started to talk. You were quite a little chatterbox talking with me. Dad wanted you to give me a break for a little while and asked you to sit down with him, but you said: 'I want mommy!' You used to cuddle so closely with me when the Wicked Witch from the Wizard of Oz would appear on TV, and you cried big tears when watching Dumbo, the Flying Elephant.

Very soon my dear, the time for little worries will be upon us once again. I firmly believe it..."

9

In cell number six, I adapted relatively quickly. In general, the roll calls were quiet. The guards tapped their keys on the cell door and – usually – shouted in a normal voice that it was time to wake up. Just like Section D, we only had to raise our hand to show that we were present – and still alive.

Also, in this prison, the cells were open from 9:30 to 11:00 a.m. and from 3:00 to 5:00 p.m..

Thomas and I were practically inseparable. We started each day with some exercises. We did push-ups, leg training and ran laps around the courtyard. Then we took a shower in the section's shower room. With cold water of course, as there wasn't any hot water.

In the morning, afternoon, evening and at night, we ate together in small groups in the cell. The journalist was organizing things pretty well. No one had to eat the daily prison gruel from the large metal pans. The food from the prisoner's families was collected and distributed to all the inmates. Every month, my mom sent money to the journalist's wife, so I was also included in the group.

Once a month, Thomas was visited by his parents from Germany which allowed him to be part of the group as well. I was somewhat surprised, but Thomas' parents were rich and I was happy for him that he was able to see them so often.

I was getting along pretty well with the other inmates. I was friendly with everyone, answered when someone asked me something. So far, everything was going pretty well...

In the cell, I read as much as possible. With my music on, I would get lost in the pages of books and magazines – especially my favorites: *Men's Health, Quest* and *National Geographic*.

The days went by very slowly, and so my birthday arrived.

10

Happy birthday to me!

Happy birthday to me!

Happy birthday to meeeeeaaaahhhh…

Yawn, sigh, moan, groan.

There I was, sitting on my bunk, still puzzled, just after the morning roll call.

"September tenth," I said quietly to myself. What day of the week is it today? I wondered. After a few seconds, I knew: Saturday. Damn, Saturday. That was right. The weekend. As usual, we had to stay inside.

It was day 261 in captivity and I had just turned twenty-five years old. I looked at my watch and stared: a quarter to nine. I relaxed for a moment and yawned once more. Rubbing my teary eyes, I jumped off the bed to prepare myself for the day. In the cell, a broadly smiling Thomas congratulated me, followed by the journalist. The rest didn't know it was my birthday. I didn't want them to. How miserable, celebrating your birthday behind bars. Still, it sort of felt like my birthday.

Based on the mountain of birthday cards that I received throughout the days around my birthday, a lot of people back home were thinking of me. A few days earlier, I received a card that must have been at least three by three feet in size from my mom, Fouza, William and his dad, and Amber and her family. I laughed heartily. I didn't know they made cards that big. In the card were pictures of balloons, in which everyone had written their own personal message. I had received many other cards as well, there were so many names. Including people I didn't even know! In total, I counted exactly one hundred and seventy cards!

"These things make me feel special. Thanks everyone!" I wrote in my diary. *"I would love to call the whole world right now to have everyone close to me."*

But making calls was still difficult. On the weekends it was nearly impossible, because the spots where you could receive a signal were full of people waiting for their turn to call. Only a few guards were on duty on each Saturday and Sunday, so the spots were hardly ever checked.

With the journalist's phone in my hand, I made my way through the crowd in the hallway toward the isolation ward. After some difficulty, I managed to find a spot. I was squatting between a few rowdy inmates and held the phone against the wall – apparently, at some places the wall actually worked as a GSM signal conductor. It was very crowded and people were constantly pushing each other. It wasn't easy talking to my mom, but when she picked up the phone, I was so happy to hear her voice.

"How are you, kid?" she asked.

"Fine, mom."

"What is that noise in the background?" my mom noticed.

I explained the situation to her.

"Today, I miss you even more..." I continued.

"We feel the same way, son. Especially now, your absence is so unfair. But unfortunately, these things cannot be undone. I know it will be okay, my dear."

"I know mom, but it's just difficult now."

To brighten me up a little, my mom talked about the day I was born.

"You know it's lovely weather here now! Twenty-five years ago, when you were born, it was just as beautiful outside as it is today. The temperature was nice, right around sixty-eight degrees, a little breezy with a refreshing morning smell."

"It was?"

"Yes, it was. Exactly twenty-five years ago, around half past eight in the morning, I was ready to go to the hospital. Here we are, a quarter of a century later, and thank goodness we didn't know then what we know now. If I had known, I would have put you back inside!"

I had to laugh at my mom's expression "put you back inside". I kept putting my finger in my ear so I could hear her better. She told me that she had been taking a walk along the river, near the water tower in our village. "For a moment, I had this feeling of pain," she said. "I wanted so badly for you to walk with me there, so you could enjoy nature again, everywhere around you, instead of all those walls. I hope you can see the beautiful skies when you're allowed to go outside, then at least you have something."

I assured my mom that I was still able to enjoy the sky, even though it was only for a few hours a day.

My mom congratulated me on behalf of grandfather too. "He thinks it's horrible what's happened you, but for Amber as well. 'Such a young girl,' he said, 'and to have a boyfriend who's in prison, and innocent.' You see, I thought that was very sweet of him. Of course, most people think of you, but many forget that it isn't easy for Amber either."

I was completely taken in by my mom's voice, when suddenly, I saw the inmates around me quickly hiding their cell phones. They were jumping all over the place, like a herd of antelopes startled by a lion.

Shit, the guards! Why now?!

"Mom, I have to go," I said quickly, while she was still talking.

I quickly hid the phone, and saw a guard coming toward us. I moved as quietly as possible with the other inmates as the guard walked past me. Thank God. I wasn't his prey. Four others were. Why those four, I didn't know, we were there with dozens of people. It was totally random.

For a minute, I felt bad that I had to cut my conversation short, but I didn't let it ruin my day. I focused on the best part of my birthday, a special gift from my mom that I had received by mail exactly one day before. It was a book named *Tell me, Mom! Because you're so special to me.*

"My sweet Joseph, for your 25th birthday" she wrote on the first page. Below her beautiful handwriting showed an ugly red prison stamp as proof of receipt. The book had more than one hundred and thirty pages with questions that my mother had answered. Questions about her life and mine. About the past, present, and the future. I read about things I never knew. Breathtaking. Hours later, I had finished reading the book, some parts with laughter and some parts with tears in my eyes.

Inside the back cover were a few blank pages. After the phone call with my mom, I couldn't resist using them to express with words, the feelings I had in my mind. Words about my mom. Words that would serve as a thank you to her, for her love for me...

II

"Mama,

I'm using these pages to try and express my gratitude for the best gift you've ever given me.

At this moment, it's September 10th, nearly one o'clock in the afternoon and I can't stop thinking about you, mom.

With great admiration and appreciation, I read your story. It's so wonderful to have a piece of you with me now. Something I will have forever. Something that has revealed many things that I never knew, even after twenty-five years.

I laughed about the five guilders birthday present, 'work of art' made out of cork that I bought for you at the local market as an eight-year old little guy. I had forgotten about that for a long time. It's funny how others remember certain events. I often think of what you wrote about what's most important in life: having, receiving and giving respect, remaining compassionate to people, animals, and culture, being content with the things you have, having the strength to develop your talents, standing up against injustice and trying to be a good person. I agree with all of these things.

There are two pictures in the book, one where I'm still in your belly, you were very pregnant, and the other with me as a baby on your lap. You looked beautiful and happy. As a son, you want to see your mom happy.

The pictures of you, your brothers and grandparents from the past were a big surprise. I had never seen those before!

However bizarre this may sound, what if I had never been imprisoned here? Would I have ever received such a book from you? Would I have ever received so much visible love from the people surrounding me?

I feel happy. Deep down inside. Surrounded by so much love. Surrounded by a mother, who would give her life for her son (I will never forget when you randomly said that to me on an average afternoon).

Despite the fact that as of today, I have lived in captivity for exactly 261 days, and I have missed many things already, especially now, having to 'celebrate' my birthday in this desolate environment, I know that you're all here with me and I'm with you. In my thoughts, I am everywhere and constantly with you.

Mom, this book is unforgettable. This book gives me strength.

I'm proud of you. Proud of how strong you are. I got this from you, this strength. That's obvious.

I love you so much, mom.

Thank you ... for everything.
Joseph (2005-09-10)"

12

Amber's birthday was two days after mine. We always celebrated our birthdays together. Last year, I gave her a balloon flight for her birthday. While she was enjoying the view from the air, I drove in my car chasing the balloon to the landing spot to meet her.

"It was fantastic!" she shouted afterwards suddenly jumping into my arms. She wrapped her legs around my waist and I instinctively held her bottom. I laughed at her enthusiasm. Amber looked at me with big sparkling eyes and started laughing too. She grabbed my cheeks, pushing them together to pucker my lips, and started kissing me.

This year wasn't quite as good.

"I'm not celebrating my birthday," she told me on the phone.

"Why not?"

"Just not in the mood."

"Oh?"

"If you can't celebrate yours as you want, well, then I won't either."

I was quiet. I didn't like to hear Amber talking this way. She was completely consumed by my situation.

"I love you," she suddenly said. "I can't tell you enough."

She giggled and I smiled. Before I could say that I loved her too, she continued.

"This week, I dreamed about you twice. In the first dream we made love beautifully."

"Oh, really?" I asked with a sense of wonder and pride.

"Yes. You're not the only one who dreams about that," Amber laughed. "It was wonderful! In the second dream you were back in the Netherlands and I suddenly saw you on the street. We ran to each other, embraced and kissed passionately. Nice dreams, don't you think?"

"Very nice! Dreams can be so perfect. I dream a lot, about us of course, but as soon as I wake up for morning roll call, I fall back into reality. It makes me sick being aware that I'm here."

"Aah, my poor Joe! I want to hold you so badly. You know what I'm thinking about right now?"

"No, tell me," I said curiously. It was heavenly to hear Amber's voice, so I tried to talk as little as possible. She started talking and in my mind, I followed along.

"We're at your mom's house, eating in front of the TV. I'm already finished, but you still have a huge plate of course..."

We both laughed as Amber continued.

"... You're sitting on the wooden floor at the low glass table in the living room. I'm behind you on the couch, clamping you carefully between my knees. I calmly pat you on the head, as you gently stroke the skin of my lower legs. Together, we are watching an episode of Family Guy and I enjoy your laughter at the stupid jokes of that cartoon." She laughed and then sighed. "Those little moments mean so much to me now, Joe. I can totally picture them. Phew, I miss you so much! Sometimes it makes me crazy!"

"I miss you too. I'm longing for you," I answered and abruptly stopped talking.

"Our time will come again for sure! I'm packing my bag to go work out. I have to look good, of course, for when you get back!"

"You always look good," I said almost drained.

"I love you unimaginably. But you already know that."

"I know."

"Kiss!"

"Kiss."

We hung up and I felt horrible.

Sigh... Sigh! Siiiiiiiiiigh!

I wanted to leave. I wanted to be with Amber. I needed her, here and now – I mean, over there and now!

13

Since my dad's visit a month ago, Uncle Samir hadn't yet returned. I hadn't heard anything from my other uncles and aunts either. I had an uncle who worked as a diplomat at the Ministry. I didn't know exactly what he did, but someone in this type of position got a great deal of respect in Morocco. When I had to travel to Casablanca for work, I would visit him and in the summer of 2003, William and I stayed with him and his family. When I was in the prison of Berkane, he promised me that he would come to visit as soon as I arrived at the prison of Salé.

But nothing, I heard nothing at all from him or the other family members. I couldn't understand why. My father mentioned that my uncle might be afraid to visit me in prison because of his job and status as a diplomat.

Afraid? What the hell is that? Afraid of who? Of me? Of this country? And what about my other uncles and aunts? They only lived a few miles away from the prison.

Nobody really seemed to understand why they never came. My mom tried to explain that she thought it was because there was never any real love from that side of the family. I never understood why she felt this way, as my uncles, aunts, nephews and nieces had always welcomed me with open arms. They cheered and jumped every time I arrived as if I told them they won the National Lottery.

Initially, I had a real problem with their actions, and my father was even more upset. He told me that he was disappointed in his brothers and sisters.

The negative energy wasn't helping, so I tried to shake it off and think more about all of the letters and cards that I had received so far. I went through some again and came across the Bible story about Joseph of Egypt, one that my mom had described extensively. I knew this story well. It used to be my dad's favorite; albeit the story he knew was from the Koran where Joseph was called Youssouf in Arabic. The stories are almost identical and I read how Joseph, the favorite son of his father, was abandoned by his own brothers and one day even ended up in jail. Well, it looks like I have a few things in common with this Joseph.

A magnificent story that ends beautifully, when, after his appointment as the viceroy of Egypt, Joseph confronts his brothers over what they had done and ultimately forgives them.

I fantasized that, just like Joseph in the Bible, I would be admired someday too. Rather than waste time feeling depressed over the people who let me down, I focused on the people who stood by my side. It was there I found my strength, my joy for living. *Always remember what you have.*

14

In the Netherlands, my mom and I were also supported by many strangers who sympathized with our situation. One of these people was a man named Abdel. He was a journalist for the NOS, a public broadcast station established under Dutch Media Law, and reported all the news related to Morocco. Through a Moroccan colleague from Sword fruits, Abdel learned about my unjustified captivity. For a few months, my mom and Abdel made contact by email and phone. However, that would soon turn into something specific, because something "big" was about to happen.

The counselor to the King of Morocco, Mohammed VI, was coming to the Netherlands for a diplomatic visit. He was the right hand of the king and was often on TV and in the news in Morocco. Abdel had successfully managed to arrange a brief meeting with him. My mom was going to speak with him personally!

It was on Thursday, September 22nd, 2005.

Later, she wrote to me about this highly exceptional meeting.

"It was a day that seemed like a dream:

At eleven o'clock, I got into my car and hastily made my way to Sword fruits. I had some coffee there with Wilko from Sword fruits and then he and I drove together to the 'Media Park' in Hilversum. There we picked up a reporter and continued on to Amsterdam. Abdel went over to greet the king's counselor and his entourage. After that, the gentlemen entered a museum. We were anxiously waiting for them on the outdoor terrace, when the company walked out. Abdel called us over and introduced me to one of Morocco's most powerful men. I was permitted to hand him the letters about you, your diplomas, testimonials, and court documents stating the accusations against you. He took the documents while he was surrounded by a delegation of important people. I stood there amongst them, an ordinary female citizen and exchanged a few words. Afterwards, we went for dinner at a Moroccan restaurant. I also spoke to the President of the World Jewish Community. He lives in the capital of Israel and is an extremely nice man, very charming. 'Madam,' he said to me, 'you're a very beautiful woman, you're very pretty and you have a beautiful strength about you that can be seen in your face.' His comments made me blush and I was a little shy. The man to whom I gave the documents was also very thoughtful. Later that evening, after Abdel had spoken with you, he started to cry a little. He finally got to speak with the boy whom this was all about: you. So, Joe, now you know what an incredible day this has been. We'll keep hope alive and wait patiently to see what happens."

15

Everything and everyone was focused on one single goal: bring back home Joseph Oubelkas. Apparently there was a lot of activity going on about me, but within these walls, I didn't notice much. My days consisted of living the prison life: morning roll call, getting up, working out with Thomas, taking a shower, afternoon roll call, reading, going "out" on the courtyard, lock-up, evening roll call, more reading, writing, doing other useful things, and sleeping. Needless to say, in between all that, I also did the normal everyday things like eating, drinking, using the toilet, burping, laughing and talking. Yes, I did a lot of talking. With people in the courtyard, in the hallways and in the cell. My Moroccan was improving, which helped me communicate better with the guards. They were amazed that I actually took the time to learn their language.

I also talked a lot with the foreigners in our section. They came from all across the world, from England, France and Denmark, to Venezuela, Canada, Nigeria and Pakistan. And almost all of them were in jail for the brown stuff: hashish.

After a few months in Section A, people started to recognize me.

They noticed the way I carried myself differently from the other prisoners, even I hadn't realized it until my mom wrote me about it.

"Joseph, right now you're allowed to get on your high horse for ten minutes only. I heard the representatives from the embassy visited you and that you're doing well and what you're doing to spend your days. The representatives have also met with the prison board and both parties are very pleased with you. They think you're very philosophical and intelligent. The Dutch Ministry of Foreign Affairs has also heard this.

The Ministry ordered an independent investigation by their own lawyers, to examine the facts listed in the judges' verdict.

Keep it up, my son! I have lots of reasons for being proud of you. You leave a trail of courage, joy, honesty and integrity... Now get off your high horse again."

After reading my mom's letter, I stretched my arms into the air as if I had won the Super Bowl. I leapt from my bunk and danced across the floor. First, the king's counselor, and now the Dutch Ministry of Foreign Affairs is looking into things with their own lawyers...

Thomas saw me swinging my hips like Shakira and asked what the problem was.

"The problem? The problem? There is no problem!" I laterally said half in Dutch, half in German and I made another pirouette. Thomas had no idea what I was doing and just laughed at my spastic dancing.

16

Thomas stood in the visitors hallway waiting for his parents' monthly visit. Normally, after the visit, Thomas came back to the cell in a great mood – shining brighter than ten stadium lights put together –, but today he was pale as a ghost. I was lying on my bed reading a book about the life of Gandhi and just finished one of his proverbs: "One cannot win by responding to evil with evil."

I glanced over the edge of the book, chuckling at Thomas' terrified face. I was so used to see him smile, so now he looked like a bad actor in some sort of B-movie horror flick.

"What's wrong with you, man?" I said, teasing him a bit. I closed the book and laid it down beside me. The sad face just didn't fit him.

"Scheiße, Scheiße!" Thomas cried, stressfully pacing back and forth from my bunk to the cell door.

"What's *Scheiße?*" I asked and sat up.

"Scheiße, Scheiße, Scheiße!" Thomas cried again. He started to panic.

"What are you *Scheißing* for? Tell me what's wrong!"

"Scheiße –"

"Yeah, I know that now," I cut him off and called out to him, "just relax and tell me what's wrong."

Thomas was standing next to me and looking up. Sitting on the top bunk I looked about three feet taller than him.

"They... They found a thousand dirham on me." Thomas looked at me, waiting for me to say something.

His parents always gave him money when visiting him. Money to survive, for cigarettes, to buy goods for the other inmates, to pay the guards. Even when something was broken in the cell – a light, socket, valve, pipe, toilet, etc. – we, the prisoners, had to pay for it. Besides repairs, we had to pay out-of-pocket for the interior things as well, from tables and chairs to pans and cooking sets. Even still, money was forbidden. The only things provided by the prison were dry bread, tap water, glop from large iron pans, a steel bed frame – with no mattress or blankets – and a roof with jammers, lined with barbed wire.

"Hmm, that really is *Scheiße,*" I said quietly while thinking of a response. "Who found it on you?"

"A guard at the exit of the visitors hallway," he said, his face white as snow.

"Where did you hide it?"

"In my sock, here." Thomas lifted his foot and pointed to his ankle.

I shook my head. Thomas turned around and continued pacing back and forth. I jumped off the bunk and asked him what he thought was going to happen. Thomas shrugged, he didn't know. The money had obviously been taken away from him. I told him to calm down, it just happened and we needed some time to think.

“They’re not going to put you in front of a firing squad or anything,” I said, in an attempt to change that weird sad face of him back to his usual smiling face.

“Yeah, I know that!” Thomas said irritated.

Attempt failed.

“I’m afraid they might send me back to Section G,” he continued. Thomas had been in Section G for two months and it was just as miserable as Section D, where I had been. It seemed so long ago. I understood now why they called those sections the Colombian Area of Morocco and understood only too well the fear that Thomas had of returning.

A little while later, a guard called for Thomas to report to the chief of staff. With the look of an abandoned puppy, Thomas stepped forward and glanced at me for a moment. He then walked with his head down following the guard.

17

Thomas got off relatively easy with five days of solitary confinement that would start immediately.

Each section of the prison had their own isolation ward. Thomas was placed in our section and we were able to give him food daily. I knocked on the iron gate, the same gate the journalist and I would use when calling from the cell phone every time, and gave the food to the guard, who then gave it to Thomas. Thankfully he didn’t end up in solitary confinement in another department, then he would be left alone and have to live like Jeremy and I did, in the “rookie space”: prison soup, stale bread and tap water.

I missed Thomas. His bed sat eerily empty across from mine. Working out together was impossible now, so was hanging out, laughing, eating and everything else.

One day, the guard let me in the room with Thomas for a few minutes, at the cost of a pack of cigarettes.

The isolation ward was a dark, musty room with six cells. There were two rows of three cells standing opposite of each other. The cells had massive iron doors with small sliding windows. I bent over slightly to look through the window and saw Thomas lying on a blanket on the floor. He was lying on his back, reading the German Quran.

"Hey, crazy German," I said cheerfully.

Thomas laid the Scripture of Islam on his stomach and looked over at me surprised.

"Hi, Joooseph!" Thomas said happily – with his familiar face again. He stood up and walked over to me. His eyes filled the sliding window and we looked at each other.

"Are you holding up?" I asked.

"Jawohl," he answered sadly, almost cynically. I looked past Thomas and examined the cell. He stepped aside to observe his temporary room along with me. A place of about six by nine feet. Apart from his blanket, it was completely empty. At the top of the ceiling, a narrow barred window let through some faint streams of sunlight. Just enough to see how filthy the cell was. I made a face.

The walls were a peculiar dirty green color, mixed with brown, and right next to the door, I saw a three feet high wall with a hole in the floor in the front of it. There was a bottle stuffed in it, to try and stop the stench from this medieval toilet. It was in vain.

"The toilet stinks, man," I said.

"Yeah," Thomas said, "the water is always out in here."

"Nice and fresh!"

We both just smiled about it. Thomas was amazingly positive. That's why I liked him so much, that's why I liked to hang around with him.

"Do you actually have light in here?" I asked.

Thomas shook his head.

"So it's completely dark in the evening and night?"

Thomas nodded glumly.

I thought the place was terrible.

"What are you doing here anyway?" he asked suddenly.

"Visiting you, of course! I miss you, man!"

"Can you just walk in here?"

"No, but a pack of cigarettes opens doors, doesn't it? Our Kabran knows the guard who works here now."

"Ah, I see."

"Two more days, Thomas," I said, trying to encourage him.

"Yeah, I know. Thanks for the food by the way!"

"Forget it, you don't have to thank me for that, monkey!"

The guard began tapping his key on the iron door.

"I have to go, Thomas. See you in two days!" I tried to stick my hand through the window, but couldn't get more than four half fingers inside. Our fingers barely touched.

"Okay, tschüss und nochmals danke für alles[10]!" echoed through the hallway of the isolation ward.

"Don't worry about it, *kein Problem[11]*!" I shouted back. Poor Thomas. He looked pitiful in that dark hole.

But his time there would pass, just like everything else.

18

"Outside it's cloudy and calm. Even a bit stuffy. The early autumn is a beautiful sight. The leaves on the trees are slowly starting to change colors, from green to tones of yellow, brown and red."

---

10. German for "Bye, and thanks again for everything".

11. German for 'No problem".

As summer turned to autumn, something quite unexpected happened.

A friend and former classmate of mine, Ward, was with his girlfriend on holiday in Morocco and wanted to visit me. I heard this from my mom and told her that this was impossible. She agreed, but Ward's gesture made us happy.

In passing, I mentioned to the journalist that a friend of mine was in Morocco. He immediately offered to talk to the director to try and give Ward access.

"Now that you're better known within the prison walls, something might be possible," the journalist said.

And to my surprise, he was right!

The director promised that Ward could visit me for an hour! He heard stories about my good behavior and perhaps this was his way of rewarding me. I was thrilled and told my mom that the director had given the green light for his visit. Awesome!

In college, while studying Computer Science, Ward and I would grind away at assignments for many hours, side by side, and we became good friends.

It was weird to see him in the big visitors hallway, but a very welcomed sight! Someone who knew me, who knew who I was and had no doubts about my innocence, was sitting there across from me. The first one of my friends that I saw, and could actually touch, since my arrest. It was like a dream. The freedom he had, the freedom that all of us had taken for granted, was so close to me now. The hour was much too short, but it was an hour they could never take away from Ward and me.

A month later, my mom would visit me too. Finally! Because of her health, the colostomy – "poop bag"– and her finances, it wasn't possible until now. And William came as well! After the good outcome with Ward's visit, it should work this time too. The journalist confirmed it. Everything was set.

"Joseph, will you hold on just a little longer, dear? William and I will be with you in about four weeks. It will be so nice to see you again and touch you. Then I can tell you myself how proud I am of you. Many people carry you in their hearts and accompany you in their minds on your path. Lots of love, mama."

19

Wednesday, November 9, 2005, day 321.

The four weeks my mom was talking about went by slowly. With the help of the journalist, the director had arranged to let William come to visit as well, just like with Ward. Now, as fate would have it, the director would be away the week that my mom and William came to visit me...

I described my mom's visit in my diary:

"This morning I got up early to get ready for the visit. Once the cell doors opened, I got my visitors card. With five letters hidden under my T-shirt, I walked toward the visitors hallway. I had the letters stuffed around my waist to give to my mom. One for my mom, for Amber, William, Fouza and one for grandpa. I prayed the guards wouldn't search me. They looked sternly at me as I walked up to them. Please, don't search me, please don't search me, I kept thinking. I nodded at them, they stopped me and asked if I had something on me. I raised my hands and shook my head hoping they wouldn't notice the letters. I tried to breathe lightly... "Okay, go on," they said. Thank God. My letters were safe! Otherwise, I would have to send them through the administration office, and that could take months...

I scanned the hallway, looking for my mom. The room was relatively empty, so I found her sitting down almost immediately and could no longer maintain a normal pace. I almost ran over to her. My mom saw me too and stood up. Smiling, she walked slowly toward me. Again, I saw in my mind the images of how she would pick me up from the daycare center when I was a little boy. I remembered how I waited after school by my mom's car in the parking lot of the hospital where she worked. Every time she threw the same smile at me. A smile that gives me a warm feeling inside, a feeling of total protection, of pure motherly love.

In the middle of the hallway, my mom and I warmly embraced each other. Finally, a sincere hug again, I was wrapped in love. People in the room were looking at us, making sweet gestures for the most part. These people understood what it was to miss a person whom you loved. Mama let a few tears go that she couldn't hold back. My mom.

We walked together to our little place, two garden chairs, one with a broken seat. There were bags with items for me that she brought with her. I quickly handed her the letters and she hid them in her handbag. We sat down and she grabbed a tissue to wipe away her tears. I struggled not to do the same, I didn't want to cry. I wanted to be her big brave son.

But my mom was alone. Where was William?

My mom said it didn't work. They wouldn't let him in.

Oh no, not again! Just like with Amber? Why did the director have to be away right now?!

I told my mom to wait for a moment, I stood up and walked over to the guards. I asked if they could please allow my best friend to come in. They referred me to Chief Bin Abdi, but he wasn't there either, and the guards wouldn't dare give approval on their own. They were all afraid to do something that was against the rules, even though I told them the director had already given his approval. They said that might be true, but the director wasn't there, so they couldn't do anything. Bunch of cowards! How frustrating! I wanted to rip my hair out! This place was so corrupt! The simplest things were made the most difficult. First Amber and her dad, and now William. To see them was simply impossible! All that work and such a long trip, all for nothing.

William got emotional, my mom told me. As we talked, she told me how the people at home had such respect and admiration for me,

I couldn't hold back the tears any longer. There we were in that big hallway. Mother and son, sitting opposite each other on plastic garden chairs.

While I had my head down, my mom held her hands against my cheeks. With her thumbs, she wiped away my tears. "All this, in the land of my father," I said. I couldn't understand what happened. My mom didn't either. "It's so unfair. Again!" I cried.

It felt nice to be so physically close to my mom. Her warm hands clasped my cold hands. I saw brown spots on them.

"What's that?" I asked sniffling.

"Age spots."

"Age spots?"

That's right, my mother was turning 57, but she still had a young, energetic appearance.

In response to seeing the age spots, I told my mom that I only had one wish, that we all live to become very old, healthy and happy. She smiled. I enjoyed every second with her. This couldn't last long enough.

We were sitting for a little more than an hour, when that terrible siren went off to signal the end of our time together. My mom was startled by the loud noise.

"Should I go now?" she asked. I was touched by her expression. It was indeed time again. I felt powerless. I couldn't do anything for my mom, for William, or for myself for that matter.

I had to go back to the cell, and let my mom go again..."

20

My mom and William had tried everything, going through the Dutch embassy, Foreign Affairs, Abdel, through other contacts, but nothing helped. The director wasn't there, hence, our entire plan fell apart.

Later on, William wrote to me in a letter about his experience:

"When we left Morocco by plane, your mom was having a hard time at first. The idea of leaving you behind was getting to both of us.

I'm having a hard time now too. I know I have to be strong, but leaving you behind there really does hurt. I'm fighting back my tears now. I was so angry when they told me that I wasn't allowed to see you. I felt particularly bad for you, but I immediately told your mom that she had to go inside quickly and not to worry about me. We were there for you and that was all that mattered.

She patted me on my face just before she went in. I watched her go inside and then I found a spot under a tree in the shade, and closed my eyes. I did nothing but hope that your mom would stay away for a long time, because that means she got to stay with you for a long time.

When she came out, it was fantastic to hear how well you were looking. She gave me the letter that you had written to me. That gave me a lump in my throat! Just know that you're in my heart and I will always be there for you."

21

Outside, they kept working on my freedom. Regarding the appeal, everything was prepared and filed for the Supreme Court. We had to have patience until the date was set.

The lawyer for the Dutch Ministry of Foreign Affairs had finished his investigation and his findings were especially good for me.

In his report to the Ministry, he came to the conclusion that there was no evidence whatsoever that implicated me. It was a confirmation of what we already knew, but now, in light of this report, they couldn't ignore my mother and me anymore.

"I don't know why that boy is in there, because he doesn't even deserve a speeding ticket," the lawyer said.

Our hopes had lifted once again.

22

My mom kept writing me long letters. She wrote about everything, often referring to it as "tittle-tattle", but for me, the tittle-tattle was more than welcome.

She wrote about the weather, work, the neighbors and people who came to visit. She gave me full reports on the lectures she gave, which always ended with a dedication to me.

My mom also wrote about the questionable actions of various people with different agencies and companies.

One time, she wanted to transfer me money through the post office. They wanted my address, no problem, but then she explained that I was in prison and asked what she had to do in this case. "Well," they said at the post office, "you just transfer it and then he can get it at the nearest bank..."

Uhm, what part of my-son-is-in-prison did you not understand?

My mom had the same problem with the bank in our village when she wanted to manage my account. Even after explaining my story to them, they told her: "...your son will have to come by and sign the forms."

And the same with my student finance. They told her that her son simply had to call them to stop the monthly debits.

Just call them? Right.

It was nearly impossible to get in touch with my mother, let alone with them.

As for the tax authorities, my mom had to pull out all the stops to prove that I was actually behind bars. It was only after she provided them with a detention statement from the Ministry that things got easier.

"Apparently, if your problem with a particular authority or company does not show up on their little square electronic screens, then the problem obviously doesn't exist," my mom said. "These days, you have to show up in person at the front desk in order to convince people that the problem is real."

Getting these things done, cost my mom a lot of blood, sweat and tears. Especially the latter.

23

A few weeks before the arrival of my mom and William, rumors were spreading that there was going to be a pardon. "A big pardon, allowing all foreigners to go home!" was constantly said in the hallways and in the cell. A pardon, given in honor of Morocco's fifty years of independence. It didn't mean much to me, and I wasn't going to let the inmates' euphoria affect me either.

"How can I be happy when I know they gave me ten years for nothing?" I kept telling the people bumping into me with excitement.

On a phone call with my mom, I told her that if there was such a pardon, I would refuse to accept it. When she heard in my voice that I meant what I said, she started to cry.

"Think of us, at least do it for your family! We want you home, why can't you understand that?"

I thought for a moment about what she said, and realized that I wasn't the only one going through this nightmare. She had written so many times: *"I'm beside you, every hour of the day."*

"Okay, mom," I said softly. "I'm sorry for being so selfish. Of course I would accept the pardon, there is nothing I want more than to have this all over with."

It was November 16th, 2005, five days after my mom and William left, the news was on TV and they officially announced that there would in fact come a pardon. There was complete silence, in the cell, in the section, throughout the entire prison. Silence. I had never experienced this before. Every single person was glued to the television. Some people were sitting on their beds, some on chairs, others were standing. They were all staring up at the little TV in the cell. They hung on the newscaster's every word. I looked around at my cellmates and became overwhelmed by the intense silence. All you could hear was the newsperson's voice reverberating throughout the prison. As they continued speaking, it remained deathly quiet. Everyone was waiting for the moment when the newsreader would announce how many people would be pardoned. It was more exciting than the decisive penalty kick in the World Cup soccer final!

And then the announcement came: ten thousand people would be pardoned!

A wave of cheers went through the prison. In the cell, people were jumping on top of one another, rushing into each other's arms, congratulating each other and already saying their goodbyes. I thought it a bit premature, but had to laugh at their exuberance. The pardon also covered 336 foreigners and everyone told me to get my belongings together. I told them I wasn't packing up yet. Seeing is believing.

For the rest of the evening, all they talked about was the pardon. In the morning, the circus of those leaving would begin.

24

Even before the morning roll call started, a planto from the hallway shouted the names of those who were allowed to go home. Most of them were still sleeping, but soon enough everyone was awake and the excitement began. Who were the lucky ones? Who gets to go home?

First, they released the foreigners. French people walked by, British and Pakistanis. I greeted them from behind the cell door. They were overjoyed and were hardly able to grasp the reality that it was over for them. My cellmates told me that I would surely be leaving too and that I should pack my things. For the first time, I started to believe that they might just be right. I hesitated and looked at Thomas, who shrugged. Thomas was waiting for his extradition to Germany, so he couldn't be pardoned anyway.

After a little while, they started calling for Moroccans to go home and everyone was staring at me. Going home wasn't going to happen for me, even though some said that maybe I would be considered for pardon as a Moroccan.

Fifteen minutes went by and many names were called through the hallway.

"Joseph Oubelkas!"

Suddenly, I heard my name and it was as if my heart leapt into my throat. Could it really be...?

My cellmates patted me on the back and wished me luck. With some difficulty, I squeezed out a smile. Now what?

The cell door was opened and I was ordered to report to the main courtyard. There, I ran into some of the other inmates and walked over to a Canadian whom I had spoken with a few times before. He was sentenced to eight years in prison – for smuggling hashish, of course.

Two uniformed men – who weren't prison employees – sat behind a wobbly desk with large sheets of paper stacked in front of them. When it was my turn, they sternly asked for my name and prison number. After arrogantly looking me up and down, they took a pen and scanned the lists of names, as if they didn't want me to get a pardon. In a cold, emotionless tone, they looked up at me and said that I had received two years reprieve from my sentence. I stood there like a robot, unaffected by what was just said, and signed the paper as confirmation of the pardon.

Without saying a word, I turned and walked away from the table. After my turn, the Canadian went through the same procedure. I waited for him so we could walk back together and talk. To my surprise, he told me that his sentence had been reprieved four years.

What? Four years?

I told him about getting two years and he frowned with uncertainty: *"Weird!"*

"Yeah, you can say that again."

While my sentence was longer than his, I later learned that a few other people with ten year verdicts also received three or four year reprieves, while others got nothing. What kind of a system would operate so inconsistently? Was it just purely random? I was quite upset over the unequal treatment I received. I couldn't make sense of it, just as I couldn't make sense of the entire justice system in this country. Figuring out the reason behind their decision would be impossible.

Anyway, my two year reduction was real. Now, instead of 2014, I would be allowed to go home in 2012.

25

It was calm after the storm. The daily routine had quickly returned. The number of prisoners was noticeably smaller. Previously, there were about five hundred men in our section, but after the pardon, that number had been reduced to less than three hundred. A guard told me that Jeremy was pardoned and released. This was pleasant news! It was a shame I couldn't go with him. I hope he would do well.

As part of our daily routine, Thomas and I began to approach our workouts more seriously. We had four large water bottles – each one able to hold five liters – which we filled with sand from the prison yard. We tied these bottles to the end of an old steel bar. The guards let us use the bar to work out, but afterwards we had to put it away in the shed next to the shower. In the shed,

I found an old piece of a TV cable which worked perfectly as a jump rope!

To be honest, it didn't look so exciting: Thomas "the Terminator" and Joseph "Tyson" *pumping sand*, but we had to do something.

In the Netherlands, there was some kind of a prisoners-abroad-initiative going on. During the pardon, Prince Willem-Alexander and Princess Máxima were in Morocco. This was big news and as a result, my mom was approached by various media outlets.

In the TV reports, my mom and Amber were back in the spotlight again. In the newspaper an article was published entitled *With Mandela in a Moroccan cell.* That title was derived from a letter I had written to my mom in which I told her about the book I read on Mandela. Powerful!

My mom wrote to me about her recent visit. She was "so happy" that I was "so beautiful and clean" looking. *"And William was such a doll. He found it so enjoyable that you and I could finally spend some time together, even though he wasn't allowed to come in."*

Regarding my plan to refuse the pardon, she wrote that I had scared her quite a bit, but secretly she thought "it was extremely brave".

Because of the responses to the newspaper articles and TV broadcasts, my mom had "some of the craziest days in the past few months". Many people wanted to hear my story. Some even called around to different news stations to try and get in touch with my mom. They wanted to tell her personally how much they sympathized with us.

"There was also a call from a man named Jeremy, who had nothing but good things to say about you. Karim from Berkane called too. They're both free and are doing just fine. Karim literally said: 'Madam, you don't have to worry about him being mistreated. Joseph is a good guy, everyone likes him, his cellmates, the guards and even the prison directors. They won't let anything happen to him.'"

26

"This morning started sunlit. I enjoyed a stunning sunrise with pink clouds, that later seemed to shine with golden edges. The plants were glistening in the sun and there was a thin layer of ice covering the ponds."

It was winter – almost Christmas. I would love to say that time was flying by, but that couldn't have been further from the truth. I was eager to talk to Amber. As fortune would have it, Thomas woke me up early that morning with news that cell phone coverage was now available. We were able to call from anywhere in the prison!

Over the past few days it had rained continuously and it apparently led to the breakdown of the phone jammers.

This was great news! Now I didn't have to fool around at the iron gate to make a call and could just call my girl while lying in my bed.

For nearly ninety minutes, our voices and thoughts were connected. The sound was so clear, it sounded like she was sitting in the room next to me. As always, I asked how things were going with school. She was studying Occupational Therapy.

"You've really supported me in trying to pass this course. Although you aren't physically here, which is what I miss the most", Amber sighed, "you're certainly here with me in spirit."

"I'm glad to hear so. You know how important I find it for you."

After a short silence, Amber suddenly said: "One year, Joe... One whole year! That doesn't make any sense, does it?"

"Indeed, one year. It was exactly one year ago that I let my mind get the best of me when I started asking those customs officers what was going on."

"You can't help that? That was just your job. You can't blame yourself, sweetheart."

"No, no, I know that," I sighed deeply, "but sometimes I really wish I had known about those drugs."

"Why?" Amber asked surprised.

"Well, if I had known that there were two vans full of hashish on that site, the moment I saw those customs officers running around with guns, I would never have started asking questions. I probably would have ran as fast as I could to the nearest airport."

"Yeah, but you didn't know. You were just in the wrong place at the wrong time."

"You're right, but still..."

"Do you remember our conversation about how you can close your eyes and be anywhere you want?" Amber asked.

"Sure, I remember it like it was yesterday."

"I do that often with my memories of us together," Amber said lovingly.

"Nice, isn't it?"

I knew exactly what she meant. I did the same almost every day in my cell. Eyes closed and imagining flying away from this place...

"I think a lot about the sports activities we did, going to the gym, being outside together, me on my skates and you on your mountain bike riding behind me... Or about our holidays in Southern France, on the island of Texel and that unexpected overnight stay in a hotel in Brussels when I brought you to the airport but the flight was canceled."

I listened while she talked, and in my mind, I took that journey that would be in our shared memories forever.

"What I really miss, is lying in your bed with my head on your stomach, falling asleep while you read or play on your computer. I really like that feeling of being safe in your arms as you pat me on the back. You make me feel like I am the most beautiful woman on earth."

"And that's what you are to me," I said.

Amber giggled. "I want to make love to you, Joe."

My hormones were raging like crazy.

"You have no idea how bad I want you! As soon as I get home, I'm going to drag you into the bedroom, lock the door and you won't be able to get rid of me for the next two weeks."

In my mind, I was beating my chest like a sexually aroused gorilla, swinging from vine to vine through the jungle and yelling louder than Tarzan. In reality, I was somewhere in a Moroccan prison, lying sideways on a bed with my feet up against the wall and my hand halfway down my pants like Al Bundy, with Amber giggling on the phone.

At some point, our conversation had to come to an end. So did my first year in captivity.

27

"To my grandson Joseph,

I received your letter from your mother after her visit to you and her return from Morocco. You will understand that it made me very happy. I've read the letter several times and your words have touched me deeply. I have great admiration for you. I admire your courage and faith that everything will be okay, because that is what you need to stay in control of this situation. Your insight along with this experience will make you appreciate once again what it means to live in freedom. I'm glad to read how your living situation has improved a little for you.

You have heard that I am also doing well. I can do everything again, enjoying the birds in the aviary and the garden. It's something to be very grateful for at my age.

I sincerely hope that you will be coming home soon and that your willpower will not let you down. Courage and faith are the cornerstones in your life that you can rely on. Last but not least, my warmest regards to you, Joseph, my great grandson.

I love you. Your grandfather."

My mom and I planned for a day when she would be with grandpa so I could call him. She knew the procedure of paging and calling back. Something my grandfather could barely understand. It was Christmas, and he was anxiously waiting for me to call. My mom watched him: *"He constantly fiddled with his handkerchief, looking at his watch over and over, waiting for you to call. And then you called. It was so heartbreaking, Joe, to see such an old man with tears in his eyes, trembling in his legs."*

The injustice not only affected me, but everyone around me. I realized this again after speaking to my grandfather. It made me emotional.

Images appeared before my eyes. Images of my mom writing at her desk yet another letter to me, my dad sitting at the dinner table alone, peacefully smoking a cigarette. I pictured my eldest brother, standing in our parents' bedroom, crying, telling me how much he missed me. I thought of William, telling me how he constantly thought of me when cycling from home to work. I thought of Amber, sitting on the train heading home about to get into bed, alone. And I thought of my grandfather, standing amongst the birds in the aviary and feeding them with his mind on his grandson, hoping for an early reunion.

28

Besides talking to my grandfather, Christmas and New Year's Eve were corny and boring again. They went by just like every other day.

On Boxing Day, just after the morning roll call, a fight broke out. Nice.

There was an argument again between the "late risers" and the "early birds". As usual. The late risers said there was too much noise in the cell, while the early birds said there was no sleeping late, "because this wasn't a hotel". The perfect scenario for a fight. In the cell, this was the number one cause of fighting; with the second being over the toilet – especially in the morning, when the persons waiting thought that the person using the toilet was taking too much time. The third thing they fought over were the two cooking sets – hungry people are notoriously selfish.

Our Kabran, the journalist, who used to keep things in order, had been transferred to another prison. Since he left, there has been no new cell leader. The journalist had given me his bed and mobile phone in exchange for my Diesel shoes and discman. He insisted. I couldn't refuse.

Thomas was now sleeping on the bunk above me.

Despite the constant noise, I was doing much better than a year ago. My mother wrote to me: *"I'm thankful that your circumstances are a little better than last year when you were stuck in that cold dark cell at the police station and nobody knew anything yet. You had to spend those days so terribly alone. At least things are better now. There really are a lot of people thinking of you."*

My mom had another great surprise for me. Through the website freesef.com, she had started a Christmas card campaign. As a result, I received several packages with more than two hundred Christmas cards in early 2006! Thomas and I were working out, when a planto in striped clothing yelled my name in the courtyard.

"Joseph, Joseph. Immer[12] *Joseph,"* Thomas said laughing, as if he was jealous. "Why is it never Thomas?"

I laughed and felt privileged. At least twice a week I was called to pick up my mail.

Smiling from ear to ear, I was standing in front of the women in administration, who, with a red stamp in their hand, were about to stamp the cards to confirm receipt.

12. German for "Always".

They looked at each other questioningly, wondering whether they really had to stamp each card in the mountain of cards that laid before them. I looked back at them with my huge smile. "Stamp away!" I thought, since I had nowhere to be and plenty of time. After so many visits the women knew me by now and I could tell they thought I wasn't such an unkind boy.

They laughed at the obvious satisfaction I took from receiving all of these letters and told me it was okay and I could just take the mailbag with me.

"Okay! Thanks! Bye!" I said quickly and rushed out of the room with the mailbag and various packages in my hands. I walked quickly to my cell. This was even better than my birthday!

The cards weren't only for me as my mom had also written a few hundred small Christmas cards for my fellow inmates. One by one, I handed them a card as they looked back at me surprisingly.

"What is it?" they would ask.

"A Christmas card," I answered. "From my mom."

"For me?"

"Yes, for you, from us."

Then they would open up the Christmas card and – those who could – read the French text my mom had written: *"Je pense à vous tous! Soyez sûr que mon cœur est avec vous pendant ces jours. Salutations de Janny, mère de Joseph."*[13]

Sometimes I got a hug, other times a smile. Sometimes they just sat there, turning the card over several times not saying a word, stunned by this gesture. Naturally, there were a few who couldn't appreciate it, but what did I expect, this was prison and there were some heartless guys here too.

---

13. I'm thinking of you all! Please know, that my heart is with you during these Holidays. Regards from Janny, Joseph's mother.

In one of the packages, there were Christmas garlands and a gold colored Christmas tree. Several inmates stood on a chair and hung the garlands from the ceiling. The Christmas tree was put on top of the TV. They had their tongues sticking out of their mouth in their efforts. Everyone was completely grateful and wished my mom all the best from Allah. It was quite a sight! Christmas decorations in January in a prison cell, in a Muslim country!

29

"My son, how beautiful it is that all the people here in the Netherlands were able to provide you and the others a nice party during this time of year. How lovely it is that there is now a shiny, decorated tree in your cell, with garlands hanging from the ceiling. Hopefully, this will give you all a bit of Christmas spirit, even though it's a little late. Now you see that you're not forgotten! I'm glad that you felt some happiness when all those packages arrived.

I am also astonished by all these gestures.

We shall leave behind the worn out and tiresome year of 2005, ready to make a fresh start in 2006. A year in which I hope your innocence will be proven, and you will happily be walking in and out of our home again, my child."

30

"You know, I very often picture you sitting with your back against the wall, your face to the sun and your eyes half closed. Looking at the sky through your beautiful long lashes, with those long legs of yours lying straight, your feet crossed."

One afternoon, we were sitting next to each other in the courtyard, exactly like this, facing the sun and I told Thomas my mom wrote that to me. Thomas wouldn't believe me until I showed him my mom's letter number seventy eight.

"How does she know? How does she know that we always sit like this?"

"Telepathy, spiritual bonding, empathy, you name it. My mom and I have a special bond."

Despite the winter, December and January not only brought some fiercely cold days, but some very sunny days as well. Thomas and I enjoyed the sun, shining on our faces.

But we wouldn't get to enjoy the afternoons together for much longer. The year 2006 had just begun, when one evening, Thomas was told that he had to pack his things. His transfer for extradition to Germany, after eight months of waiting, had finally come. The night guards gave him fifteen minutes to pack up his belongings and say goodbye. Thomas was quite upset about leaving. He was looking at ten to fourteen years in prison, so the trip to Germany was far from positive.

Fortunately, he was still able to smile, because we had supported each other through a lot. The workouts, library visits, our talks, solitary, sharing our thoughts, listening to music together, they were all special moments that we would never forget.

He packed quickly and, as if Thomas had never been in the cell, his place atop my bunk was immediately taken by a cellmate whose turn it was to have a bed.

Just before he disappeared from my sight, I spoke to him through the barred gate. It was a proverb my mom once told me: *"He who lives without fear, cannot break."*

31

Now that Thomas was gone, I hung around with Younes more often. That was prison life: people come and people go. And every time, you start hanging around with other people. You don't choose them, but you cross paths with each other.

Younes was a Moroccan guy of my age. He had small black eyes, a remarkably high forehead and a narrow nose. Not a great looking guy, but plenty of charisma. He was from a wealthy family and very intelligent. Younes was a good man, but he had one major flaw: almost every night he got as stoned as a monkey. He regretted his hashish addiction and swore to me daily that he was going to quit, but he never did.

Younes taught me how to read and write Arabic and he also helped me improve my French. In exchange, I taught him English. This language was gaining popularity among the Moroccan youth.

We often walked together through the section hallways and he would tell me stories of the inmates we had met. One of the most bizarre stories that has stayed with me to this day, was about a guy called "Farkash". Farkash had stolen twenty sheep and had already been in prison for more than three years. Younes told me that the tribunal had "forgotten" about him.

"Forgot him? For three years?" I asked.

"Yes, he was forgotten. This is pretty common. The file of the prisoner gets lost and then he is forgotten."

Again I couldn't believe my ears. Farkash had no family, except his old mother, who occasionally came to visit him. I spoke to him because I was curious about why he had stolen the sheep.

"Well, as I walked across the countryside I saw a group of sheep without a shepherd. So I thought to myself, I'll take them."

Farkash was a simple guy, not a shred of immorality.

"But, you know you can't just take them like that," I said.

Embarrassed, Farkash looked down and scraped his foot against the floor.

"I know, but I thought the sheep were neglected. I walked for two days with them, letting them eat and drink everywhere. Then, down the road, I was arrested by two policemen. I've been here ever since."

No one even offered to help him. People could think very fatalistically in prison. They would often say "God wanted it this way" and there was nothing that could be done. Not to mention everyone was dealing with their own problems, so the willingness to help others wasn't found very often.

"Can't the guards do anything, then?" I asked Younes.

He shrugged. "Maybe someone could write a letter..."

"So, let's do it!"

Piece of cake.

Like almost half of the population of Morocco, Farkash was illiterate, so writing the letter himself wasn't an option. Younes did it for him, and – together with a few packs of cigarettes – we delivered the letter to the guards.

Miraculously, Farkash was called two months later. He was officially sentenced to eighteen months in prison and could go home immediately. The eighteen additional months he spent in prison was deemed "bad luck". He received no compensation, nor an apology.

Just before Farkash left, he came to say goodbye, embracing us with gratitude. The guards literally had to pull him away from us. All he could do was thank us and cry.

32

Younes taught me a lot, but his addiction took its toll.

One afternoon I was chatting with him in the hallway. Well,

it was basically Younes doing all the talking. He was always a talkative guy, but it never really bothered me that he spoke up in our conversations.

Younes smoked a fortune in hashish every day, and apparently he owed a lot of money to his "supplier", who was at the end of his rope. In the doorway at the end of the hallway, a black outline of a bulky figure became visible. It looked like someone had hit the guy on the head with a shovel, as his neck was nonexistent. After it stood in the doorway for a while, the dark figure started to come closer, stomping furiously. I looked up, but kept leaning against the wall in the same position. Younes aborted his monologue and his cheek blanched with fear at the sight of the brute.

"What's going on? Do you know him?" I asked.

"That's the Chinese," Younes said shakily.

"Chinese? Did you order something?"

He didn't have time to appreciate my joke because the Chinese walked right up to him. He owed the nickname to his narrow eyes. On his arms and face were numerous scars that made him frightening. The Chinese was furious and kicked a large plastic trash can ten feet into the air. A trail of debris was left behind, as the dented can rolled by. Younes braced himself and I instinctively went into a defensive position as well. The Chinese walked past me and pressed his face against Younes'. He was there for one goal: to get his money or demolish Younes.

A few words were exchanged between the two, but within seconds the Chinese's fist went flying toward Younes' face. I heard a dull thud. Younes swung back immediately, but missed. The Chinese became wild, he screamed and punched Younes in the face again. His left eye swelled up instantly. After a brief frozen moment of watching, I finally snapped out of it and grabbed the Chinese's heavy body from behind. I wrapped my arms around his waist, but like a panther fixed on his prey, he continued punching a few more times. Due to this sudden explosion of energy, I let go of him. I immediately jumped to the side. I wrapped my left arm around his thick neck and pulled him away from Younes. With the Chinese's head clamped firmly in my arms, I forced him to bend over. Like a bull wrangler, I kept him in check with all of my body's strength and weight. Younes finally saw his chance and kicked him, repeatedly cursing in the process.

"Knock it off, Younes!" I shouted, yelling for the guards to take him away.

The Chinese continued to struggle and started to punch my back. I yelled at him to keep quiet. With some difficulty, he turned his head around sideways and looked at me with his narrow eyes full of fury. I kept telling him to stay quiet and miraculously he seemed to listen. His resistance decreased and I saw two guards arrive. I let the Chinese go and pushed him toward them who then dragged him away.

In the distance I could see the Chinese being searched. To my horror they found two knives, one from behind his back in his belt and the other from his sock. He was slapped in the face by one of the guards, handcuffed and then removed from our section. He was taken to "el hadeeka" – "the zoo".

The zoo was a collective cell where they kept the prisoners who fought, were caught with a phone, drugs or anything else forbidden. Guys who went there often came back emaciated or with visible injuries. They consisted mostly of bruises on the face and around the diaphragm, as well as the marks of beatings on the soles of their feet.

At that point, I didn't know why they called this cell "the zoo", but soon enough I would come to find out why for myself.

33

A day after the fight, I had some big bruises on the right side of my ribcage. Younes' left eye was excessively swollen and bruised. The expression "the first blow is half the battle" fitted well here. Younes continued telling me that he really was going to quit smoking that "devilish hashish". I encouraged it and set a number of goals myself which I would pursue during my imprisonment. It was a list I came up with after reading the biography of Malcolm X:

"In the hectic pace of the world today, there is no time for meditation, or for deep thought. A prisoner has time he can put to good use. I'd put prison second to college as the best place for a man to go if he needs to do some thinking. If he's motivated, even in prison he can change his life."

I let Younes read this piece and talked with him about making ourselves useful. That's what I put at the top of my list. How was I supposed to make myself useful? I wasn't sure yet, but I knew that time would tell. Under the "make myself useful" column, I wrote the words "reading", "writing" and "learning languages". I was already reading every day and writing in my diary and together with Younes, I was working on my Arabic, French and English.

The next item on the list was "working out". I was already doing this as well, however, I wanted to get Younes completely onboard with my routine, so he had to exercise with me. After a lot of complaining from his side – Younes never did any exercising – we finally took the workouts seriously. I had *Men's Health* magazines sent to me from home and the cover models seemed to convince Younes of the usefulness of sports. We also tried sticking to a diet as much as possible. We did a lot of exercises using our body weight. Our goal was to develop a body just like one of those cover models.

It didn't take long before someone asked if he could exercise with us. Sure, no problem. The more the merrier. But it didn't stop there. Cellmates started to notice us sweating and getting fitter by the day. Apparently they were encouraged to join and the group quickly grew to ten men.

I supervised the training sessions by demonstrating the exercises and teaching the men how and what to do. I pushed them to achieve their maximum results.

These were men who were more than a foot taller than me in some cases, and three times as wide. They were covered with tattoos and scars and were feared by most of the outside world. Here, however, under my training routine, they were wimps. They were struggling with the leg exercises and push-ups, and sweating like pigs during the running parts.

"Is that all you got?" I said, like an experienced drill sergeant. They responded with moans and groans. "Oh, outside the prison walls you're pretty tough, you're the man, but in here you guys are already complaining after ten push-ups! Come on guys!"

My Spartan training was remarkably accepted. It seemed as if my fellow inmates gradually respected me more because of it.

Every morning at half past nine, Monday through Friday, we gathered in the courtyard and exercised until eleven o'clock. Afterwards, we had to return to our cells, but still had some time to take a shower and wash up. This way, we survived the mornings and was one-third of the day gone.

34

"Spring is in the air, there's no denying it. There are big buds on the branches of all the trees. The roses have tiny leaves, and the daffodils and tulips have grown to about two inches above the ground."

It was Easter, and instead of searching for eggs, I decided to read all of the letters and cards I had received again. The continuous stream of mail was so overwhelming that the administration had its hands full with translating and stamping all the letters and cards. Every time I stood in front of those ladies, I wore a big smile. Shrugging I said: "I can't help that I get so much mail."

They didn't know what to do. It even went so far that the director had to get involved. He decided that all mail for me coming from the Netherlands had to be sent to the Dutch embassy in Morocco. The embassy would now have to stamp my letters and cards for approval and the prison director would give his consent that there were no prohibited things inside. From that moment on, the representatives of the Dutch embassy came with a stack of mail for me every month.

"How is that possible? So much mail every time?" a representative of the Dutch embassy asked once. "Do you just call a random family in the Netherlands and ask if they would like to send a card?"

We laughed.

"No," I explained, "it's all thanks to my mom."

My mother was my personal, unrelenting ambassador, not to mention my PR agent. Through the website freesef.com she launched one card campaign after the other. They were always done in honor of some sort of celebration. At that precise moment in their lives, my mom wanted people to think of the less fortunate, such as a prisoner in a foreign country, someone like me.

Many people didn't know what to write. It was difficult, but my mom always said that it didn't matter *what* you write, as long as you *write* something.

"Include him in your life," my mom said. "Even if it's only a change to something in your garden, a pregnancy, a move, a promotion at work, your pet, a holiday or a dream."

As people continued to write, it gave me strength. This motivated my mother even more and she kept launching more and more campaigns.

"We must go on! Sitting depressed in a corner doesn't help."

My mom sent me a monthly package that weighed about twenty-two pounds. Inside were different foods such as oatmeal, canned tuna, ginger bread and peanut butter – delicious! There was always a guard with me when I picked up my package at the administration.

As I started to unpack it, I would imagine how my mom packed it at home. She weighed each item carefully and made sure that there was no empty space remaining unused.

After approval, I could take the package back to the cell. Often, the guard requested to have something from the package too, which I allowed. In my mind I said "Don't you touch my things!" but I knew I had to play the game along. I was living in their world and I knew that if I didn't give into the guards' request, they could hold back the packages. Childish games, but unfortunately, it's just the way it was.

My mom wasn't the only one to send me packages. I also received packages from many others. The fitness center "Van Drunen" once launched an awesome campaign. They sent me two packages of T-shirts bearing the slogan *keep on fighting, no matter what.* I believe I once said that in an interview, and Peter van Drunen, owner of the fitness center, remembered it.

Handing out the T-shirts was one big party. I gave them to the inmates I knew best, and I actually needed more than a thousand to satisfy everyone, but of course that was impossible. It was amazing to see my fellow inmates walking around in the T-shirts. I chuckled at the sight of a few old men, who were proudly wearing it even though they had no idea what the slogan meant. But that wasn't important as long as it came from the Netherlands. Everything that came from the Netherlands became sacred.

The thing that was sacred to me was my appeal to the Supreme Court. I had to wait, I wanted to wait, because I was innocent. I wanted the judges of the Supreme Court to realize that too. My case, however, was not yet approved to be heard. Everyone was waiting for their turn, and if the odds weren't in your favor, then it could take another eighteen months.

Eighteen months.

That would make it the end of 2007! A time that seemed impossibly far away!

Don't think of it, just live, day after day...

And so, time ticked by...

35

Twenty four hours a day, seven days a week, William was a surrogate brother to my brothers, and he wrote about it every time:

"Last time I was over, I played Mario Kart on the Nintendo with Amir. He thinks it's really fun. Occasionally I let him win, otherwise his confidence would fall and he'll think he's bad at it, when he really has improved. Yesterday, I played soccer with Amir and Malik on the field at the mill. Well, actually with Malik. Amir always asks if I want to play "soccer", but as we're standing on the field, he kicks the ball three times and then he goes running to the playground to swing and chase butterflies. By the way, he's losing some teeth. On the top, he lost four front teeth altogether and now has a huge gap between them. Every time he says something, I burst out laughing!"

Amber was having a hard time with everything and missed me very much...

"For the longest time, I've tried to keep strong, but right now, I can't help missing you and feeling frustrated and powerless. Honey, I know I

can't imagine what you have to go through each day, but please know that you are truly a hero. I'm sorry that I haven't spoken to you in a little while. I've been really busy with school. But don't you worry about me. Just know that I miss you. I miss your company, your smile, our conversations, your teasing, your touches, your love, your support."

My mom felt she had to visit me again. It had been over six months since her last visit. It was still winter when she came the last time, and she brought William with her. Now it was early summer and she was coming alone. Of course, William and Amber wanted to come with her, but we didn't dare take that chance in case they wouldn't be allowed in.

So my mom came alone.

Just like last time, it was wonderful to see her and feel her touch again. We chatted joyfully, and I was spoiled again with more goods that my friends had given her to bring.

"I enjoyed both the serious and trivial things we talked about, but it all went by too fast," my mom wrote to me the day after she left. It really was over in what seemed like seconds. It was as if it had never happened...

"It was strange to be back in the Netherlands, almost unbelievable that the day before, I was still with you and we had to say goodbye again, for who knows how long. I feel so fortunate that I was able to see you and hold you. You looked so handsome and clean! So far, your mission of keeping your head up and your chest out has certainly succeeded, my child!"

My mother's words made me happy, but I also knew that she had a hard time in Morocco. She wrote me beforehand that she had hoped this trip would be her last to this country. She didn't want to come here anymore. The trip was very expensive and my mom had to save literally every dime. Having a child in prison wasn't cheap. Shipping packages alone cost more than fifty euros, and I certainly had no income. I was forced to sell my interest in my company, but was still waiting for the money. The contact I had with my former partners sadly fell apart. The company we established now no longer existed. One of my partners left to work with an existing IT company, and the other started his own new business.

The Dutch embassy sent me thirty euros per month, but this went to buying cigarettes for the guards. I told my mom I would rather she stayed home and saved the money for her and the packages.

"The most important thing is and shall remain, that we are mentally and emotionally connected through the many silver threads of the moon."

36

I just finished taking a shower after exercising with Younes and the guys, and I was feeling fit. I look down at my watch to see that it's a little after one o'clock, and I didn't want to take a siesta. Instead, I'm sitting on my bed looking at pictures of my mother, my home, the beautiful skies and Amber and her new dorm.

Amber sent me a picture of each corner of her room. I can see her TV and comfortable sofa, the desk where her laptop sits, the sink and her bed.

Hey, what's that?

I look closer at one of the pictures. Is that a package of pills next to her bed? THE pill? As in the-pill-that-doesn't-get-you-pregnant-pill? The birth control pill? Huh? Would she still be using it? Why would she need to use it?

Several thoughts were flashing through my mind.

Would she...?

No way, definitely not. It's probably an old package.

But why is it still lying next to her bed?

Could she be involved with another guy? Now that I'm stuck here?

The thought of this alone made me feel dizzy.

Over the next few days, different questions and thoughts were still running through my mind. I caught myself at already accusing Amber when I had no reason to. According to Younes, it was obvious, but I told him that Amber would never do that. I completely trusted Amber.

At night I was plagued by nightmares in which I would see Amber with someone else and I would startle awake, gasping, staring into the dark cell.

It took a few seconds to come to my senses and calm down, falling backwards onto my bed. There I was, staring at the bottom of my upstairs neighbor's bed.

Knowing that she would never be unfaithful, gave me some reassurance. I thought of the years we had spent together. Instinctively, I thought of the countless times we made love, and where. I thought of her letters and how she described me as "sexy thing" and "beautiful, sweet, intelligent man". In her eyes, no one could hold a candle to me.

No one.

37

Amber's parents were celebrating their fiftieth wedding anniversary with a big party. It was Saturday and I called Amber's parents because I couldn't get a hold of her on her cell phone. I was standing in the courtyard at one of the new phone booths. They were recently installed to eliminate some of the congestion in the previous phone room. Normally, prisoners weren't allowed to use the phone on the weekends, and certainly not the ones on the courtyard, but I explained to a guard that I desperately needed to make a call. I gave him fifty dirham upon which he told me to be quick.

For a few days now, I couldn't stop thinking about the pills on Amber's desk. I was anxious and stressed and couldn't wait any longer, I had to talk with her today. Sometimes you get the feeling that something has to be done, right now, even though you could have done this long before.

Amber's mom picked up the phone and I congratulated her. She graciously thanked me and said that Amber was standing right next to her. She quickly handed her the phone.

"Hey, Joe!" Amber shouts enthusiastically.

I could hear noises of fun and pleasure in the background.

"Hey, Amber."

"Hold on, Joe, I can't hear you that well, let me walk upstairs."

As I was holding, I could hear Amber's footsteps echoing on the floor.

"There, that's better," she says.

"Yes, it's much quieter now. How are you?"

"Fine, busy," Amber laughs. "And you? Are you still hanging in there, sweetheart?"

"Yeah sure, it's not always easy, of course. I miss you guys, and I should be there right now at the party."

"Ah, yes, I know, sweetie. You should be here. Those bastards over there."

I ask her about the usual things like school, her sister and parents, but then I came straight to the point.

"Do you still use the birth control pill?"

For a moment, it's quiet. I could feel our talk was taking a different turn.

"I saw it in one of the pictures of your room, there was a package next to your bed."

"Yes," she answers as normal as possible, "I still use it."

"Why?"

"Oh, it's just a habit. I take it on autopilot."

I felt that there was more to it than that, I could hear it in her voice. She's trying to avoid the subject.

"Do you still exercise a lot?" she asks.

"Yes, almost every day."

"And the guards, are they still being reasonable?"

"I'm standing alone in the prison courtyard right now. The guards allow me to do things the other inmates are forbidden from, which is pretty cool."

I speak nasally. She wants to continue asking questions, but I interrupt her.

"Amber? Should I be worried about that pill?"

"Come on, Joe!"

"I mean, if there's something going on, you have to tell me."

"Now stop it, there's nothing going on."

But there is. For a moment, it remains silent.

And then she continues. Her voice begins to tremble.

"Joe, please know that it's hard for me too."

I already know what she's about to say, but I don't want to accept it yet.

"Yeah, I know, it's not easy for you either. You don't have to tell me. Just like I don't have to tell you that this place isn't always as cozy."

"I know..." Amber is speaking softly.

I keep silent. I don't know what to say.

"Life goes on here as well," she is sobbing. Silence. "And... And I've met someone..."

BOOM!

No...

I'm starting to feel sick.

"And?" I ask as mundane as possible.

"Well... I have feelings for him."

I gasp. With the receiver in my left hand, and my right arm leaning against the phone, I let my head rest on the keypad.

"Does this dude know about my situation?" I ask grinding my teeth together.

"Yes," Amber sniffles.

"Damn, Amber!" I raise my voice and squeeze the receiver. "Do you have any idea what kind of situation I'm in? What kind of fucking place I have to live in?"

"Yes, of course I know!" Amber shouts, crying. "I feel so bad and it's so hard. For a while, I wasn't sure how I was going to tell you this."

"Do I know him?" I ask angrily.

"No..."

My world was falling out from under me. On the other side of the phone all I could hear was Amber crying. She can't talk. So I do.

"Do you realize what kind of world I live in? I look around and every day I see nothing but damn concrete and bars! And then you go and do this!!"

I feel myself losing control, tears are welling up. I feel betrayed. "Don't think for one minute that I'm going to cry about this! I've been humiliated here so much already!! You know what... Never mind!!"

I slam the phone down twice. Tears well up in my eyes. I turn around and start to shout uncontrollably in anger.

"Why is all this happening to me!! What did I do to deserve this, damn it!!"

I swing my fists through the air around me, looking for something to throw, something to beat or break. I keep shouting. It's the first time I'm letting myself go this way since my conviction in early 2005, almost eighteen months ago.

I feel so alone and abandoned in this large courtyard between the high walls lined with barbed wire. I can't catch my breath. I keep crying and asking myself over and over again, why has this all happened to me.

Suddenly I look up and see the beautiful deep blue sky.

It calms me.

I breathe in through my nose and out through my mouth. I'm inhaling and exhaling very consciously, while the tears are still flowing down my cheeks. I look into the sky as far as possible. It's blue, intensely blue.

"Be strong, Joseph. Be strong. Prove that you can survive this too."

It's my mom's voice I hear in the distance. I close my eyes and breathe in the warm air.

"Never lose your dignity and hang on! Stay strong, be brave..."

38

"And I who went to sleep as two"

"Woke up as one, now only you remain"

"You'll close your eyes and travel back"

"To the time, when the light went fading fast"

"And the words you'll never, never forget, oh no"

"As you slipped away"

"Goodbye baby..."

Back at the cell, I go straight to bed without saying a word to anyone. I put on my music and listen to Fleetwood Mac singing *Goodbye Baby*. I cry and think about nothing at all and a hundred different things at the same time. I am angry, sad and furious, but I also remember how much Amber has done for me through all of this, and I'm really grateful to her. But again the rage rises, when I see her picture sitting next to me on the shelf. I grab it, walk over to the toilet tearing the picture into shreds and flush them down with a bucket of water. Of course, my cellmates now see that something is going on, but they can tell from my body language that I want to be left alone. I don't even speak to Younes. He and the rest of them will surely laugh in my face. They were right all along, even though I didn't want to believe it. They would only laugh harder now. Assholes.

If this had happened on the outside, I would have handled it a little better. I would have jumped in the car and taken a drive. I would have gone to William to pour my heart out or listened to my mom's calming words. I could go to the gym and take out my anger, or throw myself completely into my work. I could go out to a bar or nightclub, anywhere, just to take my mind off of Amber. Either way, I could have done something to take my mind off of this.

Instead, I'm lying on a bed in a cell, biting my lip and clenching my fists, imagining what I would do to this dude, this new boyfriend of hers. I picture slamming him on his face, over and over again.

Coward! How dare you? Stealing the girl from an innocent man sitting in jail. My girl!

Damn it! Damn it!!

39

Later that night, I went back to talk with the guys, they were playing a card game at a table in the middle of the cell. I was sitting behind Younes as I told my story. Everyone looked up at me and listened.

Amber claimed she couldn't control her feelings. They all thought that was a poor excuse. I shrugged, I didn't know how to feel, I didn't understand it. Why was this happening to me?

The days and weeks that followed weren't easy. Every time I thought I started to feel better, I wandered off again into a fit of emotions. Even over the smallest things, at the slightest thought, I got tears in my eyes. Every time it happened I would force myself to swallow the lump in my throat. I longed for love again, the kind of love you could touch, feel. I longed again for a woman, my woman, Amber.

There was no sex life here. Well, there were men of course, who engaged in homosexual activities, but I kept myself far away from that. Very far. I will never forget the one day after exercising, Younes and I caught two men in the common shower together. It made me retch because it had nothing to do with "love".

Married men still had the right to be with their wives once a month for conjugal visits. They would meet in a separate, guarded room, right next to the administration department. I imagined it all, how the couple's feelings were uncontrollable in the "love room", while the guards were listening at the door.

Not me, all I had were my memories and dreams, ones that always seemed to be about Amber.

I missed the embrace of loved ones even more now. The feeling of a hug or cuddle, from my mom, friends, people who know me and love me. I missed the arms of my little brothers around my neck, after they ran to me enthusiastically as I came home to my father's house. I wanted this nightmare to be over, that this trapped life, a dog's life, would close its doors behind me forever. Despite my grief, I saved Amber's necklace and kept it on my shelf close to me. I was still determined to give it back to her one day. No matter what happened. That was our promise.

My eyes began to fill with tears again, but I refused to cry. I didn't want to cry anymore, I had had enough. I was twenty-five and would soon be twenty-six. I wasn't the little boy anymore whose mom picked him up from daycare. I was now the big strong man I wanted to be when I was younger. I had to go on. I couldn't give up. I wasn't allowed to give up. I had to focus on myself. I had to look in the mirror.

"If you need to rely on someone, then rely on the one you're looking at in the mirror."

It was a proverb I think I read in some magazine once.

Yes, I had to trust myself, encourage myself. I had to go on for my mom, for William, for my dad, and my little brothers. For everyone who supported me with all that mail. But especially for myself. Head up, back straight. I've had time to be upset, now it's time to roll up my sleeves and move on!

40

"Will you please keep the faith? Will you keep taking such good care of yourself? Watch out for yourself, but also make time for others. Keep exercising, writing and reading. Keep doing the little things you do. Every cloud you see, is one that I've blown your way. When the moon laughs, I think of you boys there. Even though I'm a few thousand miles away, you'll never be alone."

As time passed, I realized that it just wasn't meant to be. Amber wasn't supposed to be the woman in my life. I started to accept it. I had to, and actually I could now understand Amber. I understood that for her it was incredibly difficult. She was a beautiful young woman who would obviously get attention from men. Who knows, I may have done the same thing if the situation was reversed. I don't know, but eventually I didn't blame Amber anymore. I closed that chapter of my life and put her out of my mind.

My friends found out that it was over between Amber and me. The letters I received were mostly asking about how I felt and that I always could count on their support. William wrote me a long letter with some inspirational words:

"Sometimes life is so different than what you expect. That's what makes it beautiful, but also very difficult. Some things you cannot control, and sometimes they require a lot of patience in order to resolve them. This helps us to become stronger, more positive, and especially

more experienced. Friends and family are also very important. Which you know all too well! I'm really thankful for the unconditional support you get from not only the people that know you, but also from strangers. That will give you the strength you need. I just can feel it!

I myself have started looking at life from a much different perspective. For example, when I get angry, I think of you and how trivial my problems are in comparison. Then I take a deep breath and just figure it out, otherwise, I walk away with a smile on my face.

It's strange living my life here normally, knowing that for you, everything has stopped. Not spiritually of course, I'm talking about the usual things, like working, going out, seeing friends and so on. Nothing should be taken for granted, you see. Fuck, there are the tears again... No matter how long it takes, no matter what happens in the future, our friendship will always remain!"

Younes saw how much mail I continually received and told me a saying that is often used in Morocco: "You can take the horse to water, but it's the horse's responsibility to drink."

He thought this saying was perfect for my situation because I had been encouraged so much. I had the choice of using those letters to help me stay alive. And I did, I drank the water, and I would keep drinking it as long as the water would come...

41

Months went by slowly in cell number six.

My mom stayed in contact with Abdel, the NOS journalist, but we had heard nothing from the counselor, the one she had handed my file to last year.

And even though the investigation by the Dutch Ministry of Foreign Affairs had a positive outcome for us, nobody could do anything.

By the summer of 2006, cell number six had already been my "home" for one year. That summer was one to quickly forget. I didn't see or hear anything at all about the soccer World Cup. Morocco wasn't participating in the tournament and therefore didn't purchase any broadcasting rights for the matches. I thought of my mom, who said that she couldn't care less about the World Cup and I convinced myself to think the same.

It was very hot in the cell and everyone was exhausted because of the heat. The main advantage of this was that no one had the strength to argue. Even with the slightest movement, the sweat poured down our back and belly. We all walked around and slept in shorts with our shirts off. There wasn't any refreshment to be found and fans were not allowed. Not to mention air conditioning. There was no escape from the stifling heat.

The number of cockroaches began to rise again. They fell from the ceiling, swarmed around the light switches, crept into the leftovers and when the prisoners shook out their blankets they fell out in clumps. The partly opened drains in the courtyard smelled horrible and were infested with rats.

Through my mom, I let Amber's parents know that they no longer had to financially support me or send packages.

"Why not?" was their reaction. "We like Joseph for the person he is and that has nothing to do with his relationship with Amber."

My mom told me this and it touched me. It was heartwarming to hear. Until the last day of my imprisonment, they continued to support my mom and me.

Birthdays passed by silently, just like last year. In my diary – day 537 – I wrote a piece for my eldest brother hoping that someday he would read it:

"Hey Amir, little brother. Congratulations on your ninth birthday. It's hard to imagine that I haven't seen you since you were seven. Bizarre.

Time just keeps ticking away and doesn't seem affected by anyone or anything. I'm sorry I missed your special day again. I really hope to be there for your tenth birthday. I heard that you're going to celebrate your day along with your brothers Malik and Kian on July 15th. How nice.

I hope everything goes well at school and that you still do your best in karate and swim class. Be good. See you soon, little man."

For my twenty-sixth birthday my mom had invited a small group of people and organized a garden party. It was a beautiful sunny day. My mom knew that I would call home and surprised me with the visitors singing in chorus *"Happy Birthday"*. I laughed and got tears in my eyes. Everyone got on the phone to congratulate me and I thanked each one of them for the wonderful singing.

"Happy birthday, my child."

"Thank you, mom, thank you."

It didn't know what to say more, as I wiped away the tears from my cheeks with the palm of my hand.

42

In prison, you experience everything more intensely. The feelings of love and grief are twice as heavy. You learn to appreciate even the smallest of things.

The packages with contact lenses, magazines and food were always welcomed, like a gift. I got excited about these things, even though there were actually very ordinary.

I started to realize that life wasn't about big materialistic things. People often measure their happiness by how big their TV is, how fast their car goes or how shiny their watch is. But in prison you learn to appreciate the small things. Things that often seem insignificant at first. Things that aren't materialistic like: a walk in the woods, a sunset, a ride on an empty highway, the views of different landscapes, that one sweet word from your lover, the pat on your cheeks, a hug when you're sad or just happy.

My mom, William and I used to pick blackberries during our walks in the woods near our hometown. It's one of my many happy childhood memories. It was late August, early September, the perfect time for picking blackberries. Every year we went there. I can still see it. My mom, William and I, courageously venturing deep into the barbed bunches. We filled our plastic bags with big ripe blackberries. It was like a paradise. And we were almost always the only ones there!

While we laughed, we got scratches that never seemed to bother us. The sunset colored our faces orange with warmth. With our bags full, we returned home to make jam. A large pan with dark blue dregs was simmering on the gas stove patiently, with my mom occasionally stirring it. I gave her the clean glass jars that used to be filled with apple sauce, honey or peanut butter. She filled each jar precisely to the top, twisted on the lid and put the jar on its head. My mom knew that this formed a vacuum so the jam could be kept longer. And boy, did we enjoy the delicious taste of it later.

43

"It was very nice and quiet autumn weather. The warmest September of the past three hundred years is behind us. Some of the tree tops are already becoming a bit bare."

I noticed little of the autumn weather here. It was almost always the same: sunny and hot. The trees in Morocco are evergreen. No leaves fall and there are no autumn colors.

The only difference from the summer was that in the autumn, it was a little less warm.

Autumn faded into winter. One day it actually snowed a lot. Snow is rare in Morocco, not to mention frost. When my dad experienced frost in the Netherlands for the first time, he was enchanted by two frozen socks left out on the balcony. He just had to show the stiff socks to my mom and took them inside. When she came home, my dad wanted to proudly show them off to her, but he was speechless. What happened? The socks had become soft again!

"They really were frozen!" my father tried to convince my mom as she laughed exuberantly.

Some of the prisoners had a lot of fun with the snow. They were throwing snowballs at each other in the prison yard and laughing loudly like children, just as I used to do in the school yard with my friends. They were rubbing each other's faces in it and stuffing it into each other's clothes. Surprisingly, it went very well and there were no fights. I watched the spectacle from a distance and smiled. It made me laugh, especially when someone slipped and fell.

But the snow also had a major drawback: it was accompanied by severe cold.

Winters brought a piercing cold wind inside the cells. The bars without glass gave no protection against it. However, I found that the cold was not nearly as bad as the heat, because you can dress properly for the cold. They say when it's cold, it's better to lie naked under the covers to keep warm. Well, not me. And surely not in this environment. So I dressed in a few warm sweaters, double socks and put on a winter hat. Then I buried myself in my bed, just like the others. We sometimes looked like the emperor penguins of Antarctica, leaning against one another and moving as little as possible to keep each other warm.

Even in the winter I continued exercising with Younes and

the guys every morning. It became routine for us, "do it without thinking". We usually worked out inside one of the rooms next to the showers. It was a big empty space, which we were allowed to use to work out.

The area was also used to temporarily store the bread cart. The plantos used the cart daily to pass out bread around the unit. The most prominent inmates were served first and got the freshest bread for a small fee – a cigarette or a dirham. The poorer inmates had to make do with the remaining pieces from the bottom of the cart.

One day, I noticed an old man shuffling into the room while I was exercising. He had sunken cheekbones and a sad look in his eyes, as if he had had enough of life on this earth. He leaned against the bread cart, grabbed one of the leftovers, turned around and shuffled quietly away again. I watched him the whole time and couldn't find it in my heart to let him go. I ran after the old man and tapped him on the shoulder. He turned around surprised.

Someone who notices me.

"Come," I said to him.

Someone who talks to me...

The little man followed me slowly. I invited him into my cell, which he agreed to hesitantly. A number of cellmates were staring him down and I noticed he was feeling uncomfortable. I walked back to him and took him gently by the hand. He looked so fragile, almost like porcelain.

"Don't mind them. Here, take this." I gave him a plastic bag that was filled with all kinds of foods, completed with things from the Netherlands such as soup, chocolate and gingerbread. I also gave him a few packs of cigarettes and told him to be sparsely with them. Finally, I gave him a sweater – his was full of holes – and long johns, for he shivered from the cold. I saw in the man's eyes that he didn't understand what was happening.

“You don’t have to do this,” he could hardly speak.

“Sure I do, here, take it. Come on, I’m going back to working out and if you need anything else, let me know.”

I found it shocking how many people were forgotten here. People who didn’t have family or friends, or someone that cared about them. My stomach turned.

To me, that’s the worst thing that could ever happen, I keep saying that: to be forgotten... As if you don’t exist anymore...

44

Younes was gone. Taken out of the cell. He clashed heads with a new cellmate, a snobbish guy who was apparently a member of the royal family.

Our “prince” was a true dictator. I tried to ignore him, and for the first few days I was able to do so, but he made his presence so obvious that it became impossible. It was inevitable when you’re that close to each other for almost twenty-four hours a day.

Whenever the prince wanted to sleep, everyone had to be quiet and the TV volume was turned down. When the prince wasn’t tired, the volume was turned up nearly the whole way, regardless of whether others were sleeping. When the prince wanted to use the toilet, and someone was already using it, he immediately had to get up, otherwise the gentleman would be upset. He didn’t hesitate to sit there for half an hour, as if it was his throne. Anyone who said something about it got an earful, and he would use insults and every item within reach as artillery.

Could this really be a member of the royal family? Apparently he was some sort of distant cousin with the same last name as the king, so he called himself “prince”.

One time it came to a big fight, when Younes was using the toilet and the prince thought he was taking too long. Younes got sick of listening to him and packed his bags. He went to the guards and told them he'd rather be sleeping with the rats in the drains than with that "asshole".

Cell number nineteen was now his new home. He said the mood was much different there, very quiet.

"There's a wealthy drug baron in here who controls everything. The guards suck up to him and the food he brings in daily is amazing."

At first, I didn't want to give up my place for some bastard who ruined everything, but then – after yet another fight – I also got tired of it and asked the guards if I could go to cell nineteen too. It wasn't a big deal – it only cost me five packets of Marlboro's.

Half an hour later it was settled and I left cell number six behind me for good.

A new stage of prison life had begun in cell number nineteen.

45

The Kabran of cell nineteen was called "Baba". When I first met him, he was lying on his bed relaxing and talking on the phone. Baba had an aura of supreme nonchalance. His legs were stretched out in front of him with his feet crossed and his arms folded behind his head. He chatted effortlessly with someone on the other end of his Bluetooth earpiece. He acted as if he was lying on the couch at home in front of the TV. Besides his talking, it was extremely quiet in the cell. Younes put his finger to his pursed lips, gesturing for me to be quiet when he saw me about to say something.

"Baba is talking to a judge," he whispered.

"Talking to a judge? Now! On the phone?" I whispered back.

"Yes."

Younes gestured for me to be quiet again, as my jaw dropped

in amazement. I struggled to keep my mouth shut and tapped him again.

"But how can he be talking to a judge right now?"

"Do you even know who Baba is?" Younes said.

"Yeah, I've heard people talk about him in the hallways..."

"Well, then you know that, as a mob boss, he has connections."

I was quiet. Yes, of course I understood. But all I knew was from the movies and books. *Every mob boss has connections, who didn't know that?*

It was yet another wake up call, that there was a man lying on the bed, talking and laughing as he was on the phone with his best friend. So surreal.

The phone jammers on the roof had been working again for some time, but Baba had hidden a mobile phone above the window sill, in a place where the GSM signal came through. With the Bluetooth device he could communicate perfectly this way.

When Baba finally finished his call, he clapped his hands together loudly, swung his legs up and sat down on the edge of his bed. Younes and I were sitting on the bed opposite his, a few feet away.

"So, Younes, so this is Joseph?" Baba asked.

I felt slightly nervous.

"Yes, Baba, this is Joseph," he answered.

"Well, welcome to our cell! I heard that you were also being bullied in cell number six by that jerk of a fake prince."

"I would rather say I left by myself," I said looking slightly toward Younes.

Baba laughed. "Come on, sit down, I'm hungry."

Three big dishes of rice, salad and fresh fish were waiting for us. There were ten of us sitting around Baba at the table, like kids around their father on Christmas Eve. The rest of the men sat on the other side of the cell in small groups.

By the way, in Arabic "Baba" means "father", and in fact, he was like a father to everyone in the cell. Every day he had food delivered from outside the prison walls. He had his "henchmen" for this.

I immediately understood why everyone respected him. It wasn't so much his height or overall stature, even though he stood more than six feet tall. Not to mention his pale cheeks, stringy mustache and small piercing eyes with dark circles. Baba had money, lots of money, and with it, he could afford anything, inside and outside the prison walls.

46

In Moroccan prisons, the "gangs" weren't based on race or color, like in U.S. prisons for example. In the Arab world, people don't judge each other based on color or origin. *Allah has created every human being equally.* It is one of the most beautiful basic principles of Islam. Racism doesn't exist in this religion. Instead of "racial gangs", in Moroccan prisons it's all about drugs, money and your reputation. Basically, it's every man for himself, although there are drug gangs from certain regions.

There are "soldiers" and mob bosses with several people working for them. The rivalry between gangs can get pretty serious, but nine out of ten times it's about money or showing respect.

In prison, the mob bosses carry on their business just like in the outside world. They are very powerful. Their associates and the people who work for them are always contacted by telephone or through the prison guards.

Every night there were guards at the door of cell nineteen and – while still wearing his Bluetooth earpiece – Baba was talking with them and negotiating. Plastic bags with small packages were pushed through the bars after which the guards would then quickly disappear. Baba's henchmen in the cell took care of the drug distribution – mainly hashish and cocaine – among the inmates. He didn't mix in with that part of the business. He focused his efforts on conducting "business" outside the walls using his phone.

"That's where the real money is," Younes told me once with a certain kind of admiration for Baba I despised him for.

The bosses, like Baba, were in direct contact with senior officials, such as judges and prosecutors. They effectively negotiated their fines and penalties. Once they reached an agreement by phone – sometimes after a lot of shouting and cursing – the hearing was held at the tribunal, followed by a verdict that everyone within the prison walls already knew.

"How were you even sent to prison, when you have all those connections?" I once asked Baba.

"It's because I have all those connections," he answered.

I didn't understand. Baba explained.

"It's expensive having so many contacts. Everyone wants their cut, so I have to pay a portion of the money I earn to each one of them. That costs a lot of money, sometimes so much that I can't afford to pay everyone. That's why I'm here. I had an argument with a police commander because I hadn't paid him yet. Therefore, he had me arrested, even though he had no reason to. I was drinking coffee in a cafe on a quiet morning, when an army of policemen walked in and kindly asked me to come along."

"And then?" I asked intently.

"Then I told the men that they had to wait because I hadn't finished my coffee yet."

I laughed. Baba stared at me. I stopped laughing abruptly and coughed.

"So I drank my coffee quietly while the policemen waited outside, then I came out and calmly walked with them."

The police knew Baba all too well and therefore treated him leniently. Finally, he agreed with the prosecutor and the judge to serve a sentence of six months. He was furious because he wanted a sentence of probation or an acquittal. The verdict was final, the "process" would be held in a few weeks.

"Well, it comes with the territory," Baba said to himself. "But that police commander isn't rid of me yet."

47

For me, 2006 went on to 2007 without any fireworks. It was the third New Year I spent unjustly behind bars. I couldn't believe I've already been in prison for more than two years. How many years would follow?

I had received stacks of cards and mail again, which made me feel much better. My mom kept organizing campaigns, and she had sent me something special this time: peas.

She told me to put the pea seeds in a glass filled with water in a place with sunlight. I did so and after a few days the first green stems came crawling out of the peas. A week later, they grew into small plants, which were noticed by one of the guards. He asked me what they were, and I explained him about them.

Most guards couldn't care less about you as a prisoner, as long as you weren't causing any problems. Some of them, however, were different. Guard Rachid was one of them.

He was standing there watching the tiny plants, impressed with how such a thing could grow in this environment. Rachid turned out to be an avid gardener and kept a lot of flowers and plants at home. It was his passion, so he asked me if it was possible to receive bags with flower and plant seeds from the Netherlands. I was somewhat surprised to meet a guard who appreciated the true beauty of nature. Such people were rare here. I happily agreed to his request, and my mom – who loves gardening too – was more than willing to send me different types of seeds. Guard Rachid was thrilled – especially when the seeds began to grow in his garden – and even suggested that I start planting a part of the prison yard.

On the opposite side of the yard there was a green strip of about ten by fifty feet that Rachid and I would use. And from that day on, I was not only the "sports instructor", but a "gardener" too.

48

It was wonderful to have the freedom to leave the unit and walk to the garden. Initially one of the guards escorted me, but after a while I was left alone. This was especially enjoyable on the weekends, because the garden was always so quiet and peaceful.

Actually, besides sowing and watering, I did little more than sit on the grass and enjoy the sky. In the first months of 2007 the plants grew very slowly. Every time I came back from the garden and walked into cell number nineteen, I couldn't get over how quiet it was. Scary quiet, like my cellmates were afraid to talk. Sometimes I heard them talking to each other, but according to Baba, even that was "too loud" and was met with unprovoked screaming and cursing. The peace was fine by me, because now I didn't have to put on my music to concentrate on reading or writing.

Baba had the typical personality of a mob boss. On a good day, they were the best. If you needed something from the guards or something from the mob bosses themselves, it didn't matter, they would arrange everything for you. On a bad day, however, you didn't exist in their eyes, just like that. The most important things to these people were their money and their children – I think in that order – and if something was wrong with either of these, everyone would bear the brunt of it. Even Younes was overwhelmed by Baba's aggression and disappeared into the background.

I experienced this for the first time when we all were eating and Baba was intensely talking on the phone with one of his "customers". The food was excellent again. We gobbled it down like ravenous dogs while Baba continued shouting as usual. But it became so heated that Baba ripped off his Bluetooth earpiece and furiously threw it in the corner. He stood up, flipped the tables with food over, and spilled everything onto everyone. Baba's helpers jumped up and immediately cleared the plates and swept the floor. Younes and I looked at each other passively as we swallowed our last bite. Nobody said a thing. It was only Baba who kept screaming "mother fuckers!" and other curses.

A moment later a guard came to the cell door asking what was going on.

That's convenient, I thought, all he did was scream "mother fuckers" and immediately a guard popped up at the door.

There was some murmuring back and forth between the guard and Baba, after which it became quiet again in the cell. I didn't know exactly what was said, but later I found out that the guard was told to bring a new Bluetooth earpiece.

49

"The sky is grayer then gray, and the clouds with various shades of the color, are chasing one another. The wind is blowing very hard and it's raining continuously. Through the bare branches of the trees, the wind has free reign. When the weather is like this, it's always homely and cozy inside. You can't do anything outside, but then again you don't have to. You can make yourself comfortable on the couch with a nice TV show or a fun movie. We used to do that all the time when listening to the

radio or with the game of the goose..."

I received letter 183 from my mom in which she talked about Emily, a woman two years younger than me, who was very committed to our case. By chance, she visited freesef.com learned about my wrongful imprisonment.

Soon after, Emily wrote a number of letters to me and communicated with my mom by email. After more than a year of sending messages back and forth, my mom invited her to meet.

"Did you know that Emily is coming to visit and stay overnight? She is such a sympathetic and charismatic young woman. Amber is pretty in pictures, but Emily really has something special. Surely there are a lot of men who would fall for that type of woman. You can feel from a distance how big her heart is. She sympathizes a lot with your situation and sent me a form from Amnesty International. Through a friend of hers, it just might be possible that they can help you. Who knows what will come of it, but the important thing to remember is that we have not forgotten about you."

I never heard back from Amnesty International again. They said because I wasn't a political prisoner, they could do nothing for me. Regardless, Emily continued to send me mail. I think, because of my mother's invitation, I was becoming more focused on Emily's letters.

50

The days in prison were sluggishly running together, where receiving mail was still a highlight. Exercising, gardening, reading, writing, listening to music, roll calls, this was my everyday routine. Occasionally, I had days where ordinary life never even crossed my mind, except from my mom. Getting up, eating breakfast, getting in the car, driving to work, dealing with clients and colleagues, having dinner with friends, going out, laughing, sleeping peacefully in my own warm bed, alone or with a lady next to me. These were things that had become impossible. For me and everyone else in this cell.

One day I saw Baba talking on the phone again with one of his associates, a judge. He hardly ever left the cell because he was always busy with his business. He lied on his bed with one leg stretched out over the other and his hand under his head. With his free hand he always tapped against the prayer beads that hung above his head. He roared with laughter. Occasionally, he turned his head in my direction, but then looked straight past me.

After the call, Baba asked me how I was doing. I was a bit surprised that he started talking to me. I think business was going well, because he was in a very good mood.

"You like it here in the cell?" Baba started the conversation.

"Well, I would rather be home, but it's not bad here. It's quiet."

"Yeah, quiet. I love silence."

You love silence? I said to myself. Then I think you've got the wrong "job".

"Do you always speak to judges on the phone?" I asked suddenly without thinking about whether Baba would get angry.

"Yes, for many years." He looked at me seriously, with a half-smile.

"I don't understand," I said, shaking my head.

"What don't you understand?"

"I thought the legal system was designed to protect people? Not to allow judges and other law men to abuse their power and walk all over everyone?"

I was expecting him to laugh at me, just like the pen man did in the prison of Berkane a while back. The pen man had explained how things work in here, but Baba kept quiet and just looked at me.

"You're right," he said.

I looked up at him, slightly surprised.

"You're right," he repeated. "They're all bastards. Don't think for one minute that any of them are my friends. Our laughter is totally fake. I'm only playing the game with them, because I have no other choice."

Because I have no other choice. Yet another person whose hands and feet were tied. I would love to tell him that he had a choice, but I couldn't. Deep inside my heart I knew he was right. What kind of a choice did he have? It was easy for me to think otherwise without knowing his background.

"What about you?" Baba then asked. "I hear all these stories about eight tons of hashish and that you're innocent. How could you be innocent when they found so much of it?"

I explained my story to him and told him that I didn't pay the judges, even though many had recommended me to do so.

"Well, money and connections," Baba said. "That's what it's all about."

"I know, I know, but I'm not sure I could have lived with myself if I would have been released because I paid them off. I never would have known if I could have been acquitted without paying them. I would always wonder why I paid when I knew I was innocent. I guess it's just the way it had to be. I'm also not sure if paying them off would have bought my freedom anyway. Maybe there was something bigger going on. Something higher up, something the court had no power over. I just don't know."

Baba listened attentively and even let a phone call go.

"I'm not sure either," Baba said. "The only thing I know for sure is that judges have power, power they like to exploit. Not only in this country by the way. I have many colleagues abroad, across North Africa, Asia, South and Central America. It's the same way there."

I found it remarkable that he said "colleagues". Baba really regarded his work as typical, normal.

"But what about the government?" I asked. "Why don't the people employed by the government get paid more in salary? Morocco is still a rich country?"

"Morocco is very rich. Even more so than the Netherlands," Baba said with a wink. "But a raise won't solve anything. There has to be a change in their mentality. That'll take generations. You must understand that Morocco has been a French colony for centuries, and therefore it is still a very young country. Everything is still growing and expanding. I'm not saying that this is an excuse to condone corruption, but it might make it a bit easier to understand..."

I kept looking at Baba and couldn't help but nod softly. I thought instinctively about one of Mandela's statements: *"I have plans, desires and hopes. I dream and build castles, but you must be realistic. We are only individuals in a society which is guided by powerful institutions with their rules, norms, morals, ideals and beliefs."*

"I keep thinking it, Baba."

"What?"

"If only I really was guilty. That. If only I were guilty, I probably would have been able to arrange something, to do something. At least I would know where I stood. I would know how to act."

"You mustn't say that. It is to your credit that you're innocent and that you're doing so well, especially in this world. I know how they act here and your time will come, trust me. Be patient and be yourself."

I never saw this side of Baba. It was as if he had taken off his "mob mask" and a real person appeared that appreciated the small things in life. Someone that I could watch a sunset with and know that there's no need to exchange words in order to understand each other. Someone who knew that money couldn't buy you happiness.

51

Younes and I had just showered after a morning workout, when a young inmate boy approached me. He asked if I would walk with him to look at something. I looked at Younes questioningly at first, but then decided to go with him.

In his cell, next to a bunk, was a closed cardboard box. The boy unfolded the top and to my surprise I saw a red and white cat with two kittens frantically feeding from her nipples. I've always been a cat lover, but the ones that walked around within the prison walls were often very skittish and poorly cared for. Especially those from the other units looked terrible with their half tails, lame legs, dirty coats with scab spots, holes in their ears, runny noses. It was sometimes almost too sad for words.

However, it was very touching to see the cat lying there in the box with her kittens. She was thin and seemed shy. When I looked at her, she meowed softly, as if she wanted to apologize for lying there with her babies.

The boy picked up one of the kittens from the box and showed me that its little eyes had become infected. They were glued shut with dark yellow puss. Not a good sign, but I wasn't sure what to do.

That evening, Baba allowed me to call my mom from his phone. A rare opportunity, but when something like this happened, it was no problem to call. I had my own phone hidden in a safe spot between all of my mail. It had become unusable since the jammers were running at full capacity again.

My mom told me to wash the eyes with cotton wool and clean water twice a day.

"But first you have to disinfect the cotton with alcohol."

"Sure, mom, plenty of alcohol here," I laughed.

Where would I get alcohol? My mom hadn't thought about it either. But for these kinds of things, I always had Baba. He laughed at first about the reason I needed the alcohol, but then arranged a bottle through the section doctor.

"You crazy Europeans," Baba said.

Over the next few days, I went to the boy's cell and cleaned the kittens' eyes twice a day, and I always took some food for the mama cat, who I later called "Pipi".

52

The more I visited Pipi, the closer we became. There's a certain bond or connection that exists in the unwritten rules of life. Just like people, that bond can also exist with animals. Of all the cats and kittens that were walking around in the prison, I found a connection with Pipi.

Don't ask me why I named her Pipi. It just popped in my head one day. Unsurprisingly, everyone looked dismayed at me when I mentioned her name, since "Pipi" in their language – of French origin – means "pee". Right. It doesn't matter, does it? I know a famous soccer player called "Kaká", which means something different in some countries too.

I've always wondered how the cats got in. They probably just walked in through the main entrance. Or maybe the majority of them were born within the prison walls, so they couldn't imagine anything else.

I always brought some food for Pipi – usually sardines or canned tuna – and water. The kittens were growing up fast. Their eyes were healed and soon they began to play in the box. The woolly creatures had absolutely no clue about the world in which they lived.

As they got bigger, their problems started when they left mommy's warm safe nest. Those little fluffy animals were an easy prey to the greedy hands of Moroccan prisoners. Somehow, they just disappeared, leaving Pipi alone and anxious. The story was that some of the prisoners used the young cats for meat in the meals at the other units. I refused to listen to these disgusting rumors.

At some point, Pipi always seemed to know how to find me. I guess by the smell of the food, or by my scent. Little by little she came around more often until I gave her a place under my bed. Baba and my fellow inmates didn't have a problem with that. Neither did Pipi.

She would stay with me for the rest of the time I spent in Section A.

53

"Although I'm staying positive about your situation, I'm being caught by a staggering feeling of nostalgia. This feeling seems to be natural after more than two years. I guess it's a kind of phase you have to go through. But Joe, we have overcome so much already, I know that we can conquer this too.

As I've said to you once before, look at the feathers of a bird, or at Pipi's coat with millions of hairs. Have you ever taken the time to stop and look at the hair structure of a cat from the nose to the eyes? It's exceptionally beautiful, but very complicated. Their hard little whiskers amaze me every time, they look like needles. Then, even in jail, you will see the miracle of beauty in everything."

In March of 2007, the Moroccan king's wife gave birth to a daughter. Stories circled of another possible pardon. But this pardon wouldn't be like the one at the end of 2005, when I received a two year reprieve. No news on TV, nothing in the newspapers, no news from the guards.

At home, it was also uncertain. To protect myself from any

disappointment, I tried to pay no attention to the rumors, yet I secretly hoped for a pardon. These mixed feelings kept me up more than a few nights. Would I go home now? Would my nightmare finally come to an end with this pardon?

"Now that the queen has a daughter, many people are doing their best to try and get your sentence reprieved. I heard your story is renowned in Belgium, and we've also heard that you're well known there in the prison of Salé. This will no doubt help your situation in the long term. I told you that in the beginning. Your strength of character will be your own salvation. Your helpfulness and kindness will make you unforgettable, I'm sure. We'll get there, my son. Know that many are with you in their thoughts, and I hope it gives you comfort that many still think of you, even after more than two years now. It's just like 'the wave'. It keeps on undulating."

54

Cell number nineteen was situated on the second level of the prison building. The advantage of this was that through the window sill behind the bars, I had a good view of the courtyard and the other cells.

During the day, a stork would sometimes fly by to its nest a little farther over by the wall. The birds always made me think of the prison of Berkane. How I enjoyed watching the stork couple while standing against the wall in front of cell number three. Two stork babies were watching over the nest, and I was admiring them with almost all of my cellmates standing around me... This thought always brought a smile to my face.

Even at night I often climbed onto the window sill and would sit there for hours staring into the darkness. Sometimes with a book, sometimes with a pen and paper, sometimes with nothing but my thoughts. The view reminded me of the time I was in the prison of Taza, and watched the people in the city swarming around. It reminded me of the text message that I sent to my mom, William and Amber in which I wrote I didn't want to be forgotten. That was almost two years ago.

Instead of the village of Taza, here I mainly watched the activities of my fellow inmates. I could look into cells number one through five. Above them were cells twelve through sixteen. On the other sides were cells nine, ten and eleven.

In each cell, something was always happening. People walked up and down, sat on each other's beds playing a card game, went to the toilet, watched TV, cooked, said their prayers, slept or fought.

With baskets tied to a rope or cloth, items were transported up, down and sideways, outside the cells through the bars. It could be anything, from food and utensils to cigarettes and drugs. Sometimes, the inmates had to swing the rope or cloth to get the goods from one cell to the other. You could hear their voices echoing in the courtyard.

"Swing a little harder!"

"I still need something else!"

"Choukran, khoya![14]*"*

There was so much activity in this small, forgotten piece of earth. This against the backdrop of an apparent stationary, dark sky where the stars never shined so bright. It was almost as if nothing had happened, like it was perfectly normal for me to be here.

---

14. Choukran, khoya means "Thank you, bro".

55

In April of 2007 my lawyer told me that I received a reprieve of two years again. However this time, I never signed off on anything. I was only reassured when the prison administration told me that my release date indicated "2010/12/23". I couldn't say that I was happy, because even with the decrease I would still have three and a half years left to serve, and still for no reason at all...

My lawyer had taken a picture of me during his visit – it's the only picture that exists from my time in prison.

"For your mom and friends back home," he said. I thought it was a good idea and smiled into the camera on his phone. I wanted to show everyone that I was still myself, that they couldn't change me or break my spirit.

Keep on fighting, no matter what.

56

Inside the prison walls I did my best to make my life and the lives of those around me as pleasant as possible.

Baba asked me if it was possible to send a pair of running shoes from the Netherlands. "They're all fake here," he explained. Of course he would pay for them. William took care of it and asked if I needed some sneakers too. A month later, the package was delivered with a pair for Baba and a pair for me. I used the shoes to exercise, Baba just wanted to show his off.

Younes wanted an MP3 player with only English songs, and another cellmate asked if it was possible to send a glucose meter and lancing device for his diabetes, all from the Netherlands.

Guard Rachid, who gave me part of the prison yard for my garden, had two year old twins. One of his daughters couldn't see that well and needed glasses. He couldn't find the right size and wanted to know if they were available in the Netherlands.

"I'll ask," I said. My mom was happy to look for this and was able to buy these kinds of things with the financial help from our friends.

Younes, the diabetic prisoner and guard Rachid were completely amazed by the gesture.

Fitness center "Van Drunen" sent me the sporting goods I asked for, including jump ropes and elastic resistors. Fellow inmates were impressed to see that, when I needed anything, it was sent to me. Therefore, their admiration and respect began to increase. They knew that I had a huge team of people supporting me and standing behind me twenty-four hours a day!

But no matter how great the support was from the Netherlands, I still lived in a tough world.

That summer of 2007, there was an ongoing sense of violent tension in our unit. I didn't know where it came from, but I had never seen so much fighting before, in the hallways, the courtyard and even in the cell.

I mentioned earlier about the quietness in cell number nineteen, but whenever something happened, it was like there was a bomb exploding!

This occurred one time, on a seemingly peaceful Saturday morning. It was an event that I will never forget.

57

It starts with one of Baba's henchmen. He's a lugubrious type with a scar horizontally on both of his cheeks. I know now that the scar is likely a result of a retaliation. He's a type who completely defies his environment and doesn't care about anything at all.

His life revolves around one thing: "scoring". Drugs have extinguished his soul a long time ago.

In the cell, Younes is listening to his MP3 player on his bed. He bops his head up and down and occasionally utters a few lyrics. I'm sitting on my bed with a book by Martin Gray, *For those I loved* – one of my favorite books – and in the kitchen I hear the lid of the kettle gently tapping over the boiling water. Besides a radio playing softly, I hear nothing else.

Suddenly I hear stumbling in the hallway.

At first it doesn't surprise me, because it happens so often. But the stumbling becomes louder with heavy dull thuds, accompanied by lots of shouting. I put the book down beside me and see some of my cellmates walking to the cell door. Shortly after, they are pushed roughly aside. Younes and I shoot up to our feet only to see a boy kicked inside, crying. He is being chased by Baba's henchman, who screams at him the crudest of profanities. The crying boy is lying with his back to the floor, he stumbles back on his elbows while taking several kicks to his legs. The two are surrounded by inmates, who seem to encourage the fight.

I know that Baba's henchman is feared by many of the other inmates, therefore, it's unlikely anyone will try to stop him. Baba isn't in the cell. I don't know where he is. The crying boy seems to escape from the clutches of the henchman and flees to a corner of the cell.

And then, something terrible happens. The henchman grabs the kettle filled with boiling water that was just simmering quietly, and swings it right past my face toward the boy, who is still in the corner, shaking. The scalding hot water splashes all over his face and body. The screaming of the boy I hear then, is so indescribably loud! Almost inhuman! He is shrieking so loud that you can feel his pain. It made my hair on the back of my neck stand up.

The boy's skin becomes visibly red, and blisters are popping up like bubbles. My stomach turns as Younes and I are glued to the floor in front of our beds.

"That will teach you ever to fuck with me again!" Baba's henchman says fiercely to the boy. He spits on the ground and walks out of the cell with big, long steps. Everyone is standing there stunned.

"Does anyone have a towel?" I'm yelling. "Younes! Grab a towel and wet it, quickly!"

And immediately, as if everyone woke up from being sedated, I see them searching for towels.

I grab the towel from Younes quickly and wrap it around the screaming boy. My hands are trembling.

"Another one!" I shout and someone else gives me a soggy towel that I put around the boy. Four towels later, the crying boy is taken away by a number of cellmates. A while later I heard that he is rushed to the hospital.

58

The actions of Baba's henchman went unpunished. Why? Because he was an important person to Baba and Baba paid off the guards. That's why.

I was angry about this, knowing that many prisoners who had done something were sent to "the zoo" while a bastard like Baba's henchman, who sent someone maimed to the hospital, could walk around unpunished.

Baba himself heard the story later on, and apparently had his "mob mask" back on. He was as cold as ice and only concerned about his business.

And his business was going quite well.

I had never seen so many drugs being dealt between the different cells. There were guys arriving at my bed constantly asking me for empty bottles, which they used to smoke cocaine. It had become the new hype that summer. My god, did those guys look bad. They literally destroyed themselves with that crap. Within a week they had unhealthy dark circles under their eyes and their cheeks began to sink in. They were pale and seemed almost desperate. Little by little, their joy for life disappeared, and like Baba's henchman, it didn't take long for the drug to consume their life as well...

Baba did nothing but sell drugs, use his phone and ensure that there was plenty of food and drugs in the cell. To me, the food didn't taste good anymore. It was all bought with dirty money. Money obtained by ruining lives. Baba didn't seem to mind. "Don't they choose this life themselves?"

Like the choice you have to be a drug dealer? I thought, but I kept my comment to myself. I was respected by Baba, but I knew, the moment I got on his bad side, I would have no worse enemy in the section. One hell of a situation to be in. How I hated living in this world.

59

It was Baba who threatened to kill a newly arrived inmate. The rookie was a man in his early sixties, placed in our section about ten days ago. The story he told us was that he was suspected of trying to issue fake checks (very common among the inmates in our section), but as it turned out, he was actually arrested for molesting young children. When the inmates found out, a hundred men gathered at the entrance to our section. Together with a few other "big" guys, Baba was grumbling to the guards. I could see the red in his face as I watched from a distance.

"If that filthy dog doesn't disappear from this section fast, you're going to find him dead in the shower one day," I heard them screaming.

"Or in pieces spread out across the section!"

"And no one will know who did it..."

The guards hushed the furious mob and immediately started working on it. They knew it was more than serious, so that same afternoon the man was placed in the isolation ward.

In cell number nineteen I still hung out with Younes, but he wasn't exercising as much. He still smoked, but not to the same extent as before. At night in the cell, we sometimes had deep conversations. He asked once if I ever thought about escaping.

"Isn't that the first thing you think about when you're innocent?" Younes asked, as he puffed on his joint. I waved the smoke he blew out away from me. "You can go to the Dutch embassy," he continued. "Won't they help you?"

"It's not that simple," I said. "Don't you think I've thought about it hundreds of times, maybe thousands? Of course I did! I even asked the embassy if they would take me in, if I really did escape and was standing at their door... "

"And?"

"The answer was a resounding 'no'. Escaping isn't the problem, there are several ways to do it. There was even a guard who told me as a 'joke', that for a certain amount he could provide me a uniform and would walk out of the front gate with me. I'm pretty sure he would have done it if I had agreed. So it's possible to escape, but then what? I can't go anywhere, and fleeing to Europe would be deadly. I'm not going to risk my life like other people do every day, and then die somewhere off the coast of Spain. Even if I could make it to the Netherlands, I would be a fugitive forever, because the government would be obliged to send me back."

I felt the anger welling up inside me and wanted to cut the conversation short, because there was no use talking about it anymore. Damn, how absurd is it that I am sitting here thinking about escaping, when they should just let me go!

Then I told Younes the story about a group of refugees, captured during my work in the port of Casablanca. After supervising a ship loading, the captain called me to come aboard. In his room were four boys, sitting, looking sadly to the ground with guilt. They were found hiding in the ship's engine room, they had hoped for a better life "on the other side". They were wearing gray overalls covered with black oil and with cans of sardines attached to them. They smelled of urine and feces. I was shocked. Those boys were the same age as me. Just looking for a better life. They didn't know where the ship was going, but anything was better than staying in their homeland. And why couldn't they come? Why couldn't they have a decent life like me? I felt just as guilty as the boys and wanted to apologize. In fact, I wish they had succeeded, but if they weren't found then, they surely would have been found when reaching the Netherlands. Dead. They would never have survived the boat trip in the blistering hot engine room.

Younes felt bad about the boys, and a little later he started telling a story about one of his best friends who was arrested together with him and was also in our section. I had spoken to the boy several times and he told me about his sick mother.

"His mother died yesterday," Younes said, but his friend didn't know yet. Younes was looking for a way to tell him. I was quiet for a moment, then I told him that there isn't a good way to bring up such terrible news.

"He needs to know," I said. Younes told him the next afternoon, in the courtyard. I was watching from a distance and couldn't hear what they were saying, I only saw their movements. Younes' shoulders were shaking as he held his arms out. His friend stood frozen, looking at him with sagging shoulders. He then started crying and fell into Younes' arms. A cold shiver ran through my body and tears welled in my eyes. The next few days, Younes' friend was brokenhearted, and I felt powerless. His mother was everything to him. Just as my mother is everything to me.

I felt so sorry for the boy and I understood his sorrow. He moped around with thick red eyes wandering aimlessly, not knowing what to do. He couldn't even attend the funeral. He had nowhere to go except back to his cell.

I prayed, begged, hoped that such a thing would never happen to me, especially here, not here, please not here... It was perhaps the most intense fear that I had felt over the years...

"I think often of you, my child. In everything I do, I pray that you'll soon be able to see the wealth of beauty that is here again. Such wealth that you can only see in pictures now. I just looked into the garden and it's so calm that there isn't a single leaf moving. Even the brightest feathers and leaves are standing motionless out in the open, as if they were painted. My laptop is facing toward the south, so when I'm writing you my letters, it's as if I'm looking straight at you. It often feels that way, like I can almost sense your every move. It's weird to think that you're so far away, when sometimes I feel like you're so close.

I hope there's not much fighting going on there. It's terrible that you just can't escape it. But we're thinking of you here. Know that I carry you in my heart and that I love you very much, my son."

60

In the summer of 2007, I was having a very rough time. The harsh life of prison had started to get to me. I felt like I was the walking dead: you exist, but you're not there, people think of you, but you're physically unreachable. This wasn't my world, yet I was forced to live this life.

I heard nothing about the appeal, except that it was still "pending".

When Christmas time came, I looked forward to the summer

and dreamed about celebrating my release. But when summer came to nothing, I looked forward to Christmas again. That's just the way it was.

To make things worse, I got sick that summer. I was diagnosed with dysentery. Without warning and at any given moment, I felt nauseous and had to run to the toilet and throw up. I also had severe diarrhea which was laced with blood. I don't think I've ever felt so sick. I just lied on my bed, and the guys in the cell took care of me. The prison doctor helped me as well, as he knew I would compensate him later by paying him extra. I had no problem with that, as long as they helped me. After several shots in my arm and butt, the doctor wanted me to go to the infirmary, but I refused. I didn't want to lie in a dirty strange bed in an unfamiliar room with other sick people. I just wanted to stay in my bed, in my cell. My request was granted, and the doctor visited me twice a day to check in. Every time he came I gave him a pack of Marlboro and "thanked" him for his visit.

For two weeks I lied in my bed and lost almost fifteen pounds. All that time, Pipi the cat was constantly at my feet. Every now and then, she came right up to my face and sniffed at me with her nose. She sensed that I wasn't doing well.

I didn't want to worry my mom and everyone at home, but still wanted to share my feelings with someone. That someone was Emily. I sent her a text message:

Prison life has caught up to me for the moment. Don't worry, it will be fine.

Emily answered immediately, saying she would be thinking about me.

Then I thought of the book by Martin Gray that I had just read. It was the first book where I had to wipe away some tears while reading. What this man had endured was so terrible, but every time, he found the strength again to carry on and said: *"To be a man, you must hold on."*

61

"You and me, we were the pretenders, we let it all slip away..."

"[...] I just want someone to talk to, and a little of that human touch... Just a little of that human touch..."

I listened to music a lot. I often put the song *Human Touch*, by Bruce Springsteen on repeat – beautiful intro. I had just recovered from having dysentery and slowly I began to resume the routine life of prison again. But what I truly longed for was a hug, the warmth of someone you love. *That human touch...*

Some days I felt great, and I felt as if I could handle the problems of this world. Other days were miserable and the bars keeping me here seemed bigger and more threatening than they actually were.

On the good days, time seemed to go by faster, but on the bad days it was as if the clock was ticking backwards. The weekends were especially tough. The time spent locked up in my cell seemed endless, even though I was able to visit the garden in most cases. Of course, I kept myself busy by reading or writing, but I didn't always feel like it. We were extremely limited in what we were allowed to do. It was during these times that the feeling of being locked up became overwhelming. I felt my body temperature rise and within a few seconds, I got so anxious that I felt like I was suffocating. Realizing that there was nowhere to go made me sad. The grief that overwhelmed me was also caused by the continued dishonesty, powerlessness and injustice.

Sometimes it's good to let a feeling of sadness overcome you.

Let it happen.

Then I went to bed, I buried myself under my sheets and pulled my knees up in an attempt to make myself as small as possible. I wanted to disappear. My thoughts of home and my friends made my tears run gently down my cheeks.

"I guess it isn't always easy with my letters always ending with 'hold on, my child', another 'hold on' and 'keep your spirits up' and 'everything will be fine'. Even though we are both convinced that everything happens for a reason, sometimes the tougher questions overcome you, like 'why', 'for what' and 'how much longer'. You ask yourself how something so unfair can go on for so long. I could write you nice things and help you think of home, which would make you feel better, but on the surface there is always the sad reality that they've imprisoned you. Why have they punished someone so trustworthy, who truly had no idea what was going on. Why have others been released and you're still there. It makes me angry that you ended up there because of your goodness. Everyone knows that you've done nothing wrong. But we can talk about it for hours and that's still not going to help your situation.

So, my child, just breathe and move on, however difficult it may be. Don't be discouraged by the resigned behavior of others. Take the path that has been laid before you and come back home as someone who's become stronger because of it."

62

After reading my mom's words, I realized that there are three important pillars in life that you can build your happiness around: health, love and freedom. As long as you have these, you can withstand anything that life decides to throw at you. If one begins to disappear, then you can rely on the two remaining pillars for support. If two should go – or all three – do your best to draw energy and courage from other sources, however difficult that may be.

I focused on the pillars that I possessed – my health and the love I could find in my surroundings – not on the pillar I was missing: freedom.

63

I received a letter from my mom in which she surprisingly brought up Amber. She had broken up with the boyfriend who had caused the end of our relationship at the time. She wrote that Amber was in contact with her again and had also met Emily.

"Amber wanted to come over on Sunday afternoon. I told her that she was welcome, but that Emily would be there too. I asked Amber to stay for dinner and she appreciated that. I think she was relieved that I didn't wish her harm in any way. Emily is so generous, she had no problem with it, but I thought it was best to tell them both ahead of time before they actually met each other.

Neither of them have a relationship with you, but both are emotionally connected to you. You've got your adopted cat Pipi, well, let's just say I'm having dinner with my two adopted daughters.

That Sunday, while I was working relentlessly in the garden, Amber stopped by. So I updated her on our situation recently. I think Amber wants you back, and I'm pretty sure I'm right. She said it was over between her and the other boy and started crying. She kept saying that she never got closure with you, and she can't get over it. Just then, Emily came by, two hours earlier than expected. I kept her busy for a while because I didn't think it was necessary for her to see Amber crying. A little later, the ladies finally met and they were chatting with each other.

The three of us had a nice dinner in the garden. It was lovely outside in the warm sun. After dinner, we went to watch the sunset at the river.

After Amber had left, she called to say thank you and that she enjoyed stopping by. Emily and I talked about when you return home, how she wouldn't be surprised if you'd still take Amber back. I didn't know what to say, because I have no influence over that.

In any case, sweetheart, keep holding on, every night there's a bead added to the chain, and one day, the chain will be complete and that will be the day of your freedom. Believe me, it will be the best news that anyone could ever get... Many people will then sigh in relief."

64

Emily and Amber. I was glad they met and got along rather well. My mom wrote to me that Amber might want me back, but I didn't let that get to me. I had already closed that chapter and wanted to see where life would take me. I had made the conscious choice to move on, because no one can see the future.

Fortunately, the long summer of 2007 was almost over. I learned that my appeal would be heard on September 12th. Two days after my birthday!

Until then, I focused on my "pillars" of life... and of course on the sky, always that sky.

I experienced one of the most beautiful moments of nature on a late-summer afternoon, just before evening roll call. It was time to be locked up again. But that moment, no matter how short it was, will always be with me.

I was sitting under the roof of the courtyard stretching my legs out and leaning back on my hands as I looked up at the sky. Pipi was lying next to me, curled up and peering quietly into the surroundings. The sun began to set. It had become a little chilly and I felt the soft wind through my shirt. The sun was reflecting on the prison walls, with their white paint peeling off they stood out in a bright orange hue. Above me, deep gray, almost black clouds were threatening the beauty of the sunset. The contrast was brilliant as I sat there with my mouth open.

The flying seagulls and cattle egrets shined like white pearls against the dark background, completing the picture.

It was in times like these that I was most aware and appreciative of my life, my health, and the love and happiness that I felt deep inside, of the beauty and splendor of nature. I was in awe at the impressive work of the Almighty, whether He is called God, Allah, Dieu, or Bog. The most important thing was that He was able to create this.

Time seemed to stand still, but soon the guards whistled me back to reality. “Take your place! Take your place!” they shouted again.

“Are you coming?” I said to Pipi, who immediately stood up and hopped along with me.

We walked past the screaming guards and like always, I couldn’t resist saying to them: “This isn’t my place.”

I smiled, knowing that I had just experienced a true moment of consciousness. One that would be with me for the rest of my life. A time when I truly felt alive.

65

The prison had a little store where basic foodstuff was sold, such as milk powder, canned fish, rice, pasta, mineral water, tea, coffee and sugar. Each inmate could open a private account where his family could deposit money. I was hardly ever there, because the grocery deliverer who came by every Tuesday, especially for the foreigners, provided me with everything I needed.

Every Wednesday it was Section A’s turn to go to the prison

store. Occasionally, I went along when I needed something extra.

On the way to the prison store I passed my little garden, and to my great joy, I saw that three "special" groups of flowers were blooming. My mom had written to me: *"At the garden center I bought three extra bags of flower seed, deliberately in the colors red, white and blue."*

There they were, shining in all their glory, the three colors of the Dutch flag.

When I arrived at the prison store, I watched the shop keeper sweating profusely as he eagerly worked to meet the demands of the inmates. Those in line kept complaining that it was taking too long. I was standing with them as their complaining started to bother me. It's easy to complain, the trick is doing something about it.

"Do you want me to help you?" I asked when it was my turn.

The shop keeper looked at me like as if he saw water burning, but after a few seconds, he accepted my offer. After that day, I would help the guard in the prison store on every Wednesday. It started with offloading things, unpacking boxes and stocking the four racks – which reminded me of how I used to stock the shelves at the supermarket when I was a teenager. Later, I would deal with the "customers" while the shop keeper handed me over the items. My life within the walls actually became busy.

Of course, Pipi never left my side while in the section. She had become quite the classy cat. I loved it when she would look affectionately at me with her eyes half shut. All it took was a few taps with my hand against my leg and she would jump in my lap. She would purr loudly and playfully dig her paws into my leg.

It was strange, but seeing Pipi so happy, filled my heart with happiness as well. The prison didn't seem to bother her one bit, and for that brief moment, I felt the same way.

"Is that cat yours?" someone asked once.

Flexible like a prima ballerina, Pipi was licking herself with her legs wide in the air.

"Uh, yes," I said, a little embarrassed at the sight of Pipi giving herself a bath.

"She looks very well cared for!"

I thanked the man for his compliment as she finally stopped washing herself. She was sitting on her little round buttocks now, looking up at me with split little eyes. She was hungry. I knew that look.

I took out the four-pound bag of Whiskas biscuits that I ordered from the grocery man every week and filled Pipi's plate. The man looked at me with his eyes growing larger.

Yes, this is how we treat our animals. We care for them and respect them, I thought to myself.

Thanks to her beauty and groomed appearance, Pipi stood out among all of the other cats. At least I had made one cat's life a little more pleasant.

66

It was a few weeks before Baba was released, when there was a massive raid in cell number nineteen. Shortly before 7:00 a.m., dozens of men in black uniforms plunged inside. I was frightened to death from their glaring screams. Around me, my cellmates were roughly seized, some literally kicked out. Dazed, I was sitting on my bed in my boxers and a T-shirt. A man in a black suit was standing in front of me. Behind him Younes was being dragged along. Baba was surrounded by four men and was handcuffed.

Handcuffed? Why?

Other men in black immediately began to search thoroughly a number of beds, including Baba's.

"What are you looking at? You, get up!" commanded the man

opposite of me. He grabbed his baton.

"Yeah, no, sorry, I'll go with you, just let me grab my pants..."

Before I could finish my sentence, I was grabbed by the arm and forcibly removed. In the hallway, my cellmates were standing in their sleepwear, side by side in a row. They were standing against the wall watching, with sad, tired eyes. I was placed between them and we were not allowed to talk.

I hated it. A few minutes ago I was in a deep sleep, walking through green pastures. I saw kids in the distance playing with inflatable balls among the corn as I heard them laughing. I couldn't remember if my brothers were among those children, but I knew that I felt extremely happy as I watched them smiling.

But that was a dream.

This was my reality, standing in the hallway in my boxers, on my bare feet, like a piece of garbage put out against the wall.

The men in black came from Casablanca. It was a special unit of the Moroccan Ministry of Justice that would invade prisons unannounced. They searched for any and everything that was forbidden.

"Then they can bring truckloads," I said softly against Younes, who was whispering to me about who those men were. Younes only had one week to go before his sentence was up, so he didn't care anymore.

"They can take down the whole tent for all I care. Next week, I'm lying on the beach again!" he said smiling.

I was jealous, but very happy for him. Despite his arrogance, I could still appreciate him as a person. We did a lot of exercising together and learned a lot from each other. Thanks to him, I could finally read and write Arabic. That is something that no one could ever take away from me. Thanks to me, his English improved in leaps and bounds. We almost forgot the fights we got involved in. Although Younes was still addicted to hash, it wasn't nearly as bad as before. I would certainly never forget him.

Cell nineteen was stripped from top to bottom. Baba was taken away and had to spend the remaining weeks of his sentence in isolation. We were ordered to pack up our possessions and await further orders. Cell nineteen was being closed down. That same morning, I found myself in cell number twelve.

67

"Good morning, my child. You're just getting out of bed for roll call and I've just finished painting the kitchen. The weather is lovely and the sun is shining. The sun's dim rays of a descending summer make it seem like there's a silk robe laid across the garden."

My mom couldn't possibly know how bad my morning was, a hundred times worse than normal roll call as I was moved again.

Things like that always happened on such short notice in prison. At 6:55 a.m. you're still in dreamland, and at 6:58 a.m. you're awakened by screaming and shouting. An hour later, you're in another cell with your belongings piled around you wondering what's going to happen this time, where you will sleep, who you will become friends with, and with whom you won't...

The guards had awakened the Kabran of cell number twelve when they brought me in. The man was slightly taller than me and even though he was still half asleep, he welcomed me with friendly eyes. He politely told the guards it wasn't a problem that I was being moved into his cell. He had a memorable face with chubby hamster cheeks. When he smiled, each cheek had two small dimples that gave him a likeable appearance. His name was Abderrahman, meaning "Servant of the Merciful". All Arabic names starting with "Abd" have a similar meaning.

Because of his sincerity, Abderrahman was well respected inside the prison walls. I noticed that he took good care of himself, nicely shaved each day and carried himself very well. We already knew each other because we had spoken several times in the hallways and in the courtyard. Abderrahman didn't like the fact that someone like me was being held in cell number nineteen with anyone like Baba.

He apologized for not being able to offer me a bed right away, but said that he would arrange something with one of the cellmates later that day.

I immediately got along with Abderrahman, whom I began to call "Abdul". I was starting to feel like this switch of cells wasn't so bad after all.

68

Pipi soon realized that cell number twelve was "our" new place to sleep. Thank God for her highly developed sense of smell, and my Whiskas. Pipi wasn't there during the raid. Early in the morning, she was often strolling through the empty courtyard. I think she enjoyed the peace there. Once the courtyard became crowded after morning roll call, she came back to the cell for her breakfast and spent most of the day inside.

I never felt strange in cell number twelve, it seemed like I had been here for years. Probably because I already knew most of the people. Abdul had arranged a cell phone for me. My previous phone that I had hidden in my mail for so long didn't work anymore. He explained to me how to hide the phone. He kept a blender in the cell, which he used to make a fruit shake every morning. The bottom of the blender could be removed with a small screwdriver. Abdul gave the screwdriver to me. He had an arsenal of handy things hiding under his bed. Inside the blender, next to the engine was a small space for the phone which I secured with a piece of folded cardboard.

I only used the phone in the evening. Cell number twelve had a few places with good reception, where the jammers couldn't block the GSM signal. Every night around midnight, I hid the phone carefully in the blender.

"There's no better place to hide it," Abdul said with a wink. He had hidden his own phone cleverly inside a shampoo bottle, keeping it in his bag between his wet bath stuff. Abdul knew that during their searches, the guards hated to dig around in wet things.

The cell was relatively clean. Abdul kept a tight schedule in terms of cleaning and our responsibilities. Late that summer, we even held a big cleanup where we pulled all the beds out of the cell and took them apart. With cans full of bug-poison, we launched the war against the countless cockroaches running around and hiding in the tube frames of our steel beds, the TV and other places. They were everywhere. To avoid inhaling the poison directly, we tied T-shirts around our head to cover our nose and mouth. We looked like the stone-throwing boys of Palestine.

Occasionally, we gagged at the smell, but we kept spraying away. Afterwards, the cell floor was covered with a thick black layer of dying cockroaches. It was disgusting to see, but very rewarding to sit in a clean cell at the end of the day. I loved the feeling, like when my mom had just changed my bed sheets. Then I couldn't wait to jump between the fresh smelling sheets at bedtime.

But however many of them had actually died, these creatures are notorious for surviving the harshest environments– even an atomic bomb explosion – and they would prove it again. The next summer they would seemingly return in bigger numbers. But for now, we survived.

69

"Happy birthday my child, and many, many years to come when you can really enjoy life. I would have loved to be there for your special day, but the trip is just too expensive for me right now. Of course, in my mind I'm with you, and I hope that you're still able to celebrate, even for a little."

I turned twenty-seven years old. Huh? Now let me see, I was just twenty-four when I entered prison, William was twenty-six, and now I'm older than he was then... I remember my first birthday behind bars like it was yesterday. I received the book *Tell me, Mom,* a great gift from my mother. No gift could ever come close to topping that one. I smiled and picked up the book again.

"Dear Joseph, for your 25th birthday." I flipped back to the first page and began to read until I had finished the book. I came to the very last, self-written pages and re-read my reaction:

"I'm proud of you. Proud of how strong you are. I got this from you, this strength. It's obvious.

I love you so much, mom.

Thank you... For everything.

Joseph (2005-09-10)"

Last year, my mom sang me a birthday song along with friends over the phone. Something I wanted to do for her this time. So, on my twenty-seventh birthday, I arranged that Abdul and the guys would stand in a circle around me and sing *"Happy birthday"*. I was sitting in a corner of the cell where the GSM signal came through. The phone rang as I glanced up to see all of their faces staring back at me.

"Hi son," I heard my mom say. I gestured to the men to start singing.

"Happy birthday to you!"

"Happy birthday to you!"
"Happy birthday to Jooooseeepphh!!"
"Happy birthday to you!"

It was loud and raucous, and they didn't know the words exactly – of course it was supposed to be "*dear* Joseph" in the third line – but it sure was fun. I heard my mom laughing and I laughed too. She told me that she loved all of the men singing for me.

It was moments like these that made the prison walls and bars melt away around us. Moments like these when I was thankful not to be alone.

70

Diary, Day 1001 – September 19, 2007.

"More than a thousand days in this mess. I had expected that day 1001 would give me a special feeling, but there was nothing, no emotion or anything for this day. Ramadan is in full swing. Many are praying and reading from the Quran, but there's just as much fighting. Nothing back yet about the appeal. I would've had to appear on September 12th, but I was never called."

Diary, Day 1013 – October 1, 2007.

"It's been a while since I've written. Maybe it's because the end is near ...? Or...

I don't know.

Today my lawyer came by. The case was postponed to October 10th. Could it now, after almost three years, be over? I wonder how it'll be when I get home. I'm looking forward to my life again... I'm so excited. Especially seeing how everyone I know in the Netherlands has been developing their lives, while I am here, day after day. Anyway, I have developed myself spiritually and that will certainly benefit me in the long run."

Diary, Day 1021 – October 9, 2007.

"A few more days have passed. Ramadan is going well. There's a lot of stress among the inmates and quite a few riots daily, but these guys aren't exactly sweethearts.

Tomorrow is tribunal. I try not to think about it too much. Every time, I force the idea out of my head that tomorrow, maybe, just maybe, I might go home. But in the last few days, my longing for home has grown stronger.

I just got a text message from my mom: 'Dear Joseph, tomorrow we'll keep our fingers crossed for you again. Lots of love. Mama.'

A smile appeared on my face... Mama... Mama... For me, it's the most beautiful word that exists."

Diary, Day 1023 – October 11, 2007.

"I haven't been to the tribunal. The lawyer came by. Another delay. Until the twenty-fourth of October. We shall see..."

Diary, Day 1035 – October 23, 2007.

"Today, I have spent exactly thirty-four months in prison. Tomorrow, we'll know more if all stays as planned. The uncertainty each time, delay after delay, is very exhausting, yet extremely exciting. Last week, my lawyer told me that they were very busy with my case. He said before that the level of concern is higher than normal. He insists on having the others there (the owner of the packing station and the 24-hour guard who were also convicted to ten years in prison), and doesn't want me to go alone. I'm so curious what the final result will be after

such a long time...

I just got another text message from my mom: 'Dear Joseph, fingers crossed and lit candles from everyone here. Love you, mom.'

So sweet. My mom already told me that everyone in the Netherlands sympathizes with us. Last Friday, I received a large stack of mail. Letters from my mom, of course, along with those from friends and belated birthday cards. This kept me busy and happy all weekend :).

The storks are flying over the high walls and into the blue again. The weather was beautiful today. How unfortunate it is that we are locked up so early for evening roll call. Every day this gives me a reason to be upset and longing for home. Today, the word 'home' is one that has become comparable with words like 'heaven' or 'paradise', something unattainable, yet the thought of it is so beautiful and nice..."

Diary, Day 1038 – October 26, 2007.

"Last night, I called the lawyer anxiously to find out the court's decision. It would be announced today. I was surprised again that I hadn't been called to court. My heart was pounding in my chest and throat when I heard the phone ringing in my ear. Please, let the lawyer tell me that I can go home, please.

The lawyer answered as I gasped for words. He came straight to the point, but I couldn't understand him, or rather, I didn't want to understand him. Based on my reaction, the lawyer could tell that I wasn't getting it, and therefore he stated it differently: 'The Supreme Court has confirmed the judgment of the Appeals and therefore rejected your appeal...'

Rejected... rejected...

'Hello? Joseph? Are you still there?' I heard him asking.

'...This can't be...' I answered in disbelief. 'This can't be, rejected?'

'Yes,' the lawyer said dryly.

'So that means I've exhausted all of my legal procedures? That I just have to serve out my sentence here?'

The lawyer replied that other pardons would surely come. He had a tone as if he was speaking about people handing out hotcakes. It irritated me. I replied that I wasn't eagerly awaiting clemency, I wanted justice!

'I just have to go home, it's been enough!'

It was an unbelievable shock again. The Moroccan Justice system had brought me to my knees with my conviction. Over the past few years, I slowly built up a feeling of hope again, only now to give me another smack in the face forcing me back down...

But I refuse. I will stay strong, even if it is unbelievable and I need time to process this.

The rest of the night, I was stunned, watching TV, imagining how I wouldn't be leaving for some time. I was terror-stricken by the thought of staying here for another three years... I quickly shook that thought out of my head again, because I no longer wanted to be weak."

Diary, Day 1084 – December 11, 2007.

"I've hardly written for some time now, occasionally on loose paper. The last few weeks I haven't slept very well. My morale has sunk to a new low. Home had seemed so close.

I'm starting to become a little insecure. Every time, I keep telling myself that it will be okay and I draw on all the words from the letters as strength. But what if it doesn't work out? Until now, everything has gone against me. Every chance, a false hope.

Is this all for nothing?

I had secretly hoped to be home for Christmas, but it looks like I'm going to celebrate the Holiday season behind bars for the fourth time..."

71

"Oh, my child, I was so sad when I heard about what happened. I wish I could make your life more bearable, but we are so far apart. It was so bitter. Still, I can only say one thing: hold on my son, you have done nothing wrong and everyone knows that. Never say that you've been going through this for nothing. It's true that you're there for nothing in the way that we know you've done nothing wrong. But, dear boy, just think about how many people you have inspired during your days there. How many you have managed to cheer up, how many you have given strength and courage to go on in their own lives. They call you the 'sunshine of the cell' for a reason. Have you ever thought about how you inspire the people here too, like you once wrote you want to do: inspire people. You do this daily, not only among inmates, but here as well. Your courage and endurance, your life vision and ability to endure this burden that apparently has come your way and this awakens the respect and admiration in all of us. People are start to think when they hear your story and they are inspired to act. This isn't a pep talk, it's the truth. It has given me strength as well during this difficult time."

72

Everyone has a time when they feel depressed, it typically comes during a difficult situation when they are down and seem to have lost themselves. Everything, absolutely everything, seems to be going against you. What I keep telling myself is that I may be sad for a while, but the sadness and doom-mongering will disappear again. Like a good cry, the tears relieve the stress and the sadness goes back to where it once was.

I may not have my freedom, but what I do have is my health and the endless love from home.

The pillars.

It wasn't easy, but I had to take action again! Think positive, allow my shoulders to bear this burden and take the wheel again.

What options do I still have?

In Morocco, I had exhausted all my legal procedures, so the only options left were either to be released on a pardon, or acquire a transfer to the Netherlands.

A transfer to the Netherlands falls under the ECJL: Enforcement of Criminal Judgments Law. This law means that a Dutchman imprisoned abroad, may serve his or her sentence in the Netherlands.

It was late 2007, and I knew that an application for transfer under the ECJL could take anywhere from eighteen months up to two years. That didn't keep me from writing a letter to the Dutch embassy. The paperwork had begun.

Listen to this.

The embassy forwards the application to the Moroccan Ministry of Justice. The Moroccan Ministry of Justice will then consider the application. Upon approval, the application is then sent over to the Netherlands. In the Netherlands, the Dutch sentence will be decided. The document containing the sentence is then sent back to Morocco, where it is either rejected or approved. Upon approval, the document is again sent back to the Netherlands and a date is scheduled for the prisoner to be transferred. All of this apparently takes lots of time...

At least the letter had now been sent. I could do nothing but wait. I was busy again on the inside with all of my activities. Exercising, studying languages – besides French and Arabic, it was my goal to learn Spanish one day – maintaining the prison garden, working in the prison shop and taking care of Pipi. I think she was the only one who was glad that my appeal had been rejected, she kept grunting happily in her box under my bed.

Meanwhile, despite the difficult times, I began teaching English for the past couple of months. My "students" had heard from Younes about how I taught him English. One by one, they asked me if I would teach them English too. There was a classroom in the section, complete with benches, a blackboard and chalk. After proposing my plan, the chief of staff gave me the key to the classroom, and I became "Teacher Joseph" to a class of petty criminals ranging from five to fifteen men.

73

Unbeknownst to me, I rose in the hierarchy of the section. I started to become a member of the Old Guard.

"Let life come to you like the waves breaking on the coast," my mom once wrote me. And I did. I let it all come to me.

I talked a lot with Abdul. Our beds were caddy-corner to each other in the corner of the cell. He hadn't mentioned why he was in prison, and I never heard him complain.

One of the reasons that he never wanted to talk about it, was because "no one believes you when you say you're innocent". But one day he told me anyway.

He was an honest police officer, who always worked with integrity, but was sabotaged by corrupt colleagues. One day, Abdul was stunned when he was falsely accused by his commanding officer of being behind an organization of car thefts. He fought hard against this injustice to no avail, as he was sentenced to four years in prison.

"Know that I do believe you, Abdul!" I said at the end of his story.

He looked down and smiled.

"I know," he said. "I appreciate that, but to be honest, I don't need to convince anyone. I know, my wife knows, and most importantly, Allah knows."

We were sitting together when Abdul began to talk about his dream. A dream he had cherished for a long time. He wanted to go to Germany. His homeland didn't offer him anything to live for anymore.

"First, I'll send my wife and son to Germany. I'm already working on that. Once I get out, I will follow them," he said, staring up into nothing.

I looked at Abdul quietly and could see his eyes were filled with pain and hope. My thoughts were with him and his family, and I wished for nothing more than for his dream to come true.

74

I began to feel strong again, that I had control of my emotions. My optimism had once again overcome my depression in recent months. But just before the dark year of 2007 would come to an end, I would be put to the test. I was now going to be placed into what was known as "the zoo". The prison's most brutal community cell.

75

The hiding places for our mobile phones had survived every guard's invasion. But no matter how good they were, there was always tension, we were always on guard and aware of jingling keys in the hallway at night.

One evening we heard the jingling again, combined with the sound of heavy footsteps. Abdul and I looked at each other nervously. "We are caught!" We quickly turned off our phones and in a desperate attempt, threw them in a corner under our beds. We could feel the palpitations pounding in our ears.

We heard a loud click of the lock, and a few minutes later, lots of shouting: "Everybody out of the cell! NOW! Hurry up, hurry up! *Jallah!*"

The sound was coming from the cell next to us...

Thank God.

The feeling of fear was instantly replaced by a sense of relief. It was not our time.

But the stress remained, like a prey animal that constantly has to be on guard from attacks. Every night before bed, I checked everything. Had I closed the blender properly? Did I hide the screwdriver well enough in the edge of the bed above me? Was my money properly hidden? Was there anything else they could catch me on? The knife? The phone charger? Everything had to be hidden. Suppose they found something, you had to go through the whole process: first the zoo, then solitary and even a possible switch to another department. And that doesn't include the debris left behind by the guards after a cell search. All our belongings, sheets, blankets and pillows were thrown together on the ground.

How nice it would be, just to carry my wallet and mobile phone in my pocket without being punished.

76

It was on a cold December night, late in the evening. I was lying in my bed reading a book as I buried myself deep under my duvet cover. I was even wearing my winter hat and gloves.

"JOSEPH!" they shouted. There was a guard at the cell door. He motioned for me to come over, gesturing with two fingers at his mouth that he needed some cigarettes. I shrugged my shoulders and told him I had nothing left – which really was the truth. This particular guard was a grumpy guy. He had a long sharp nose and a bald, egg-shaped head that was now covered with a knock-off Nike Cap. He motioned again but I didn't feel like moving. Just when I was about to tell him to come back tomorrow, he left.

I had always hidden my phone carefully in the blender every night, but that night it was so cold that I didn't want to go through the whole process of using the screwdriver again. And of course, the next morning, just before roll call, four guards invaded the cell. The grumpy guard was there, deviously grinning at me, as if to say, "I'll get you". As I walked into the hallway, I glared back with my eyes half asleep at the other inmates. I knew what would happen.

How could I be so stupid not to hide my phone just now? It was lying in my bag, stuffed in a wad of socks – a known hiding place. The guard had combed through my entire sleeping area. He walked out of the cell and asked very demonstratively whom "this phone" belonged to. He walked past us one by one, holding it at arm's length, looking at me and my cellmates. I put up my hand, sighing. "It's mine," I said. *As if you didn't know, asshole.*

I was so disappointed in myself. I should have seen this coming.

Later that day, I checked with the other three guards who I knew a little bit better. They found it strange that that grumpy guard only wanted to search my area.

Unfortunately, they couldn't do anything about it because he had already taken my phone to the director. And that's how I ended up in the zoo with a few of my cellmates.

77

I've already told that the Arabic word "hadeeka" stands for "zoo". Inside the walls, this word was used daily among the inmates. I heard it time and time again, "he's in *el hadeeka*" or "he has to go to *el hadeeka*". I got used to hearing it, and when you're used to something, you start to become less concerned with its true meaning.

The zoo was a large community cell near the entrance of the visitors hall. The cell went unnoticed for the most part because the entrance isn't easy to reach. You first had to enter through a small hallway before reaching the actual cell door of the room.

The room was square and had a total area of about thirty by thirty feet with a filthy, vile toilet in the corner without a door. There was a constant dripping from the water tap. Against the walls, narrow wooden benches were attached and the cold concrete floor was littered with trash and debris. There was nothing else in the room.

It was freezing cold. After the cell door was slammed shut with a bang, I looked at the six men who were already there. Two of them were chained to the benches by one hand. One had a blanket around him and was singing to himself, the other did nothing but bob up and down, as if he came straight from the psychiatric ward. His left eye was closed thanks to a visible scar. The handcuffed men had a plastic bucket on the floor beside them where they did their business.

After three years of imprisonment I thought I had seen it all, but I was now experiencing something I never thought was possible.

A little later, I found out why this cell was called "the zoo".

I heard the siren in the visiting hall roaring as I watched the prisoners sprint over to the cell door. I didn't know what was happening until I heard them calling out.

"*Khoya! Khoya!* Please throw us some food!"

"We are hungry, please give us something!"

"Can you afford something, anything, it doesn't matter what it is! A banana, some bread, milk?"

They pushed each other aside like animals, with their arms through the bars.

A minute later, I saw a boy running back to the bench with a carton of milk and some fruit, while the others kept begging. The inmates who were coming back from the visitors hall would walk by and sometimes throw things to the beggars at the cell door. Just as you would throw peanuts to the monkeys in... exactly, a zoo.

"Don't they give you food here?" I asked one of the boys.

"No, we only get it from the fellow inmates, who sometimes give it to us when they come back from the visitors hall."

"How long have you been here?"

"Oh, a couple of days."

"And how long must you stay?"

They answered with a shrug. I turned around and walked over to one of my cellmates who had also been caught with a phone.

"You knew about this?"

He nodded, saying that he would occasionally throw something to them when he came back from the visitors hall.

I wondered why I had never noticed this. Maybe because I didn't go there that often? Maybe because I didn't want to know? I didn't know.

The men at the zoo were abandoned.

Throwing the food was tolerated by the guards. Luckily, I didn't have to beg like a dog at the cell door like the others. Abdul would send a planto to me every now and then, who secretly gave me a bag filled with food and drinks. I would share this with the boys in the cell, as well as the man sitting under the blanket.

I tapped him and he stopped singing. He looked up revealing his weathered face from beneath the blanket.

"Here," I said, "have something to eat." I had a banana, an apple, a carton of milk and a piece of bread with cheese in my hands. The man looked at me with glassy eyes as a shiver ran through his body. As he took the food, I was shocked to see, that beneath the blanket, he was naked and covered with scratches and bruises. And it was so cold! I was well clothed, but still felt the wind in my bones.

I took a step back while the man began to eat greedily.

"Why is he naked in this cold?" I asked the boys.

No one had an answer, and it seemed to me that they could care less anyway.

"The dude is freaked out," I heard someone say. I glared at him intently.

"What would you do?" I asked angrily. "What would you do if you were sitting here naked in this cold?!"

The boy kept quiet and looked away, when I suddenly noticed the other handcuffed prisoner loosen his pants. He was clumsily holding the bucket under his male member and began to pee. I quickly looked away because I didn't want to see that. But I turned only to see the naked man again. He chewed with his cheeks chubby and full of food. At the same time, the milk carton was glued to his mouth, with streams of milk running down his chin.

Sometime later, I was sitting on the bench between these two guys, staring quietly in front of me. We put our arms around our body.

How can these people be forgotten? How is it that no one is looking after them? That they weren't even given food to eat? I thought about it over and over again...

I became very frustrated because I was consistently confronted with situations that I could do nothing about. It made me angry how powerless I was, like a mouse in its hole, with ten hungry tomcats waiting for me outside.

"Let's take a walk, and get to know each other a little more," I proposed.

The two boys walked with me up and down the zoo for hours. We talked about the most diverse things. Well, I did most of the talking, a lot about home, about the Netherlands. I caught myself a few times praising my homeland, almost comparing it to heaven on earth. Suddenly, as I talked I began to realize why the men here had viewed my home country – along with other countries outside of Africa – as the "promised land".

78

It was a miserable New Year's Eve of 2007 in the zoo. I was standing behind the bars of the cell in the cold darkness. With every breath, plumes of white steam escaped from my mouth. The moon was shining on the common courtyard and let the slowly falling rain twinkle softly. Every now and then, the raindrops were replaced by flakes of wet snow.

Many New Year's Eves fade away and you forget them over the years. If you would ask me where I was on New Year's Eve in 1997, I really couldn't tell you. But other ones I can remember vividly. Like New Year's Eve in 2003, my final one in freedom. William, Amber, her best friend and I, were at a beach admiring the fireworks. And New Year's Eve of 1995, when I was hit by a bottle rocket in the face, right above my right eye. You can still see the little scar. A little lower and I would've been blind in that eye. Like the one-eyed boy at the zoo.

This New Year's Eve I would never forget either. How I spent hours and hours shackled to the bars, looking outside.

I just didn't seem bothered by the cold, or the hunger pains in my stomach. The only thing I could think of was home. My mother.

"I remember, in our first home, how I was standing at the kitchen door with you as a four-month-old boy in my arms, watching the snowflakes. With your big eyes, you watched this whirling white miracle falling from the sky. You didn't know where to look, because

this big thick cotton of snow was everywhere!

I wonder if I have ever written you about how wonderful the snow really is. I'm sure, that tomorrow morning, if the streets are still covered, I can see what has passed. Bird legs of blackbirds, tit birds and crows. Cats paws, dogs paws and prints of all kinds of shoe soles. You name it. And then it starts snowing again, very soft and soundless, and all the tracks are covered up, as if they had never been there. Just like life. Each man carries his traces through life. And again and again, these traces are covered by a new layer, which makes you forget the misery, or at least makes it bearable."

79

The nights were long in the zoo. You could barely sleep on the narrow benches. By turns, we fell asleep whilst sitting, but would startle awake dozens of times throughout the night.

It was very cold, especially at night. It's incredible to think that even our blankets were banned from the cell. We had nothing but our clothes to protect us from the bitter cold nights, and they didn't help much. We would shiver throughout the night, our eyes watering from the cold. To encourage the guys, I kept telling them that it would all be over soon.

My stomach was growling. Everyone was starving. The last time Abdul had sent some food, the planto got caught and the guards seized the bags.

The most miserable part of it all, was that time went by so incredibly slowly. Extremely slowly...

At one point, the one-eyed, handcuffed prisoner lost his patience. He continuously shouted at the guards, pulling at his wrist until it was bleeding. We stood at the cell door calling out to them as well, telling that he was injured, and finally the guards came in and picked him up. Who knows how long he had been here.

No one seemed to worry about the naked man. He just kept singing and unashamedly did his business on the floor. The bucket next to him had become overflowed. What else was he supposed to do? The guards ignored our requests to clean the floor after he was done.

Because of the cold and rainy weather, there wasn't must food being thrown inside the cell. The inmates coming back from the visitors hall wanted to get back to their sections as soon as possible.

My teeth felt dirty and I began to have diarrhea again. For a moment, I was worried that I had contracted dysentery again. There wasn't any toilet paper or soap, which made it virtually impossible to clean my bottom. Occasionally, new prisoners were brought in. Sometimes with considerable injuries. Things just carried on, as they had been doing and always would.

I spent three days and two nights in the zoo. The feelings of humiliation were starting to hit me again, and just as I wondered how long this could actually last, I was called in by the director. I left the naked man and the other guys behind.

80

The director said he "was sorry", but informed me that I had to spend ten days in solitary confinement.

"These are just the rules."

I wanted to cry out in anger about the "rules" he was referring to. All of the rules were ignored here, especially the ones concerning the treatment of the prisoners! Just then, I was reminded about the little mouse who was trapped by ten hungry tomcats.

I gritted my teeth as I stood there in front of the director.

Damn it!

He apologized again for taking so long to get me out of the zoo. As if his apologies helped any. I accepted my sentence of ten days and expected to be placed in solitary immediately, however, that didn't happen. There was actually a waiting list. I would be called automatically when it was my time.

Back in cell number twelve, the guys warmly welcomed me "home". Abdul smiled and hugged me. "Happy New Year! May 2008 bring you your freedom!"

The first thing I did was eat a cup of delicious, hot Moroccan soup – "hareera" – followed by a shower. I shivered from the cold water, but I was happy to be clean again. I felt so dirty.

My cellmates felt sorry for me and thought it was unfair that I had to be sentenced to solitary, especially considering how much I had given to the guards and others.

Abdul was very nice to Pipi. He gave her food and water every day. She was lying on my bed, staying warm. I was happy to see my adopted cat again.

"She slept constantly on your side of the cell and I think she missed you," Abdul said.

When I began to pet her, she immediately started to purr and lovingly looked up at me with her slit eyes, as always.

That same day, I started teaching my English class again, and Abdul joined us. Before his release and departure abroad, he had to learn at least a few words in English.

A fellow prisoner had given me a few English textbooks. He had them at home, and asked his family to bring them to him. In the cell, I created homework exercises and tests for my students. As I checked them, I was proud to see that they were progressing slowly.

My work in the prison yard had stopped for a while because of the cold, wet weather. I would begin again in the spring.

I continued working in the prison store every Wednesday, and on other days too when it was busy. After work, I occasionally brought a plastic bag with some food for the prisoners in the zoo. The men thanked me. I told them it was no big deal and apologized for not coming more often.

My work-outs also continued every day, rain or shine.

Abdul taught me how to cook. He cooked very well with the minimal resources at his disposal. I feasted on the chicken and fish he had seasoned so deliciously. And Pipi ate with us as well. She sat down next to us, begging, typically by cooing over and over.

Every time Abdul prepared something I wrote down the recipes in a separate little book. This way I tried to cook it myself next time. We ate a lot of rice and spaghetti, and salad almost daily. It was cheap and easy to prepare.

Sometimes, when we needed something at night that we didn't have in our cell, we asked our neighbors. We communicated by holding mirrors through the cell doors, this way we could see if any guards were coming. Communicating through the hall way with your neighbor wasn't permitted. I used the mirrors without thinking. Suddenly I realized that this was exactly how they did it in the movies. Bizarre.

On the weekends, there was often a shortage of meat and vegetables because there were no visitors. We sometimes had extra food left over, but if there wasn't any, we asked others to see if they had any extra. I told them that they would get their food back on Tuesday, after the grocery man had come.

Whenever there was no food for the weekend, it was often "lentil time". Lentils were long lasting and easy to prepare. They are full of iron and protein, which I was happy about for the most part. However, there was one major disadvantage: I had tremendous gas. For that very reason, I no longer ate white beans because it started to get out of hand. I wasn't the only one having problems with it. Every time a fart popped through the cell, everyone began laughing loudly and – literally – answered by “stepping on the gas”. Even grown men like these still had their boyish behavior.

Even after the terrible things that I saw and went through, these rare moments of shared laughter would remain with me forever.

81

Two other Dutchmen were brought to the section, and it was wonderful speaking Dutch to them. One of them was named Maurice – he too proclaimed his innocence.

It may seem like everyone in here was innocent, but that was certainly not the case. The other Dutchman had actually done something wrong, and he openly admitted it. It was a trait that astonished me, not only about the Dutch, but almost all foreigners: they were honest about their guilt. I have great appreciation for inmates who simply say: “You made your bed, now you have to lie in it.” I am also convinced that any sense of a false innocence will never endure within these walls. Sooner or later, you'll be exposed. This was often the case with those who initially claimed their innocence, only later having a lot to answer for.

Maurice was a quiet and sensitive man in his early forties, slender and just about my height. His dark eyes possessing a certain confidence.

He joined the sports group, read a lot and tried to serve his time as uneventful as possible. He was in prison because two Englishmen had started a fight in front of his house. These men had come to discuss selling his house. It was a large villa in one of the most expensive neighborhoods of Rabat. After the police arrived, the men and Maurice were taken away for questioning.

Later, they explained in court that they had started the fight – for reasons still unknown – and that Maurice had nothing to do with it. But the judge thought otherwise, and sentenced both of the men to eight months in prison. Maurice received two-and-a-half years.

"But the two Englishmen admitted that they'd started the fight, and that you had nothing to do with it?" I asked surprisingly.

"That's right," Maurice said with his eyes in disbelief.

The feelings of injustice and frustration twisted in my stomach again.

Imagine you're driving through a green traffic light, but the police decide to stop you and give you a ticket for ignoring a red light. Of course you tell them that the light was green, but no matter what you say or claim, you're still ordered to pay the ticket.

We constantly fought these feelings of injustice and powerlessness. The feeling you have when no one believes you. Only a thousand times stronger.

82

"Joseph, you're on the list to go into solitary now," the section head said just after morning roll call.

"Now? What section?" I asked.

Most of the men were still asleep, but Abdul and I already had our workout clothes on.

"Section B."

Damn. That means it's going to be hard to get any food from Abdul and the guys.

Maurice came to our cell asking whether we were going to work out or not, but Abdul told him I had to report to solitary.

A few moments later, a guard was there to escort me. I was

only allowed to bring the necessities. I grabbed my toiletry bag, some books, mail, clean clothes, two blankets and a pillow. With everything stuffed under my arms, I followed the guard. Throughout the hall ways and different cells, I could hear the voices of inmates repeatedly saying how ridiculous it was that I was being sent to the hole. The guard answered them in agreement, saying that there was nothing he could do about it. I smiled the entire time, graciously thanking them for their sympathy.

"I'll be okay," I said, "and I'll be back before you know it. Don't worry."

I had prepared myself mentally for ten days of isolation, bitter cold and hunger. I actually considered these days as a form of rest, after being constantly surrounded by people for such a long period of time. Looking at it this way helped to soften the punishment.

I thought about Thomas and how I had visited him in solitary confinement before. How will he be doing? I wondered. After being transferred to Germany, he was so afraid that he would be sentenced to at least ten years by the German courts...

With my blankets under my arms and plastic bags in my hands, I was standing before the head guard and two of his men. In the meantime, head guard Bin Abdi, who knew my uncle and had me transferred from Section D to A at the time, was replaced by the man who worked beneath him. I got along well with him and his two colleagues. The three men were now standing in front of me when I saw the head guard smiling. I smiled back.

"So, are you ready?" he asked.

"Yep," I said, "let those ten days come."

The head guard looked at his colleagues and began to laugh out loud.

"I like this," he said. "I like it!" He clapped his hands loudly.

I was slightly confused and looked at the smiling guards.

"You know what, at least you're a man about it," he continued. "That's why I like you. You're not crying or begging, you just accept your fate. Bravo, boy. Really."

He put his hand on my shoulder laughing again. Then he spoke to the guard of my section who was standing behind me. "Take this boy back to the section. It's okay."

I looked at him surprisingly.

"I don't have to go?"

Another roar of laughter as the guard looked at his colleagues again. "You see, it really doesn't matter to him." He looked back at me and said: "Joseph, if all the inmates were like you, we would have the easiest job in the world."

83

I walked back down to the section again, smiling to myself. The guards looked at me while my fellow inmates in the hallway stopped for a moment.

"It's okay," I said, continuing on my way to the cell. I quickly put my workout clothes back on and went to the courtyard where Abdul, Maurice and the other guys were exercising. Their faces lit up in awe when they saw me.

"Did you think you could get rid of me that easily? What kind of female exercises are you doing?" I barked while smiling.

They smiled back.

I noticed a new prisoner and Abdul introduced him to me.

"So you're Joseph?" He asked, and shook my hand.

"Yes, that's right, why?" I replied while shaking his hand.

"I heard about you in the prison of Casablanca. I've been there a while and came here on transfer. When I arrived, I asked the guards if I could be placed with you in your section. And now, here I am!"

I looked at him and then looked over at the guys.

"Is that true? Nice to hear!" I smiled.

"Do you mind if I join in?" he asked.

"Sure. But you better keep up!"

The boy saluted me as if I was his superior officer about to give him orders again. So I did.

Back to exercising!

84

Abdul, Maurice and I got along very well together, like "The Three Stooges". Training, eating, discussing, philosophizing, dreaming, we did almost everything together during the day. It was a pity that Maurice wasn't with us in the cell – the guards wouldn't allow two Dutch prisoners to be together in one cell.

We constantly promised to meet each other on the outside, when we became free men.

Abdul was completely focused on his dream, speaking almost every night on the phone with certain people, trying to secure safe passage for his wife and son to Germany.

Abdul was someone who never asked for anything. Not even in the worst of times. One night, for the umpteenth time, he was repairing his sneakers with a needle and thread that he kept hidden away with his other "forbidden" things. I couldn't stand the look of his shoes anymore and Maurice and I decided that we would order a new pair from the grocery man. Abdul was over the moon about our gesture, although he immediately added that we really didn't have to do it. The black suede sneakers with white vertical stripes were his pride and joy. After each training session, he cleaned them thoroughly.

"A gift, because you taught me how to cook," I told Abdul later as a joke.

I often cooked for myself and the guys. They were surprised at how much I ate. It may have seemed like I was hungry twenty-four hours a day! Abdul seriously questioned whether I had a tapeworm and, to my annoyance, would even catch me eating while standing up. Every time I got caught, he spoke to me in a fatherly tone and informed me that eating while standing isn't good for the stomach. "Take your time to eat, go sit down. Please remember next time!"

"Yeah, yeah, I know," I said sighing, and sat down again.

We had quite of few happy moments together, like watching TV, especially the program *Wipeout* which, to my surprise, was broadcasted on TV and dubbed in Arabic.

"Those people must have nothing to do over there?" he said with tears in his eyes from laughing as someone fell into water on the show. Abdul had a very contagious laugh, and every time I would start to laugh with him automatically.

But we also experienced some very sad moments. Especially Abdul – most of the time during Islamic holidays – and Maurice – whenever he spoke to his children on the phone – and afterwards we would always comfort each other. It had been quite some time since I shed a tear. Sometimes, I felt like I wanted to cry, but I just couldn't.

Not even when I cut my thumb trying to making a salad. The knife was razor sharp, it had been sharpened on the stone step of the toilet. I didn't even notice what happened until the salad started to turn red. Blood? My blood!

I can stand the sight of blood from someone else, but when I see my own blood, I become a first class wimp. My head quickly begins to swim and I get the feeling like I'm about to pass out.

There was a slight panic as we had no first aid supplies. With toilet paper and tissues, Abdul helped me to wrap my thumb. Later, the night guard asked the doctor to disinfect and rewrap. No, it wasn't until my mom visited me for the last time that I began to cry.

"Fortunately, we'll see each other in a few weeks and I can finally hold you again. Wonderful. I'm looking forward to that feeling, even though I don't like the idea of returning to that country. We'll have a lot to talk about again. I think of you often and I'm very curious about how you look these days. Perhaps I won't ever have to come there again after this visit, because you will be home. Lots of love from mom."

85

"Whatever happens, even if your appeal is rejected, I will somehow make it to Morocco. A fever of 100 degrees couldn't stop me!"

This is what my mom wrote to me just before my appeal was again rejected at the end of 2007. Now she was planning to come visit me on her birthday in April. I was very excited to see her again after such a long time. Oddly enough, I couldn't remember exactly when the last time my mom had visited me was. Was it in 2006 or 2007? Was it during the summer or winter back then? The concept of time had become indefinable to me. Later on, I looked it up in my journal, and realized that the last time I had seen my mom was in the early summer of 2006. Almost two years ago!

I told Abdul and Maurice about the visit my mom was planning, and how I wanted to give her something for her birthday while she was here. But what? It wasn't exactly easy to find gifts in here.

"Flowers from your garden?" Abdul suggested.

"Good idea," I said, "the only problem is that there aren't any nice ones growing right now. I still have to prepare the garden for the upcoming season."

We pondered further.

What do we have here?

People... Lots of people!

"Yes! I got it!" I cried.

Abdul and Maurice looked at me waiting for the answer.

"She will definitely love this!"

I took several A4 papers and a pen, and began to draw circles on the pages. Their eyes were intently following my actions. When I finished drawing the circles, I grabbed my yellow, blue, green and orange markers and started outlining them.

"Those kind of look like balloons," Maurice said.

"Right!" I said, as I continued drawing, "and in these balloons I'm going to have each one of you write something for my mom."

86

"Are you the mother of *the* Joseph?" She said with shining eyes. "That's what the guard at the prison gate asked me!"

"No. Are you serious?" I asked, grabbing her hands.

We were in the huge visitors hall again, sitting on two chairs at a table that was covered with old food and dirty cups.

"Yes, really. They immediately let me inside and another guard accompanied me from there. I even got to skip the long line of people waiting to get in. Pretty VIP huh?"

"How cool! Which guard was it? Is he walking around here now? "

My mom sat up straight and looked around the hall.

"Him!"

I turned around to see to whom she was pointing.

"That's guard Rachid!"

"Do you know him?" she asked.

"Of course! He's the one who gave me the prison yard for my garden!"

"Is he the same man I gave the glasses to, for one of his twin daughters?"

"Exactly!"

Guard Rachid saw us and waved. My mom and I both waved back. We laughed and looked over at him, then looked back at each other again.

I was thrilled that she had met guard Rachid and he had helped her.

"Oh, before I forget!" I said. "Happy birthday!"

We both laughed and fell into each other's arms again. "Next year, I really hope to finally celebrate your birthday at home, mom."

"I hope so too, my boy. We'll just wait and see what the procedure from the ECJL brings. The last I heard, is that your papers were sent to the Netherlands. Now we have to wait for them to be returned to Morocco again."

I sighed, but at the same time I was happy that the first step toward getting home had been taken.

"I've got something for your birthday, mom."

"Really?"

"Yeah, hold on."

From the plastic bag I brought, I first took out a present that one of the female guards from the administration department had given me. It was a porcelain rose that she made herself.

"Oh, how beautiful!" my mom said.

"Nice, isn't it?"

"You're such a charmer. Even the ladies of the administration department have been swept off their feet by you."

"Well, I just seem to get along well with the ladies. They're always nice to me, and can't understand what I'm doing here."

"I don't get it either. No one understands," my mom said with a half-smile.

"This isn't the only thing I have for you, mom."

I grabbed my bag again and pulled out a roll of papers with

a red cloth ribbon wrapped around it. Abdul had made the ribbon for me from an old T-shirt.

"What is this?" she asked as she took it from me.

"Just unwrap it," I said with a big smile. "I hope you like it..."

She untied the ribbon, and rolled out the gift. Her eyes began to widen and her mouth fell open. She looked at the many balloons and read some of the personal words that my fellow inmates had written. The huge birthday card with balloons on the inside that I had received for my twenty-fifth birthday in 2005, had inspired me.

"Oh, it's lovely!" my mom said.

"You like it? I took the pages around the section and asked the guys I know best to write something for you."

"How many of them there are!"

"I have many friends!" I laughed.

She carefully put the roll of paper aside and hugged me again.

"Thank you for the wonderful gift, my child. I like it very much."

Finally, tears rushed into my eyes again as I felt a lump sticking in my throat.

87

"Now that I am back home, I'm so proud of how you look and the fact that you're taking care of yourself.

I got really scared on the plane again – that pesky phobia of mine – and while sitting there I realized how far away you are from me. I just couldn't help but cry about the whole situation again.

And here at home, the sun is shining as if nothing happened.

Everyone loves hearing about you, your stories about cooking lessons, your adopted cat Pipi, the English classes, working in the prison shop, your local 'gym' and the plants from your garden. It's too bad you can't be here, you would be able to see how inspired they are by your actions. William only had one thing to say after hearing about how you're doing: 'Incredible'. You're more than amazing, my child!

I show everyone the birthday presents you gave me and they all think it's wonderful. They love the things you're doing and how you're living your life in there.

Trust yourself, no matter how long it takes or how difficult it is. One day, that prison gate will close behind you and you'll be standing in the open sun. It's also important to be mindful of what you leave behind. They will talk about you for years to come, and about that mother who used to make cards for the inmates, even though she didn't know them.

I'm still desperately longing to see you again. I hope things continue to move forward with the ECJL. The thought of your freedom is all so exciting again.

Back here in the garden some daffodils are blooming; the small ones with stalks about three inches high and very yellow. I hope, my sweet boy, that you will be able to see them again next year. We will never give up, my son. We'll keep on going as long as it takes."

88

Guard Rachid and I were preparing the garden again in the prison yard. My mom had given me new seeds, including some from my favorite flower, the sunflower. As a little boy I loved this flower, especially when we would drive through France on our way to Morocco. We passed huge, vast sunflower fields. I would stare at the fields through the rear window of the car until the last moment.

Guard Rachid handed me the seeds and I carefully knelt down and planted them. The sun kept shining throughout the mild spring weather and helped the plants and flowers grow quickly. One by one, they showed their little faces to the sun.

That spring, the prison yard was blooming beautifully again.

A wealthy Frenchman in my section was apparently impressed by my garden so much, that one day he came over to me and mentioned that he had given guard Rachid some money to buy rose bushes. Four plantos all came walking up the path with their wheelbarrows in a row, as if it were a little train. We planted them immediately.

Later, the Frenchman came by to admire the roses. With a twinkle in his eye, he mentioned that when he was in his twenties, it was "le miel de la vie" – the honey of life – and he felt sorry for me. So sorry, because I had to spend those years of my life behind bars. I said I could never really know how these past years would have been for me had I been a free man. Those years were gone forever, but at least I knew that I had lived a nice and carefree life up until I was twenty-four.

I told the Frenchman that I felt sorry for him as well, that he had gone to jail as an older man.

"Don't worry about me," he said. "Just make sure that you get your life back in order once you're on the outside, and enjoy the years to come."

I looked at my garden and saw the roses standing motionless in the sun. Guard Rachid watered them and the only thing on my mind was my mom, and how she always talks about "her inseparable roses". They are her favorite flowers and I wanted so badly for her to see these and the other plants. Truth be told, I would much rather be working and helping with her garden back home, and afterwards drink tea on the terrace together, while the spring sunshine warmed our faces.

When I was working in the garden, Pipi would often visit me. She loved spending time with me in the peaceful setting it was. She had become a thick snooty cat of about 11 pounds dressed.

She was gorgeous to see, so trim. I wanted to take her home with me, but I didn't know when or how that was going to happen. Even if my transfer request was approved, it was impossible, because they would never allow a cat on the bus. Should I be pardoned one day and released, she had to be near, because once you're free, they kick you out of the prison as quickly as under a minute. We would have to wait and see.

The guards and fellow inmates also noticed Pipi's beauty and were surprised at how well kept she was. They were even more surprised to hear the story of how I gave her the birth control pill and then burst out laughing while I kept on staring at them without changing the expression on my face. The laughing then stopped quickly. I explained how much I hated the fact that kittens would either starve or disappear all the time. These creatures didn't belong in this cold confined world. They didn't fit in with the harsh way of living.

I gave Pipi the title "princess". Princess Pipi, who took birth control pills, was clean, thick and sometimes snooty, but also very sweet. Sweet to me, because she would never let just anyone pet her or pick her up. The behavior of a real lady, hence the title.

Regarding the pill, it first had to be examined by the doctor. Initially, the guards wouldn't believe me that this pill really was for Pipi. Thankfully, it also came with a description written in French.

Apparently, the "pill story" was so bizarre that people even came from other sections to visit my cell to see Pipi – and her strange owner who put her on birth control.

I could understand their disbelief, considering it wasn't very common to keep pets in Morocco. Animals are used for work or food. That's what my mom found out when she just got together with my father. Kept in a cage in the living room, she had a big beautiful rabbit for a pet. One day, she came home from work and my dad had surprised her with a delicious meal: rabbit.

“Tadaaa,” my dad said proudly with the roasted feast before him.

My mom looked over his shoulder at the empty rabbit cage.

“Flappy!” she screamed, running to the cage with tears in her eyes.

“What’s the matter...?” My dad turned around, following her with his eyes.

He was completely surprised by her reaction...

89

“Wow...what’s that smell?” I said.

“They’re painting,” Abdul responded.

“Painting?”

“Yes, they’re painting the walls in the hall ways, the common shower, everything.”

“Why?”

“They’re expecting some French delegation, so everything has to look good.”

“Typical.”

Thanks to this, just before summer began, Section A was turned into a model prison as if representing how all prisons should look. We were ordered by the guards to behave decently. “Otherwise there will be severe penalties.”

The majority of inmates responded to these threats with a “pff” or shrug. They hated being used like puppets.

The section was consistently a picture of poverty, but for the few days that the French delegation was there, one would hardly have guessed. They toured the prison surrounded by numerous guards, the chief of staff and the director himself. Some of the inmates were questioned, including me. The French representatives assured me that anything I said would be considered confidential. At first I was suspicious, but I decided to tell them my story. In French, I explained the truth of it all to the two men and the woman standing opposite of me. How corruption runs rampant, how quickly everything was painted over ("can't you smell the fresh paint?"), how not even a week ago this section looked like the others, and that they should see for themselves.

But of course, that would never happen.

Everything I said was written down in chicken scratch by a man in a tight suit. The guard nodded, seemingly satisfied with my answers. I knew he didn't speak French, so I could say whatever I wanted. I couldn't do anything other than tell the truth about how everything works.

The visitors thanked me sincerely, as I secretly hoped they would do something with this information. However, deep in my heart I knew that their sheets full of illegible notes would end up somewhere lost in a big stack of papers. But who knows... Maybe someday they would be found...

Back in the cell, Abdul told me that the "mailman" was looking for me. Nowadays, there was a small, thin man responsible for the distribution of the mail packets. He was always nice to me, but this time was different. He was specifically looking for me because in addition to my two packages, he was delivering a personal message.

"Best regards from the entire staff at the post office," he said after I finally found him.

"Best regards?" I asked surprised.

"Yes," he smiled. "They told me that I had to give that certain 'Joseph Oubelkas' their best regards, because 'he is getting mail and packages so often.' Every time they see your name pass by again every month, so they guess what kind of good guy you must be for all of those people to constantly send you things. I agreed with them, and promised to give you their regards."

For a minute, I was overwhelmed at the thought of them thinking of me, and I just had to laugh.

"How nice of them! Well, then you certainly have to give them my best regards back!"

"I will!"

My mom always told me that receiving lots of mail would have a positive effect on my environment. She noticed this through our supporters at home, and I among others in this way.

90

Working with the numbers in the prison store was a good distraction for me. I've always liked working with numbers, and I love everything about math. While working in the shop, I was forced to do mental calculation, which reminded me a lot of elementary school. I remember well, how in the seventh and eighth grade, I was always ahead of the class in our exercise booklets along with one other classmate. The teacher allowed me to work through the next chapter on my own and I got an A in math almost every time. It also reminded me of my love for mathematics through high school and college. There was a math teacher who would bring extra books for me, as we would go through them together after class. After school, I would even tutor some of my classmates who didn't understand the lesson. School, it all seemed so long ago. Like something from a previous life.

Every time I walked out of the section, to go to the prison store for example, or if I was visited by the embassy, I would walk by my garden and smile at the flowers and plants that were flourishing quietly. The sunflowers grew tall and very fast! Guard Rachid had arranged some planting sticks, and together we put them in the ground and tied the stems of the sunflowers to them.

Every time I glanced at the garden, I thought about Abdul and his dream. He always said he'll succeed, with a smile on his face and his eyes shining.

That day finally came as he walked up the path toward me. I was kneeling in the grass trying to thin out the carrot plants in the garden. With his arms spread wide he came over to me. I saw Abdul's typical smile with dimples in both cheeks. I got up and went to dust off my knees, but didn't get the chance, as he grabbed me and gave me a huge hug. I wanted to pat him on the back, but my hands were still dirty, so I tapped him slightly with my wrists.

"I'm so happy, I'm so happy!" he said. "It's been approved! My wife and child are moving to Germany! And once I get out in two weeks, I'll follow and be with them!"

Abdul grabbed my shoulders and looked me straight in the eye. "It's happening, my dream is finally going to come true!"

Just like him, I became excited. We hugged each other again with tears in our eyes. I was so happy for him and told him that I always believed in him.

"Thanks for believing Joseph... And thanks for being here, right now at this moment."

"Well, thanks to you too, but I don't want to be here!" I said laughing.

A few moments later, he laughed as well, realizing how misplaced his last "thank you" actually was.

"No," I said, "I'm really, really happy for you and wish you all the luck in the world!"

"I know," Abdul said. "I know... Thanks again! I'm going to tell Maurice and the others now!"

"Okay," I said, while he turned around.

I knelt down and went back to work in my garden, softly shaking my head in happiness.

"Do you hear that, Pipi? He did it!"

Pipi looked at me askew and flicked her ears.

"He did it... His dream came true!"

That's what everyone thought at least.

But Abdul's dream would never come true.

91

Abdul was released and I soon began to miss him. I missed exercising together, making our protein shakes, cooking, his laughter. I just missed having him around. Our farewell was emotional. We hugged and looked at each other promising to meet again one day in Europe.

When Abdul spoke out the word "Europe" it was like he was describing some sort of fairytale Utopia. And then "Africa" somehow sounds very shabby.

In the end, he had been unjustly imprisoned for nearly four years.

It was a hot summer in 2008. But when isn't it hot during the summertime in Morocco? Again, the heat melted us like M&M's in the clammy hands of a toddler.

Something remarkable had begun within these walls: the prisoners began injecting oranges with vodka. During the daytime in the courtyard and at night in the cells the inmates were constantly eating oranges. The guards must have thought that everyone had suddenly decided to make healthy choices, but when fights broke out amongst the drunk prisoners, they quickly realized what was going on. Oranges and any other fruits that could be injected with alcohol, were then banned for a while. They were allowed again later, but tightly controlled by the guards.

The scorching heat also brought the cockroaches back. We thought we got rid of those creatures during spring cleaning last year. But there they were, crawling around everywhere again, as if they were resurrected from the dead. And yet, every time I saw one, I had to smile, because they made me think of a part from one of my mom's letters.

"You can make up all kinds of stories about cockroaches to make them seem less filthy: The story of the cockroach brothers Cedric, Charles and Chuck. Try to see the humor in it. Together, with their neighbor Christian, Chuck was the smart aleck of the family, and of course you have the adolescents Carla and Chloe cockroach, who would walk around with food dangling behind their legs to try and seduce Cedric and Charles, but where then caught by Boozer cockroach who was always a blind drunk and did nothing but telling stories, especially to Coffin cockroach, who worked as a gravedigger..."

How fun those stories could be, I would prefer not to have the Cockroach family hanging around me.

A new trick that we often used to catch them, was putting sweet yoghurt in a plastic jar at night. We would place the jars on our beds, the TV and the kitchenette. The next morning, the jars would be filled with cockroaches. We poured them into the toilet, sprayed poison over them and flushed the suffocating cockroaches down.

In the courtyard, Maurice, myself and the boys were always exercising, most of the time in shorts with no shirts on. We had come up with some new exercises because the guards allowed us to use the frame of an old bunk. We turned it sideways on the short side so we could do exercises like "dips" and "pull-ups". We also did the typical exercises like push-ups, squats, jumping, running and sprinting.

I learned how to do some interesting things from a fellow inmate: Lee "Lightning" Murray, a former fighter in the UFC – Ultimate Fighting Championship. He came from England and was arrested in Morocco by order of the English, because of his involvement in the largest robbery in UK history, where no less than seventy five million euro was seized. For Scotland Yard, Lee was at that time "public enemy number one".

Lee spent twenty four hours a day in the isolation ward and I would often act as a translator for him. As we began to see each other more, I would spend time with him in the isolation ward where he did his sports exercises. Lee was my age and built like a giant. He was slim, tall, but very strong and muscular. He showed me exercises I never thought I would be able to do, like handstand push-ups. A very difficult exercise, but practice makes perfect.

We communicated a lot on paper and I made sure he got extra food. I kept many of those notes, which I had received through the guards, as a kind of souvenir. To thank me, he gave me one of his fight photos with a personal message written on the back. I told him several times how I thought it was a shame that such a talented fighter ended up here in this place.

That summer, the fitness center Van Drunen sent me something extraordinarily fun: towels with names embroidered on them. I could give thirty names and it certainly wasn't easy, but eventually I chose the guys from my exercise class with whom I hung out with the most. I also got Abdul a towel, but I never got the chance to give it to him because of his release. Nevertheless, it was fun to see the inmates' faces when they received them.

"I would have loved to be a fly on the wall in their cell when they got their towel. You're now someone they will never forget, each person

taking that towel home with him, will think of that boy from the Netherlands every time they look at it. That boy who received so many letters and whose mother sent us cards every year. You should know, my boy, people will come to respect you a great deal for the manner in which you're dealing with your misery. Sitting in that cell in that prison, under such miserable conditions, and you're still able to put others before yourself. People admire the courage it takes to be proactive in that type of environment. That's what defines you. You've always been someone who shined when it came to leadership and responsibility. I'm glad you listened to the advice from your mother. Embrace life as a gift, no matter what happens."

92

After Abdul was gone, cell number twelve had no leadership, and my cellmates turned to me asking if I wanted to become Kabran. With some hesitation, I gave in.

The prison machine kept growling relentlessly as new inmates continued to arrive. As a Kabran, I had to instruct them on the rules of the cell. Every time I saw their tired looks, whether from the exhausting days spent in the "rookie space" or after any transfer. I knew what they were going through, how they sometimes felt lost and disoriented.

From the moment a new inmate stepped into the opening of our cell door, I could tell what type of person he was. Basically, there were three groups: "pitiful – submissive", "quiet – respectful", "authoritarian – troublemaker". I was right nearly every time when it came to the future of these new inmates.

The "pitiful – submissive" type was typically treated like a doormat or drudge. The "quiet – respectful" type could go either way, but in most cases they were well taken care of by the group. The authoritarian types, or troublemakers were often given a rough time. They were the "tough-guys" who thought they were something special outside of these walls in the streets, but they were treated harshly by the older inmates. "You might think you're hot shit on the outside, but in here, you start on the bottom of the ladder, boy. Now shut up!"

It quickly became clear to them, that this "wasn't Kansas anymore", and they were now within the walls of a different world.

One of the guys from the "quiet– respectful" category was a Spaniard named Fernando. I saw him looking around with big disturbing eyes when he and other new inmates walked through the main entrance of the section for the first time. One of the guys from my cell was standing beside me and noticed the section head was reviewing the information on the newcomers. He told me about the Spaniard, and I jumped at the opportunity to finally learn Spanish! I went to the section head, and told him that I wanted that guy in my cell. He was fine with it. Fernando was too, even though he didn't know where he was going. I reassured him that everything would be okay.

Fernando was fifty-two years old and fit the stereotype of a Spaniard: he loved pork, soccer and bullfighting and couldn't speak more than a few words in any foreign language.

He had been sentenced to eighteen months. Guess what for. He explained to me with his hands and feet how he had stuck bags of hashish to his body just like they did in the movie *Midnight Express.*

"You know... the movie?" he asked in the few words of English he did know. I nodded.

Fernando had successfully crossed the border with drugs many times before, but this time he got caught.

Good, I thought to myself, because now I was able to learn Spanish. Initially, it was very difficult, but by referring to the things in our surroundings, we were able to get started.

Later on, my mom sent me a Spanish-Dutch dictionary, and

after that things moved faster. Just like I learned the Dutch language in elementary school, I was conjugating Spanish verbs in a notebook. To thank Fernando for his help, I arranged the top bed on my bunk for him and showed him the ropes of the prison.

My prison.

93

When fighting broke out, I still kept my distance. I didn't care enough about it, not even as the cell's leader. Except for one moment, when one guy went too far. He was short, but broad. His nickname on the outside was "Pit Bull" and the typical problem kid. The type I would classify as an "authoritarian – troublemaker". Even so, I still had the feeling that there was a sensitive boy underneath it all. The look in his hazel colored eyes betrayed his true nature.

"Those faggots at the tribunal gave me a year for nothing!! For nothing!" he shouted over and over. He would take his anger out on others, pushing chairs and tables aside and provoking fights.

"What are you looking at?" Pit Bull shouted at a man.

"Can't I just look?" the man answered calmly. The man was sitting in the corner on top of a bunk. "I find it amusing, to be honest, how you're walking around here acting like a baby, not realizing how much you're getting on our nerves. Pussy."

The term "pussy" didn't sit very well with Pit Bull. He immediately grabbed a glass from a table and threw it toward the man, barely missing him. It shattered against the wall.

That was the limit for me.

I jumped up, pushed a table aside roughly and walked over to Pit Bull, grabbing his shoulders with force.

"Just take it easy, man! We're all in the same situation here, for crying out loud!" I shouted. The boy looked past me.

"Hey... Look at me!" I said. "Back in 2004, they gave me TEN years in prison for nothing!"

Pit Bull looked me right in the eye and I saw that look, the look of a sensitive guy. His actions and body language were quite misleading.

"Listen," I said, putting my arm around him. "See that man?"

Pit Bull breathed heavily.

"He got five years for a robbery he didn't commit, and he ..." Pit Bull watched as I pointed to each person that I was speaking about, "he got eight years for allegedly falsifying of documents, and believe it or not, he got even thirty years for a murder he didn't commit, okay?"

I continued pointing as the eyes of the men in the cell were directed at me. "You're not the only one who's falsely accused here, we know how you feel!"

I almost wanted to say "be happy that you only got one year" or "you're lucky you only got a year", but those kind of statements never come off well in prison. If you really are innocent, you don't want to hear someone telling you to "be happy" or "you're lucky".

Pit Bull dropped his arms, breathing calmly again as a tear ran down his cheek. He nodded and apologized.

"So pull yourself together! Nobody wants to be here, but it's just the way it is. I hate it too."

"Okay, yeah, you're right, sorry."

"Good. Now apologize and act like a man. You're not a kid anymore. How old are you?"

"Twenty-four."

I looked at him, nodded and then let him go. He walked over to the man on the bunk he had just hit with the glass. I kept watching with a little smile, like I had just taught my own son a lesson. But my smile faded instantly. Pit Bull outstretched his arm to the man in order to apologize. The man pretended he was going to shake his hand in return. However, he had wrapped a cloth around a shard of glass in his hand and lashed out toward Pit Bull's face. The blood began to gush in milliseconds from the boy's cheek.

"That will teach you never to throw another glass at me, fucking kid!"

Pit Bull grabbed his face and collapsed as the man jumped off his bunk.

"Damn it, NO! What are you doing!" I screamed and ran over to him.

"He has to watch his mouth, the spoiled fucking kid. How dare he throw a glass at me!"

"He didn't know what he was doing! Leave him alone!" I pushed the man aside.

Suddenly, it was getting serious in the cell. Most of the men had gotten up and were standing around us. Pit Bull was lying on the ground pressing his hands to his cheek. He didn't cry, but kept surprisingly quiet, although the blood kept coming.

Then the man grabbed me.

"How dare you put your hands on me!" I shouted.

While he was holding my arm, a number of cellmates grabbed him, and he let the piece of glass go.

"Hold him until the guards come!" I cried. I asked them to call for the guards and a doctor.

Two guys lifted Pit Bull up and another gave him a T-shirt to stop the bleeding. In the background echoed the shouting of the men at the cell door screaming for a guard. They eventually came and took Pit Bull with them. A little later they took the other man, who was brought to the zoo.

The blood spots and pieces of glass were cleaned up by some helpers in the cell.

I lied down on my bed and stared at the bottom of the bunk above me, Fernando's bed. He was speechless by what had just happened. So was I. I didn't see it coming. That man, he was always so quiet. How could he do this?

And Pit Bull, the boy was only twenty-four, the same age I was when I ended up behind bars. Soon I would turn twenty-eight.

Both men were reassigned to another section. I felt sorry that Pit Bull wasn't around anymore. I had the feeling I could've taught him a lot.

But now he was gone and he would be scarred forever.

94

I had the best intentions in the world when performing my job as a cell leader, the Kabran, but after a few weeks I was completely tired of acting like the middle-man for everyone and everything. From fighting to being held responsible during cell searching, making cleaning schedules, checking, telling people that they are no longer allowed to smoke after midnight, arranging new glow plugs for the stoves, having the broken water lines repaired, finding the culprit who was leaving all the pans dirty, finding out who had stolen a pack of cigarettes from someone else, and so on, and so forth.

Find out for yourself!

I buried my nose in my books and letters again. Something I hadn't got around to since a while.

Abdul called me every week to see how I was. He always asked about Pipi and how things were going in the cell. I told him I was tired of my "leadership" role and how much I missed having him around. He wished and prayed that I would be released as soon as possible. He gave me courage to believe that my day would soon come.

Abdul told me every time how happy he was that he would soon be leaving for Germany. It had been two months since his release and he often reminded me of our times together. He also made sure to mention that once you got on the outside, life and its many obligations would easily overwhelm you.

"But anything, anything is better than being there," Abdul said. "Just wait until you get out, all that time you spent in prison will feel like a never-ending dream, actually, more like a nightmare. I sometimes even get the feeling like I was never really there at all."

"Well, I'm looking Abdul, and everything I see around me seems pretty real," I said.

I heard him sigh and I sighed with him.

"You're right, I know it really happened, but you know what I mean. I have to go, my card is running low. I just heard the beep before it hangs up. Say hello to everyone there and take care of Pipi. Give her a pat on the head from me."

"I will Abdul! *Choukran.* And best of luck with your trip to Germany. Life is waiting for you there."

I could hear him laughing as he thanked me. Then we hung up. It would be the last time that I – or anyone else – would ever hear his voice again.

95

It's early. My clock radio says half past seven. My bladder wakes me up.

As I come off the toilet, I stop at the cell door for a minute and glance up through the bars. The weather outside is beautiful. It's a bright blue sky with a peaceful hanging tuft of cloud here and there. It's calm, quiet and everyone in the cell is asleep, in their beds or on the floor. The whole prison is still asleep. Only the birds are awake, tweeting busily to one another.

I'm sitting on the edge of my bed, listening to the chirping. It sometimes appears as they are screaming at each other. I breathe in deeply. It's Sunday and that means I probably won't make it outside today. Well, maybe I'll try to go to the garden.

Yesterday, when I talked to Abdul on the phone, it was late in the evening. He told me he had borrowed a car and promised the owner he would return it to Marrakech that Sunday morning. From Rabat to Marrakech was a two hundred and fifty mile ride, most of them on local roads. Although it was late, he really wanted to return the car. "A promise is a promise." Abdul was a man of his word.

"Drive carefully," I said.

He laughed telling me that I had nothing to worry about...

I am watching the twelve o'clock news when the reporter announces that there had been a terrible accident. A head-on collision on one of the local roads between Rabat and Marrakech.

Sub-consciously, I held my breath and jump up to my feet.

No, it couldn't be?

It's a taxi carrying five passengers, and a dark colored car with one man inside. The bodies are placed under a white sheet next to the totaled vehicles. The feet are sticking out.

That's when I see it.

Under one of the sheets, two feet are sticking out; one with a torn sock, the other with just one shoe on. It's a black suede sneaker with two white vertical stripes. The same exact shoes that Maurice and I have given to Abdul before he left.

He took such good care of them.

It is Abdul's shoe.

It is Abdul's body under the sheet.

Abderrahman's body. Abderrahman is gone.

96

I'm squatting down on the ground in the garden as I carefully remove the plants, one by one. My mom told me to repot them as soon as they got too close together.

Behind some tall blades of grass, I notice Pipi observing me closely, following the movements of my hands.

"Remember Abdul, Pipi?"

She looks at me as if she can actually understand my question, only to reply: "Of course I remember him. Why do you ask?"

"Well, he's gone..."

I'm starting to feel sick. The injustice, unfairness, I can't understand why. Why?

These kinds of things always seem to happen to good people.

Every time I look up, I see Abdul's smiling face in front of me with those dimples on his cheeks. In the distance, I hear his contagious laugh. I see him sleeping, almost always on his back with his hands folded on his stomach that was slowly going up and down. I hear his voice and think of how he always warned me not to eat while standing up, because it was bad for my digestion. I think of the last time we were in the garden, hugging each other, talking about his dream, his happiness, and how everything had worked out so well for him. Now everything was over. Just like that, in one blow.

No one can do anything about it. Nothing. It is over.

I sit down on the ground, crossing my legs, and staring up at the sky. It's still a clear blue. The shade provides a pleasant refuge. Breathing in deeply, the garden smells fresh. I moisten the soil to repot the plants. All the bugs seem to be very contented about that.

Many small creatures are crawling through the flowers and plants. A woodlouse is walking through a column of ants, I must have disturbed her nap. A little further away I see two spiders running after each other, just missing a snail that seems to have all the time in the world, as she glides slowly forward. Nature is so beautifully put together.

The images of Abdul keep coming. It really was his body on TV. His sneakers. The sneakers he cared so much for were now smudged with sand and dried blood. He leaves behind his wife and child that he had already sent to Germany. Do they know? How horrible this must be for them.

I'm starting to feel sick again. How awful this all is. He had just been released after being locked up for all these years... And now he's dead.

Her husband, his father, he is no longer there.

"Come on Pipi, let's go back to the cell."

97

"... It's wonderful weather here at the moment. What really stands out are the young green plants in the yellow light of the evening sun. So very green, so beautiful, almost surreal, it gives you the feeling that something like that isn't supposed to exist in a world like this. One which is dominated by injustice and atrocities committed toward humans and animals.

I've had a restless heart for the past couple of days, but I'm feeling better now. I'm guessing you weren't feeling well. I always seem to get this sad feeling when you're feeling down.

I almost forgot to tell you that I had a dream about you last night. I put my arms around you, you were home, and a bit too skinny. You loved being home and you rested a lot. I thought everything was perfect, but then I realized I had forgotten to call everyone and tell them that you had been released. I felt ashamed, so I started calling immediately ... But then the alarm clock woke me up...

Despite the fact that you were having a wonderful time in my dream, I sensed the notion that you were missing something. Perhaps the people you left behind whom you had started to care for, or Pipi who would surely be looking for you, or maybe it was just the fact that things are very different here.

After these dreams, I'm always upset because I long to show you how beautiful it is here. I just get so frustrated because I can't get you out of there. I can't wait to say to you: "Son, come home with me."

You know what? I actually feel more like a mom now, even more so than when you were little. Sometimes it seems that you need me more now than you did back then. Well, don't forget that I'm here for you. But you already know that.

By the way, I think it's amazing that you're still able to see greenery and flowers in your little garden. I know it's weird, but that's important to me. I feel like the people there couldn't really care less, but then I reconsider because you told me how excited they were at the growth of a pea plant back in the beginning... I don't think they realized how it actually works. That a root can grow out of a hard pea 'just like that and that this root becomes a plant.

Do you keep taking care of Pipi? Your little princess. Are you still watching the birds fly inside the walls? Please my boy, pay attention to how wonderful their feathers are put together, and how it's possible that such a large animal can be carried by such small feet that look like matchsticks. Make sure to keep to yourself, but be sure to also take time for others. Keep exercising and writing. You're truly privileged within your community. You have the ability to bring something good from all of this. Remember that we'll never forget the unfair injustice causing you to be there. We don't sit around thinking "oh, Joe is in there and it's fine" because of your ability to adapt so well. No. You're still in a prison, and you're still innocent.

Remember what I said when you were in Berkane? You can see the warm wind that you feel around you, as if I was holding your face in my hands. It's still true, and it's never going to change."

98

My dad, Fouza and my brothers were coming to visit me!

It will be the first time seeing my brothers since all of this started. Of course, I now had three instead of two!

How they must have grown!

Would they still recognize me? Would they be scared, wondering who I am?

My oldest brother Amir was seven, Malik, was three and the youngest, Kian, hadn't been born yet when I was thrown behind bars. Now they were, let me think about it, eleven, seven and three.

Has it been that long?

I had a plastic bag in my hand with three toy cars and some drawing materials. The grocery man brought it for me. When I walked into the visitors hallway, I was nervous, but that disappeared immediately when my brothers came running up to me.

They still recognize me!

I laughed, leaned over and spread out my arms to try and scoop them all up. They were of course bigger than they used to be, but to me they will always be my little brothers. We hugged each other in the middle of the hall.

What a wonderful feeling to have the four arms of my brothers wrapped around my neck. I stood up and lifted my middle brother Malik with my right arm as I held hands with Amir on my left. His little hand had become larger, but still sank into mine. Malik pecked me on my cheek the whole time and giggled.

"We've missed you, Joseph! When can you come home?"

"Are you coming with us now?"

"What's in the plastic bag?"

As we walked toward my dad and Fouza, Amir and Malik asked me all kinds of questions that I tried to answer the best I could.

A few moments later, I hugged my dad and Fouza and looked down at my youngest brother, Kian. He clung shyly to his mother's leg. I squatted down next to him and put my hand on his back. He felt warm. It was still warm for being late summer.

"Hi, Kian," I said. "I'm Joseph, your big brother."

He was too shy and turned his head away like most boys his age. It was quite different from my other brothers. They bounced around the visitors hall faster than at the play palace where we used to go back home.

My dad, Fouza and I talked nineteen to the dozen. After watching his older brothers for a bit, Kian became slightly more talkative. I held my arms out and asked him to come see me. He looked at his mom briefly,

"Go on, he's your big brother, Kian," Fouza said.

He walked up to me with little steps and I locked him in my arms. I picked up my plastic bag. "Look what I have for you."

Kian grabbed the toy car with both hands. Then my other brothers sprinted toward me with their faces red from running around. They took the cars. Amir was hesitant, he didn't like toy cars that much.

"Oh, okay... Maybe you like this?" I asked, handing him the drawing materials. Fouza told me that Amir loved to draw and he was very good at it too.

A few moments later, Malik and Kian were busy with their cars as Amir sat next to me drawing a deer. I was happy to see that they weren't afraid and didn't know of the injustice taking place as we spoke.

My youngest brother was a funny little guy, but he had also dropped something funny in his diaper. The air near our table was filled with the smell of his full little pants. We had to laugh, but Kian looked at us, pouting his lower lip.

"Don't worry, Kian, I'll take care of it," I said gently, motioning to one of the guards I knew well. He came over to us and gracefully introduced himself to my dad and Fouza.

"Is there anything I can do, Joe?" he asked.

"Well, actually there is," I said smiling. "My little brother here left a nice pie in his diaper and we don't have a clean one."

"No problem, I'll get you one," the guard answered quickly.

He went to the women's department where diapers were always in stock. The imprisoned moms were often visited by relatives who brought their small children.

Fouza changed Kian on the toilet as I continued talking with my dad. I answered my brothers in turn as they continued to ask me questions.

The clean diaper worked like magic on Kian, when he came back with Fouza he was in a much better mood. I lifted him up and held him high in the air, like a plane. My brothers wanted me to do that to them as well, but they had become quite heavy. Therefore, we played hide and seek together.

While I was sitting on my chair talking with my dad and Fouza, I looked around every so often to make sure they were still there. I tried to divide my attention between all of them. I loved sitting there, it was like the old days, but just then, the alarm whistled loudly as if it roared: "Remember, you're a prisoner, you have to return to your cell now!"

My brothers were shocked by the loud noise and the oldest asked if someone had escaped. Amir of course knew that this was a prison, but he didn't think I was one of the prisoners. He was still under the impression that I was here for work.

One day, he'll understand.

It was time to go back, but my brothers wouldn't let me go. Malik was clamped around my leg, I carried Kian in my right arm and Amir was holding my left hand again. I shuffled along with my dad and Fouza toward their exit. I wondered what would happen if I just kept walking with them, right out the door...

The time came for me to return to my cell when the oldest

said, "You've been gone long enough."

Little wise guy.

"I know, Amir," I said. "Can you forgive me for being away so long? I'll make it up to you as soon as I get home, okay?"

"When will you be home?"

I thought for a minute, and said: "Next year, I'll be home, definitely this time."

99

"Your dad and Fouza were at a loss for words," my mom wrote after their visit. *"They said it was fantastic to see you. They couldn't believe how great you looked. I told them before they left that you looked amazing, but now they've seen it with their own eyes."*

My mom's letters kept coming, just like Maurice and I were tirelessly keeping the rest of the guys from the unit on a strict exercise schedule. We were in excellent shape and could easily run laps around the courtyard for at least an hour. As we ran, we imagined ourselves in the woods, or in the mountains, or running through our own neighborhoods.

Maurice and I often talked about Abdul. We couldn't believe that he was no longer here.

In the afternoon as we sat in the courtyard, we watched many planes flying in the sky above us, wondering every time where they were going. Freedom was so tangible for them. The people on the plane didn't give a moment's thought about us, sitting down here in a prison courtyard somewhere in Morocco.

We fantasized about holiday trips and places we would like to visit one day: Italy, Norway, America, Japan, Australia, the Seychelles. We dreamed about our lives in the Netherlands, and how someday it would all be real again. We thought about

Abdul's dream, for most of the men here, that's as much as it would ever be. I told Maurice about the stowaways on a ship during my work in Casablanca, as I told Younes at the time. Maurice and I were going through the same process under the ECJL. I was further along, and my transfer request to the court from the Netherlands had already been sent to Morocco. Now, all I had to do was wait for the approval from the Moroccan authorities. It was very exciting, but also scary. If my transfer request was rejected I would have to remain in Morocco until December 23rd, 2010. That was more than two years away! But I refused to focus on the negatives. I focused on the transfer.

My application will be approved.

I'm sure of it.

100

Diary, Day 1358 – September 10, 2008.

"My twenty-eighth birthday. My mom had sent me another wonderful gift: a digital photo book with pictures of my friends and places back home. I also received many cards, letters and text messages. It gives me a warm feeling that people hadn't forgotten me on my birthday. They are the ones who give me the strength to survive. I told my mom on the phone about the cards and texts and she said that everyone was supporting me as much as possible, but ultimately, I had to go through this myself. "That's true," I agreed. "You can take a horse to water, but you can't make him drink." Surprisingly, she had never heard this expression before. "You must have learned such wisdom in there, I'll have to remember that one," she said.

It's the people back home who bring me the water, and I drink it. It was the positive connection with home that gives me the strength to not only rise above my situation, but also myself."

101

In the last months of 2008, Emily and I talked on the phone a lot. When I got the chance, I paged her from my cell and she would call me back immediately.

"She truly is something, that Emily. Last night, I was talking to her on the phone when out of nowhere she says: "Oooohhhhh, it's your son on the other line!" And bam! She hung up. I think I'm going to have to accept that a young woman might rather talk to a young handsome man, instead of an old woman like me. For a brief moment I felt like an old pathetic mother, ha-ha."

My mom, very lovingly, said that she didn't mind me talking to Emily instead of her. Emily's sweet cheerful voice always seemed to put me in a good mood.

"You truly are the perfect man, you know," she once said on the phone.

"Oh yeah? How come?"

"Well, if you were my husband, at least I would know without a doubt that you couldn't possibly be cheating on me!"

Emily roared with laughter.

'Ooooh! You're so mean!"

"Well, am I right?" she answered playfully.

We joked about things like that a lot.

Right around the same time, I started talking with Amber again. We talked a few times, but our calls were missing the joy and optimism that I felt when talking with Emily. Amber was starting to have feelings for me again. Feelings that she could better express by writing them down on paper. In one of her letters, she wrote how every time she would think about our years together, she began to feel homesick, like something was amiss. In the letter she tried to apologize for all of the pain that she had caused in our relationship. It was a letter straight from the heart. She didn't want us to drift apart any further, but said she would understand why if I didn't want to have any more contact with her.

And then there was the question: *"Do you think we could ever be together again?"*

When I read it, I wasn't sure how to react. Different voices were going through my head, ranging from "leave me alone, Amber" to "I really wish everything could be the way it was".

But I had to let it go. I didn't want to think about it anymore. Not now, not here. I wrote her back that she shouldn't wait for me, that she needed to look for happiness with someone else. I truly hoped that she would find peace in her heart once again.

"When you meet someone, speak from the heart, but leave me behind as your beloved. I would still like to be friends with you, but the love we had is gone. I gave it a special place in my heart that I will always cherish. I'll always be grateful for the years you've given me."

102

Letter 356.

"Dear, dear son,

A great idea it is, that at Christmas, many people will hear the carol "Silent Night, Holy Night." To me, the greatest Christmas song of all time. Just for the melody. All who know you and hear this carol, are undoubtedly thinking of you and your situation. I know, because this wonderful song always makes me think of those who are less fortunate. Not only people like you, but also homeless people, and those who suffer from hunger or loneliness. I don't know of any other song that has that kind of power.

As you know, I am collecting Christmas cards from people who didn't use them in previous years. I wanted to collect five hundred cards so each man from your department can receive a Christmas card from

"Mama Joseph". They are welcome to it, whether they are fools or not, guilty or innocent. Somewhere deep inside them or perhaps closer to the surface, they are and will remain human beings who enjoy receiving this kind of attention.

And wouldn't you know, I received nearly seven hundred and fifty cards! It made me so happy to see how people adopted my message of collective action on freesef.com and how they went on to publish it on the internet through their own website or blog. For me, it's a confirmation that you can also get attention for a cause by doing good things. I've packed all the cards in a box full of Christmas things which will be sent to you.

I'm hoping with a never-ending optimism, my child..."

Letter 358.

"... The final day of the year again. Unfortunately, another year has gone, taken with it the hope and dreams that didn't come true. I think again about the terrible cold you had when you were just imprisoned in the jail of Berkane and late last year in "the zoo". It's terrible that people are living that way. I find it awful to think of you in that situation. Horrible.

But 2008 was also a year of positive things. You, working in the garden, the store, Pipi the cat, lots of mail and packages with snacks, magazines and books, the conversations we had. The help I received from many people and another important thing: I haven't been sick. Not a single illness this year!

As I wrote before: experiencing the mystery of life is a great gift, even though you're an innocent man in prison and how financially difficult it has become. We will simply go on. I keep believing that everything will be all right. We are surely heard, my son.

But I'm so tired now that I'll stop. Tomorrow, on the first day of the new year, I will write you another large piece.

Lots of love, mom."

PART III

2009

Sweetheart, it makes me feel good knowing that you can be so patient. Everything's going to be all right, for sure. Regardless, I am very proud of you and always consider myself fortunate that you of all children are my child. For a mother, that's the world! Take care, my son. In our thoughts, we are always with you. One day, you will leave this evil and be able to walk through the sunny green meadows again. Keep hoping and dreaming about your future outside the four walls.

Every night, the final day is getting closer, just like counting the nights as a child, waiting for your birthday to arrive.

I

"Is there someone who can translate for me?" the director asked the guards in his office.

The prison recently hired a new director. Every number of years, the prison directors are repositioned throughout Morocco.

Our new director asked this question because more and more foreigners were being assigned to "his" prison. They came to him with their problems, but he couldn't understand any of them unless they spoke in Arabic.

"Well, Mr. Director," the head guard said, "for several years now, there's been a young guy here from the Netherlands and he speaks different languages."

"Bring him up here," the director ordered.

A little later, I found myself standing in the office between the guards and the new director. I didn't know what was going on. *What could I have done?*

"I'm sorry, Mr. Director, I apologize for my appearance, I was exercising with some of the guys."

I was a little embarrassed to stand in front of him in my sweaty clothes.

"No problem, no problem," he said. He stood up and walked past his big shiny desk. He was no taller than five and half feet, but I had learned that a man's height had nothing to do with his power. The director sat down on the edge of the desk in front of me. He folded his hands and his lips were curled up, making his thin white mustache inch up slightly.

"I understand you speak several languages," he said.

"Uhm, yes, I can speak fairly well in several languages, sir."

I glanced back and saw the head guard looking sternly at me, but not in a bad way. Normally, we greeted each other informally, but in front the director, everything had to look official.

"Fine," the director said. With a little jump he landed back on the ground with both feet. I watched him as he walked to the leather chair that was beside his desk. He hit it with his hand firmly and said: "From now on, this will be your place whenever I need you, okay?"

Again I glanced at the head guard. He nodded slightly.

I quickly realized the director's question only had one possible answer: "Yes, of course, sir."

2

After I started to work as a translator, it was as if all doors within the prison had been opened up for me. I could go wherever I wanted, except outside the walls of course. The big prison gate next to the principal's office was the only door that remained closed.

Most of the guards were already pretty friendly to me, but now it seemed like every guard was going out of their way to say hello. Wherever I wanted, I was allowed to go anywhere without asking or explaining why; the infirmary, the departments in "Colombian Morocco", the visitors' hallway, the isolation wards, administration. I was even allowed in the guarded room where Lee "Lightning" Murray, the UFC fighter, had monthly visits with his family.

"You're allowed to go anywhere, it's like this is your home," Lee told me once laughing.

At the end of the afternoon, I was no longer required to attend roll calls. I could even walk the hallways or go to the garden far after evening roll call. Also, on the weekends I often spent my time far outside of the unit. I would walk in the "general" courtyard among its palm trees, lemon trees and many red flowers. The covered paths that surrounded it provided shade from the sun, or protection from the soft rain. As I walked there, I remembered the first time I arrived at the prison and saw this garden. I thought of the horrible weekend I had to spend in the "rookie space", where Jeremy and I were crammed in together. I remembered Soufian in Taza. How was he doing? And Karim and Chief Nordin from Berkane? It seemed like ages since the last time I saw them.

I usually walked my rounds alone or with a guard – he wasn't there to guard me, usually just to make small talk – or sometimes I walked with the doctor who had helped me when I had dysentery. There were several inmates who were allowed to stay outside after roll call. Some worked for the administration, others for the guards, but everyone knew that I worked for the director. It gave me a status which initially I wasn't aware of, but nevertheless used to my advantage.

During my walks, I still couldn't believe how beautiful the trees, plants and flowers bloomed here, against the backdrop of high walls, bars and barbed wire. I pretended I was outside the prison walls, I imagined getting in my car and going to see William or my grandfather, or heading out just because. Maybe to do some shopping, or something else mundane. But that was, and still remained impossible.

3

I came to find out that working for the director did have its drawbacks, two to be exact. First, I became so busy that I couldn't continue my English class. However, Maurice came to my rescue and took over the class for me! Awesome!

The second drawback was when I noticed that some of the inmates started to behave differently toward me. They began to avoid me, and one day I took the opportunity to talk to the guys.

"What's wrong with you?" I asked the group of men who were typically responsible for getting drugs into the prison. There was no answer, they just glanced at me.

"I know what it's about," I said. "You're acting like this because I'm working for the director now, right?" Some of them began to shuffle, while others were looking the other way.

"Hey, guys!" I spread open my arms. "What is this? You know me. Don't tell me you're afraid that I'm going to tell on you to the director about your business? I don't care what you guys are doing here! That's your thing, something I can't change no matter how much I hate it."

Their eyes slowly glanced back at me, one by one.

"I understand that this is your life," I continued, "and I would like nothing more than to take you all away with me in a big plane, so you can get out of here and live a normal life." I looked down and struggled for a minute. Society saw these men as scum, I used to see them as scum and that broke my heart.

"What I just want to say is, even though I don't approve of what you're doing, who am I to judge you? I just want you to know that I respect you, and that I want to serve my time here in a peaceful way."

One of the guys stepped forward and looked at me.

"You're right, Joe." He turned around to the group and then faced back at me again. "I'm sorry we were thinking about you in this way, but there are many betrayers in here."

"I know, but that's why I didn't expect this from you. You know who I am, right?"

After these words, the situation cooled off and everyone stood around me to apologize.

"It's okay," I said, "but if you're worried about anything, if you have any doubts at all, please promise me that you will come see me right away, okay?"

They stood around me nodding, and apologized again.

We shook hands and went our separate ways again.

4

Possessing a cell phone was no longer a problem for me. The guards left me alone. Hiding the cell phone in the blender was history. The fact that I could easily be reached by phone was soon known amongst my friends. I found all the attention to be enjoyable! Now, besides the sustained flow of mail, I was getting a lot of phone calls and text messages every night.

Hi Joe! Just a quick message. Right now, I'm sitting in a gym with 30 toddlers, driving myself crazy from the noise, and suddenly I thought of you... Just saying hello. Greetings from me... There's another package on the way! X Dagmar

Hey Joe, I really enjoyed our conversation. We should do it more often. Anyways, you get some rest and I'll talk to you soon, love... X Farida

Joe! I just wanted to tell you that in my mind, I am with you. Damian

Hey Joe! Just ring my phone if you wanna chat, I'll call you right back! X Ferda

Just wanna say that it was super nice talking to you. We're keeping our date! Don't forget me of course :-) Big kiss, Sandra

I sent you a little something today. Straight from the heart!! In case you want to talk, let me know! Jean Paul

Hey sweet Joe, it's been too long since we talked. Hope everything is going well with you. I'm still crossing my fingers that you get to come home as soon as possible. Next week I'm going to write another letter to you to keep you posted about my life. Thinking of you. Love,Amber.

I just realized that we have been best friends for over 20 years! :-) Greetings! William

Can't sleep and can't stop thinking about you. I'm so sorry that you're still in there. I know we need to stay positive, but now I think it's just bullsh*t. You're one of the few people who really impress me! And no, I'm not just saying that. Sleep well, Joe. X Emily

I also got text messages from my fellow inmates in the other cells. Especially Lee Murray and Maurice. I was on the phone so much that they could hardly get a hold of me.

You could be the Dutch world champion for talking on the phone! Lee.

Even though you're a lot younger than me, I want you to know that I look up to you, and how you're dealing with all of this. I'm glad you're here, one day we will go home together. Maurice.

5

Maurice and I came out of the showers and put our sweaty gym clothes in our soap bucket again. For a long time, it had been our daily routine. We let the clothes soak in the bucket until around noon, then we washed them out at the water tap on the toilet. When the cell doors opened up again in the afternoon, we hung the clothes on a rope in the courtyard.

"This little light of mine... Lalalalalalalala... I'm gonna let it shine!"

"What are you singing about?" Maurice asked.

"Oh nothing, I always have that song in my head when I'm hanging up laundry."

"The Seekers?" Maurice asked and roared with laughter.

I tied the laundry rope at one end to one of the poles of the shelter, then stood on my toes to get it as high as possible while Maurice held the laundry bucket behind me.

"Yes, The Seekers. And? I think it's a fun song."

"Ha-ha, that's not like you, man!"

"What do you mean, not like me?"

"I mean, The Seekers!"

"Well, it's not like I've got all their albums or I'm sleeping out for one of their concerts in front of the hall twenty-four hours before, I just think it's a fun song. What's wrong with that?"

"You're nuts! I thought you were more rock n'roll and that sort of thing," Maurice laughed and I laughed with him.

"True, but I actually like all kinds of music. Did you know that my mom interviewed a Dutch folk singer, for a TV program she was working on? He turned out to be a very likeable guy."

"TV program?" Maurice asked.

"Yeah, my mom was the editor of a successful TV program at Brabant Broadcasting, a local broadcast station.

"Wow! Cool."

"Yeah, my mom is cool, Maurice."

"I know. I still think it's incredible that she sends you so many letters."

I smiled and felt a spark of happiness flow through my veins.

"JOSEPH!!"

Maurice and I turned around. A planto stood on the other side of the courtyard waving at us. "THE DIRECTOR NEEDS YOU!"

Maurice, can you finish this?" I asked as I was about to tie off the other end of the rope.

"Sure, no problem. Go ahead."

I walked with the planto, assuming that it was about another translation job. But it was something completely different. It was the best news I had heard in a long time.

6

"What's this?" the director asked, as I sat beside him in "my" chair.

The director gave me a look of satisfaction.

"'What's what?" I asked and smiled back.

"I have the papers here for your transfer to the Netherlands."

I grabbed the armrests of the chair, and felt the urge ready to leap into the air.

"And? Is it approved?"

The director nodded. I leaped into the air anyway.

"Really?! This is great news! I have to tell everyone! My mom, William, my dad, my brothers…"

I kept going on and on, thanking the director many times as well.

"And the guys, I can't wait to tell the guys in the section!"

That's fine, go ahead. But you have to come back later this afternoon, because I need you to do some work for me."

"Okay, no problem! See you later!"

I stood up, nearly tripping over my own feet, as I walked back to the section. I couldn't believe the time had come, that I was finally able to see a light at the end of the tunnel!

But as I walked along the path back to the section, my excitement suddenly disappeared. In front of the chief of staff's office, a group of guards was standing in front of a handcuffed boy. I walked slowly past them and saw how badly the boy was being beaten. One of the guards evidently felt that the boy had not been punished enough, because he began punch him as hard as he could in his face. The boy's blood flew from his mouth splashing at my feet on the ground. I slowed down, pausing to watch the guards. It was the bulky guard with the bald, egg-shaped head who was hitting the boy. The very same guard who caught me with the phone that one time, causing me to be sent to the zoo!

He looked at me, expressionless.

The other guards greeted me kindly. The boy was hunched over looking up at me. Blood and drool were dripping from his mouth. I looked him straight in the eye and I was ashamed that I couldn't do anything to help him.

"Nothing to worry about here," the chief said. "Just keep walking, Joseph."

I said nothing and looked at the boy once more. I was startled when they punched him in the stomach again, and started walking away, glancing over my shoulder. I kept looking at the boy and the guards around him.

Why should I feel happy? I'm still here and so is this boy.

And here he would stay. In this world of injustice.

A world that I would soon hopefully leave behind.

7

Maurice and the guys were very happy for me that my ECJL request was approved. They asked when I would be leaving, but I didn't have an answer yet and I wasn't going to get one anytime soon. Not even during my official visit in February of 2009.

A visit from a representative from the Dutch Ministry of Foreign Affairs, together with a few people from the probation service department and the Dutch embassy.

After the director informed me of their plan to visit, I told him I wanted to welcome them in a nice way with cookies and soda. He gave me permission and so, on the day of the visit, Maurice and I carried two bowls of cookies, plastic cups, drinks and napkins to the visitors room. There, a delegation of five people was waiting. When we walked in, I could see in their eyes that they weren't expecting all of this. They reacted very excited with *oohs* and *aahs*.

"You look well, Joseph," was the first thing the woman of the Ministry of Foreign Affairs said to me. She had been following my case from the very beginning, and helped to ensure that their trust lawyer conducted an independent investigation back in 2005. She regretted that it hadn't resulted in an early release.

The woman from the Ministry was in her mid-fifties with bleach blonde hair and dark designer glasses. In one of our telephone calls, my mom told me to make myself look as "beautiful" as possible, because even middle-aged women like to look at young men. I had a good laugh at her comment, but still took my mom's advice to heart. She was right. During the conversation, they couldn't stop saying how sorry they felt for me.

However sorry they felt, it did not change the fact that I had been wrongly imprisoned for over four years. I asked repeatedly how something like this could possibly happen, and their response never changed: it shouldn't have happened, but there was nothing they could do. Eventually, I dropped the subject and asked when I would finally be allowed to go home.

"We don't have an exact date," the woman of the Ministry said, "but it will definitely be this summer."

For a minute, it was quiet in the room as everyone looked at me. I couldn't hide my smile any longer. After hearing the word "summer", my mind wandered for a moment.

"And guess what, I also know that once you've landed at Schiphol Airport, you may immediately go home."

"Really? Straight home? That would be unbelievable!"

The house I would return to, wouldn't be my mom's Norwegian wooden home. In late 2008, she moved to another house. She was forced to leave after disagreeing with the landlord, because after nine years, he still hadn't put the house in my mom's name. So now, someday soon, I would start a new life in a new house.

8

This summer I'm going home.

This summer I'm going home.

This summer I'm going home.

This summer, it's finally going to happen.

I had it on my mind constantly. Five more months. Five times thirty days. So one hundred and fifty days. It seemed so far away, nearly unreachable. But knowing that I had already spent much more time away from home than this, I was able to overcome it.

Back home, everyone was elated by the news. It caused a real boost in the amount of incoming letters I received. It was like many of them had woken up from their disbelief by the happiness of the fact that what once seemed to have no end, was finally coming to a close.

"The responses to your upcoming transfer from Morocco are heartwarming. They are truly happy for you," my mom wrote in one of her letters, which were now counting well above three hundred. She would soon reach number four hundred.

William was thrilled and had already ordered tickets for the Lenny Kravitz concert on July 4th. *"If you can't make it, don't worry, but I'm going to assume that by then, you and I will be jumping in the sun to Lenny's music in Amsterdam."*

William's notion gave me the idea to create a "bucket list". A list of things I wanted to do after I was released. I wrote down the Lenny Kravitz concert and also added a few more concerts to the list: Bruce Springsteen, Pearl Jam, Live and Nickelback.

I wanted to see a few stand-up comedians as well and one of them was Najib Amhali, whom I would have gone to in 2005. His name was written directly below the concerts.

It had always been a dream of my mother's to visit Italy and sail through Venice in a gondola. That would be nice too! There were many other countries that I once wanted to visit. Norway,

America, Japan, Australia. The countries Maurice and I talked about last year while sitting in the courtyard, staring up at the planes flying high in the sky.

But I also realized how much I wanted to see in the Netherlands. For example, I had never been to all twelve provinces. Therefore, I wrote "Journey through the Netherlands" on my list too. There was so much to do!

I imagined myself working out at Peter van Drunen's fitness center. Working out with real weights. I pictured myself among the people in the city, at the supermarket, at concerts, in the cinema. I was actually looking forward to sitting in traffic again! Among all the people who live their lives every day, lost in their own thoughts.

It would be a dream come true to help people, inspire them, and give them strength by sharing my story. The way Mandela and Gandhi gave me strength. Of course, I don't dare compare myself to them, I'm just a regular guy, but one with a special story, I think.

Every day, I thought about how I was going to tell people of my story to both acquaintances and strangers. I was sure everybody would sympathize with me. And those who wouldn't, well, that's the way it goes.

My head was reeling at the thought of doing untold things again. It was like I was a little kid again, after being told that we were going to the biggest playground in the world: I just couldn't decide what I wanted to do first. I was so excited.

It was nice to think about all these things, but right now, I was still here.

I had to wait and see what would happen in the months ahead.

I wasn't home yet.

"Remember, Joe, we all love you very much and we're looking forward to the day we'll see you again. Lots of love, mama.

9

A week after the visit from the Ministry of Foreign Affairs, the representatives from the embassy came to see me again. Much to my surprise, the official told me that the woman from the Ministry couldn't stop talking about me.

It was flattering, "Joseph this, and Joseph that!" and "He looked so good!", "How has he been able to manage this? I've never seen that before!"

My mother wrote to me that she had talked with the same woman on the phone for half an hour: *"If she was younger, she probably would have fallen in love with you, ha-ha. You were quite the Romeo, with your biscuits and juice. She did mention that she felt a little guilty because of how much money it cost you for everything."*

No matter where I was, the director's office, in the prison shop, the garden, in my bed, while cooking or exercising, every time I caught myself daydreaming for a moment. A flurry of jitters would come over me, curiosity, and an awareness that this really was going to happen. I was going home this year. Every emotion was one filled with happiness, combined with a mix of nervous tension and a touch of love. I realized that, after more than four years, I had unconsciously become accustomed to prison life.

Daily detentions, roll calls, the fear of being caught with a phone or money. These things seemed only natural.

Only after they announced that my transfer would officially go through, that I would really get to go home, did I slowly come out of this trance. Slowly but surely, I became detached from my "ordinary" prison life.

However, I also began to fear life outside the walls. I know that sounds crazy, and it is, because I wanted nothing more than to continue on with my life. I think I had developed a fear of change after becoming so adapted to my daily familiar life. A change can always bring about feelings of resistance. I was probably afraid of being thrown back into fast-paced society with all of its obligations and responsibilities.

However, the thoughts of happiness and joy made it easy to forget about the fear. Suddenly, the idea of living a normal life popped back into my head, causing butterflies in my stomach again. Adrenalin, dopamine, testosterone and every other body substance were coming together like an emotional bomb inside of me. I wanted to get out. I wanted to start again with a real life! Right now!

IO

My mother sent lots of pictures of the new house. Little by little, it began to take form. William helped with the heavy lifting and moving, Emily took care of painting the walls and doors, and Amber's parents helped with tiling and laying the laminate floor. My mother asked me what colors I wanted to have on my bedroom walls.

'Soft orange," I said, "and yellow shades." I wanted sunny colors, my favorite colors.

My mother agreed with me and decided to paint her own room with her favorite colors: green and blue, the colors of nature.

After seeing all the pictures, I began to get used to the idea. With that being said, I still thought it was going to be weird coming home to a different house.

In prison, I now had more friends than ever. Every time I walked through the hallways with Maurice or Fernando, I shook hands, waved or gave *high fives*. I greeted almost everyone by their name and everybody knew my name as well. Many invited me to join them for dinner, and if I needed anything, I only had to ask. All this attention gave me energy. The people gave me energy and suddenly, I realized that I had always fed off of the energy from the people around me. At school, work, with friends, but also here in prison.

And of course from the many letters.

I gave six large bags of mail to the "message man". I knew I wouldn't be able to take all the mail I had received in my transfer to the Netherlands. So the letters were temporarily kept safe with him, until they could be shipped to the Netherlands by a courier service. I also gave him the pens for my friends that the Pen man had made for me during my stay in the prison of Berkane. As I packed, I looked at them, one by one, and read the names. I actually couldn't believe that I still had them. I never thought it would've taken this long to give them to everyone. Another item for my bucket list: "Handing out the pens."

I kept the letters from my mom with me, along with many others written by William, Amber, my grandfather, Fouza and Emily. I would carry them myself during the transfer in my red suitcase. The very same suitcase I had with me at the end of 2004, when I unsuspectingly left home. In Berkane, the lawyer had taken my suitcase and made sure to hand it over to the prison of Salé.

Prison life went on, and just as you might expect there were many more fights. I never got involved and told Maurice and Fernando the same. We came close once, when walking through the hallway. Next to us, out of nowhere, an inmate stabbed another man in the shoulder with a pen. Maurice and Fernando were surprised and wanted to go in for a closer look, but I grabbed their arms and pulled them away. "It's better not to interfere with those kind of things!"

I continued my daily routine of visiting the courtyard and the garden. I was allowed to stay out until I told the guards myself that I wanted to go back to my cell. The roll calls, the most annoying moments of the day, had also become a thing of the past. As I walked around outside of my section, I could hear the guards shouting in the distance for everyone to get back in their places. Over the past few years I made sure to tell them that this wasn't my place. After a while, the guards stopped saying it to me. I had my personal victory.

This has never been my place.

II

"The weather outside is lovely, with an occasional rain shower. Sometimes it's cloudy, and then the sun returns, shining brightly. It's incredible how fast the trees have become green. It's like a party with the different shades of green rolling into each other. The tulips are in full bloom and the king-cups are blossoming for the second time. The beautiful leaves in the ponds have also begun to flourish, I think they're one of the most beautiful flowers I have ever seen. Just five little white petals with a second layer of leaves, almost like feathers, sitting on top, and in the middle a little red heart."

The months of 2009 flew by. With all my activities and work for the director, things weren't that bad! The only real problem was the heat, the temperature had risen again to nasty heights.

It was a Friday afternoon, just after evening roll call, when I sat back in my chair in the courtyard. I was all alone. Well, not entirely. Pipi was sitting next to me.

I closed my eyes a little. It was June and the sun was shining brightly, just before the true start of summer. All prisoners were called back to their cells to spend the weekend behind bars again. The guards left me alone, giving me a moment to myself. A moment before the long weekend started again. They knew how much I enjoyed the blue sky.

A minute ago, there were a few hundred people walking

around, now, the courtyard was dominated by the sounds of squeaky sparrows and screaming gulls. Occasionally, a rat appeared, crawling from one of the open manholes and then running to another as quickly as possible. Pipi followed the movements of all the animals closely, but wasn't good for much more than a big yawn here and there. Now and then, a stork or cattle egret would fly low over the prison. As difficult as it was for me to get to the other side of the wall, as easy it was for the birds to fly over them. To them, walls were ridiculous.

Please give me wings. Just for a day. I promise I'll never need them again.

It was an impossible wish, one of many.

I could hear a mix of television noises and voices. The voices of inmates and guards, ordering the evening roll call. They seemed far away. Pipi and I enjoyed the sun as long as possible, as I sat and waited for it to disappear behind the wall. Then I took my chair and walked to the door as she pattered behind me. I tapped a few times and a guard rushed over to me.

"Would you like to go back to your cell, Joseph?"

That weekend would be my last in captivity...

12

Monday, June 15, 2009, day 1635.

It's a Monday, a day on which I've so often said "yet another new week with new opportunities." This week is one I'll never forget as long as I live.

Around noon, I walk across the indoor path, back to my department. The path I've walked so many times in the past years. I'm returning from the director's office, where I completed another translation job, and walk past the head keeper's room.

"Joseph!" someone calls from the room.

I stop, turn around and walk into the room. I greet the guards politely.

"Everything all right, Joseph?" the head guard asks. He is sitting between two guards at a large glazed table with a cup of tea and asks me if I would like some too.

"No, thanks," I kindly say. This tea is and remains much too sweet for me.

The guards are smiling at me.

"Take a chair," the head guard says quietly. "You know why we've called you here?"

As I'm sitting down, I say that I don't know but the way they are looking at me is making me very curious.

"The day has come..."

The day?

"You will be transferred to Casablanca."

Transfer... Casablanca...

The three men in their light brown summer uniforms are looking at me, waiting for a response.

"I'm going to Casablanca?"

"Yes, and from there you will be picked up to go to the Netherlands."

When hearing "the Netherlands", a tremendous feeling of joy comes over me. I can't resist putting on a big smile.

"Really? I'm going home? Can I go home?"

I see the three guards still smiling.

"Well, we don't know how long you will have to stay in Casablanca, but it seems that the end is in sight for you."

I get up and walk to the head guard. He is also getting up and meets my embrace.

"Thank you, thank you!" I keep saying as we pat each other on the back. The other two guards also got up to wish me strength and success.

"Thank you, thank you! *Choukran!*"

I can't believe it. My time in this jail is almost over after nearly four and a half years. Suddenly, I begin thinking about a hundred things at once! My friends here, my friends in the Netherlands, my mother, Pipi the cat, my things.

"My belongings? Should I start packing now?" I ask.

"The transfer bus is waiting outside, but take your time. Pack your bags, take your time to say goodbye to everyone and when you're ready, you let us know."

I am perplexed. The bus is ready, but I can take my time to say goodbye. This is very special. Normally, the prisoners must be ready to leave within two minutes. I thank the men once again for their kindness.

"It's okay. Now go say goodbye."

13

As I walk through the section toward my cell, I'm feeling happier and happier. From my stomach to my throat, a warm, tingling feeling comes over me. I can hardly resist bouncing down the hallway shouting: "I'm going home! I'm going home!"

The day of the transfer was here. Finally, the time had come for me to go home, back to where I belong.

Home, home... How wonderfully familiar that sounds.

The hallways are empty, everyone is back in their cells like always at noon. I'm telling my news to the guard in the hallway and he can't believe it. I can't wait any longer, I have to tell Maurice immediately. The guard went to get him, and a few minutes later, Maurice was standing at my cell, overwhelmed.

"I'll leave the cell open for you Joseph, have a safe trip," the guard said.

When they heard "a safe trip", the guys in the cell began turning around, one by one.

"What did he mean by "have a safe trip?" Fernando asked.

"I'm being transferred!" I answer him in Spanish, and again in Moroccan, "I'm going back to the Netherlands!"

Now everyone is looking, I have twenty-eight pairs of eyes focused on me. I spread my arms wide, as if to say: "Group hug!", after which the first guys get up and walk over to me. Fernando jumps from his bed and joins them.

"Really?

"You're leaving?"

"To the Netherlands?"

"I'm so happy for you!"

"Finally, back to your mom!"

As we all hugged, everyone was talking at once, the only thing I could say was: "Thank you all, my time has come, I'm going home."

14

I divide my things among the guys in the cell. My clothes, blankets, pillows, food, everything. I don't need anything anymore. The only thing I'm packing are some basic toiletries and the box with Amber's necklace. I stare at the box for a while. I will keep my promise to give the necklace back. I put the things in a backpack. The letters are in my red suitcase.

After saying goodbye to the guys in the cell, Maurice, Fernando and a few other cellmates join me on my farewell round along the twenty-one cells of the department. The same guard from before is with us as well. At each cell door, I reveal the news that I will be leaving and the cellmates salute me through the bars. I will never forget the picture of all those faces together, hidden behind the steel bars.

I shake their hands and put my cheek against theirs. Now and then, I see a few watery eyes. The guys I spent most of my time with, are taken outside by the guard to join me. Everyone wants to join, but the guard only allows a few. I apologize to the ones left behind, but they don't mind. They wish me all the best.

It's taking half an hour to say goodbye. Downstairs, at the entrance of the department, I'm with some twenty other inmates and six guards, including the tall head guard. At every turn, I hear my name echoing through the halls and "goodbyes" from the guys who are still sitting in the prison cells. There is a lump in my throat. I try to squash it with all of my might, I want to be strong. But after seeing the guys in front of me, I let a few tears fall. I can't help it.

We do one final big group hug. Like a rugby team, we put our heads together in a circle. I tell everyone that they have to carry on and that one day, the time will come when they will be home again.

In the background, Pipi is watching. Princess Pipi. I call her name and she immediately turns her little ears toward me.

"Come here," I say.

Pipi's mouth is slightly opening, but I don't hear a sound. With her elegant gait she trots up to me. But then she stops and stays at a distance, there are too many people around me. So I walk up to her and squat down beside her. While giving her a pat on the head, I tell her that I'm leaving. Pipi coos and squints her eyes. She's oblivious.

"This is it Pipi, my little princess. I'm leaving. The guys will take good care of you. Will you be good and strong? I'm sorry that I have to go..."

It breaks my heart that I can't take her with me and can no longer care for her. I pet her one last time, stand up, and look at her for the last time. She is looking back with a very penetrating gaze through her intense greenish-yellow, bright eyes.

With a gentle shriek, she opens her red and white mouth one last time. I know I will never see her again.

15

I don't think anyone believed that this was finally the day I was going to leave this place. My face, my name, my appearance had become so natural to everyone. Same goes for me. This had become my life, something it never should have been.

I was going back to my real life, and I knew I would never forget the men who were standing in front of me right now, Pipi the cat and much more.

"Are you coming?" the head guard asked.

I turned around and looked at him with tears in my eyes, smiling gently.

"Yeah, I think it's time..."

16

On my way to the transfer bus, everyone was greeting me from all sides: prisoners from other departments, the keeper of the prison shop, guard Rachid, many other guards, the women from the administration and the doctor. I waved at them, smiled and thanked them for everything.

The bus was right outside the door of the director's office. I searched with my eyes to see if he was still there, but the head guard who guided me told me he had just left for a meeting at the Ministry.

"He will be sorry that you're leaving," he added.

Another guard carried my red suitcase carefully to the bus, as if he were a bellhop in a fancy hotel. While the bus guard handcuffed me, I thanked the head guard and the other guards for the last time.

With my backpack in hand, I stepped onto the bus.

There were nine other inmates on the bus and we saluted each other kindly. Some faces I recognized. The kindness on the bus felt somewhat inappropriate. Or rather, the handcuffs we were wearing were inappropriate. After all, we were just people, and who knew which of these nine men might be innocent too.

"Sorry for the wait guys," I said when I sat down.

Using different words, they were very civil and said that it was okay.

Although I felt one step closer to being home, the handcuffs quickly reminded me that I wasn't free yet. I was still a prisoner, an inmate.

The bus engine started with a loud roar and the door shut with a slam. The wire mesh on the windows prevented me from looking out. I couldn't help thinking about the first time I was brought here with Jeremy. How we observed the high walls and barbed wire of the surrounding area with our mouths open. I remembered the very first transfer from Berkane to Taza, and the letter from my mom I was reading at that time: *"Your life too, will again be as fresh as the budding spring, so you may give the deep gloomy autumn time and dark days of winter a place in your life..."*

It seemed like ages...

The bus slowly started to drive, through the big prison gate and into the outside world. I looked behind me and saw the guards disappear behind the slowly closing gate.

The prison walls were getting smaller and smaller.

Strangely enough, I felt no joy inside, only emptiness. It felt as if something was taken away from me, something I had built up over the past few years. Now, I had to leave it behind and close that chapter. In a flash, I remembered everything I had been through inside those walls: the infinite number of roll calls, the countless fights, the continuous screaming and crying, but also the working out with the guys, the English class, the prison yard, the prison shop, the visits, the translation work for the director, Pipi the cat.

Did that all really happen? It already seemed like a very long time ago.

I had so many thoughts I was starting to get dizzy. I shook my head and told myself that I had to look forward.

The prison of Salé, everything and everyone, was now in the past.

Farewell everyone.

17

On the bus, something happened that I never expected. I became carsick. I had never been carsick before! My body had probably forgotten what it was like to ride a bus, with all of those turns. I asked the boy sitting closest to the window of the driver's cab if he could ask them to drive a little slower. He did and then the eyes of a guard gazed toward me. They were familiar. It was a prison guard. He ordered the driver to slow down. "The boy hasn't been in a car for years," I heard him saying.

I noticed the bus slowed down and began to take the bends more carefully.

"Thanks," I said as I bent over a little with my hands cuffed on my belly.

"Are you okay?" another boy asked.

"Yeah, don't worry, it'll be over soon," I answered and I forced a smile on my face.

Strange, I never felt like this before. I calmed myself down and tried to take my mind off the trip by watching all of the things out my window.

The streets were very busy. Honking cars, smoking trucks,

crackling mopeds, merchants with carts and donkeys, countless cyclists and people walking. Everything was just as chaotic as it was before. It was very strange to see. As if time stood still, as if I had never been away.

Familiar images of a country that I would probably never see again.

18

From Salé we drove to the neighboring capital Rabat. We drove down the promenade along the beach, where years ago, I was walking around smiling with my family, friends and William. In my mind, I unconsciously said goodbye to the streets, the people and the country. I was amazed that the way people drove in traffic hadn't changed at all. The cars honked like crazy in the crowded streets crisscrossing each other, as if the gas they used was free. I couldn't believe my eyes. We drove past large billboards with the king's picture. He was staring out into his country like George Orwell's "Big Brother" from 1984. The king who pardoned me twice. I was grateful to him, even though he probably had no idea who I was. I wondered if he knew which judges had done this injustice to me and how many more lives they destroyed by putting innocent people behind bars?

Why are they doing this? How can people be so ruthless?

My mind wandered again with these thoughts, when next to me I saw a man trying to light a cigarette with some difficulty. Like always, the pungent smell of smoke made me think of my dad.

I understand, dad. I now know why you once decided to leave this country, your homeland.

From Rabat, we headed further south to Mohammedia. I noticed a group of women wearing modern clothing, and I secretly glanced at them through one eye. I breathed in the sultry air that came in through the open windows.

The guard who had previously told the bus driver to slow down was now sleeping. The driver was grumbling at other drivers on the road. Between them was a police officer, constantly holding a cell phone to his ear. The phone looked remarkably thin and flashy. I couldn't guess the brand.

Small raindrops slowly began to fall from the light gray sky. It almost seemed as if this country was crying over what had happened, over saying goodbye.

After almost ninety minutes of driving, we arrived in Casablanca. I immediately recognized the city by its crowds, noise, dirty buildings and the smell of oil and industry. The houses and apartments hadn't been "blanca" for quite some time. "Casanegra" would be a better name for this town nowadays. I recognized the streets in the industrial area we drove through, from back when I worked for Sword fruits. I didn't know there was a prison around here, although it wasn't easy to miss between the rest of the buildings.

As we approached the prison, I saw eight buildings looming behind the prison walls. They were very badly kept and clothes were everywhere, hanging from the bars in the windows. It was impressive for someone who didn't know the prison.

I suddenly had all kinds of feelings inside. I felt stressed, tense about being inside another prison. As we drove through the huge prison gate, I wondered: "Where am I going to end up now?"

19

I think I wasn't the only one who was nervous. When the bus stopped, everyone was dead silent. In the background, we could hear the soft rumble of the many prisoners. We looked around, waiting to see what would happen next.

An unknown guard opened the door and ordered us to step out quietly. We had to identify which luggage belonged to whom. The guard who had fallen asleep walked up beside him. I greeted him and kindly asked if he had slept well. He stretched, unashamedly and nodded. He then turned to the unknown guard and informed him about my transfer to the Netherlands and asked him if there was a better cell somewhere that I could stay in.

"I'll see what I can do," he said gruffly, ordering the other inmates along.

I thanked the guard.

"Feeling better?" he asked as he took off my handcuffs.

"Yes, everything is fine! I appreciate you telling the bus driver to slow down."

"My pleasure. We're going now, good luck to you, Joseph."

He got back in the transfer bus and it disappeared out of sight.

Together with the others, they brought me into the building.

At the entrance, there was a guard holding a large book. I gave them my name and was directed to the "waiting room". It was a long room with small benches on either side. I sat down with my backpack and red suitcase.

A little further down, there was a cell with inmates who had just returned from court. They made all kinds of noises toward us, some saying vulgar things.

"Which one of you has a cigarette and a light?"

"Hey! Why don't you guys answer? Are you deaf?"

"Or just too good to talk to us?"

"Just wait till you're in here!"

Their bantering continued. It didn't bother me much, I was used to it and most of the time it was boasting.

"Hey! You, rookie! With the red suitcase!" I suddenly heard a guy say.

When I heard the word "rookie" my body somehow shot up immediately.

Rookie? What do you mean, rookie?

Normally, I would have ignored this kind of shouting, but I couldn't resist and walked down to the cell. Their eyes narrowed, their pupils got bigger. They probably didn't expect me to come down there. I walked directly up to them. The cell smelled like old sweat and urine.

"Who are you talking about? Rookie? Don't even think about calling me that, I've been here since late 2004," I yelled in genuine Moroccan.

They were silent and I actually heard one guy apologize. I knew that in prison, there was an unwritten rule requiring respect for the people who were imprisoned longer than you. A hierarchy. At first, I was even shocked by my reaction, because I realized it was a typical response for a prisoner. But in fact, wasn't I a prisoner? To the guys in the cage I certainly was.

I accepted their apology and said it was okay. The booing and yelling from the cell had disappeared and a few minutes later, a guard began searching our possessions. I opened my red suitcase and was afraid of the guard making a fuss of all the letters inside of it. I was right.

"What's this?" the guard asked.

"These are letters from my mother."

"Letters? So many? It can't be! There must be something else in it."

"No, really, these are letters from my mother and friends that I've received over the years."

To avoid any problems, I had hidden a hundred dirham note in the suitcase. I showed it to the guard. Without thinking, he grabbed the money.

"You can close your suitcase now, it's okay."

I didn't have to open my backpack either. I could move on, into the huge hallway of Morocco's largest prison.

20

I was ordered to report to the prison's communal cell, just like in Salé when I stayed with the "rookies". I was frightened at the thought of that terrible weekend when Jeremy and I feared for our lives.

The large hallway came to a T. The signs on the wall showed me that I had to go left. Both left and right were large hallways, about six hundred feet long and sixty feet wide. The hallway was swarming with people occasionally looking at me. I then heard my name.

"JOSEPH! JOSEPH! "

At first I thought it was my imagination, but I really had heard someone calling my name from the crowd. A boy was waving at me.

"Joseph! How are you, man!"

I looked at him and told him I was doing fine. I apologized and told him that I couldn't really remember who he was.

"No problem, I understand! We used to exercise together in Salé a while back, but that was in 2005, or 2006, I can't even remember anymore," he said laughing. "My name is Rayaan."

He shook my hand, saying how great it was to see me again. I laughed with him and tried to remember him as best I could. I had seen a lot of people come and go over the years! I used to get embarrassed when I forgot someone's name, but that kind of thing just didn't matter in here.

Rayaan asked where I was going.

"The communal cell..."

"The communal cell? That sucks. Wait, let me talk with our department head, I'll try to fix you a place in our cell.

With my suitcase and backpack in hand, I followed Rayaan. He was half a head shorter than me, well-built with his head shaved. The type of guy who was never bothered about prison life, at all. “That’s our life,” he often would say.

After some tussling and bribes, Rayaan had arranged for me to sleep in his cell. The long hallway we stood in had four entrances to the left, which led to the four flats in this wing. Each flat had a separate section of four floors. Each floor had an aisle with four cells on both sides.

It didn’t surprise me one bit that the building looked as if there hadn’t been any maintenance work since they built the place. Neither did the musty smell. The walls were covered with texts and slogans, and all the cell doors had rust spots. Everywhere I looked, inmates were walking around. Rayaan dragged my red suitcase up the stairs to the third floor. He introduced me to the other inmates in the cell and spoke very highly about me. I sometimes thought it was a little exaggerated, but I soon realized that this could only work in my favor. After shaking hands and storing my belongings in the cell’s “trusty”, they showed me around a little more.

The cells were all the same size, slightly smaller than the one in Salé, a little over five hundred square feet. However, there were just as many people. Each cell had about twenty to thirty inmates.

Rayaan then introduced me to the foreigners, the French, Spanish, German, Danish, Polish and English, and every time, he mentioned the fact that I could speak their language.

“But I don’t speak Danish or Polish,” I said.

“They don’t need to know that?” he said with a wink.

I just let him go ahead.

There were two other Dutch prisoners, also waiting for their transfer back to the homeland. I talked with them about my experiences, all the way up to evening roll call, which was also announced here with a lot of noise, fuss, shouting and whistling. We agreed to continue talking the next day. But that wasn’t going to happen.

21

That night in the cell with Rayaan went by calmly and reasonably fast. I talked incessantly with everyone. There was an Irishman, a Frenchman and a Spaniard that I exchanged stories with. Rayaan took care of the food and a place to sleep. At some point I excused myself, because I realized that I still had a letter from my mom I hadn't read. For some time now, I was actually receiving her letters from the embassy unopened. I tore open the envelope.

"*... Like always, I woke up thinking of you, wondering if you've slept well, if you've made it through the day again or if you've met someone you get along with. It all still seems unreal, you being there; not some sort of weird, bizarre dream, but harsh reality. Hang in there. We're almost there...*"

Although I could hear talking all night long, I fell asleep. I was exhausted by the day's events.

22

Tuesday, June 16, 2009, day 1636.

"Joseph Oubelkas!"

"Joseph Oubelkas!!"

I sat there leaning on my elbows, half asleep with one eye barely open. I thought I was dreaming hearing my name called, but there actually was a guard standing at the cell door. I looked at my watch, it was half past five. There was a slight odor in the cell – a mixture of cigarettes and hashish and everyone around me was still asleep.

"Joseph Oubelkas!"

"Yes, yes, I'm here," I said putting my hand up.

"Pack your things, you're being transferred!"

Transferred? Right now?

"To the Netherlands?" I asked.

"Yes," the guard answered. "The police will be here to pick you up at six."

My eyes flew open.

"I'll be back to get you in 15 minutes."

"OK!" I said while getting rid of my blanket.

Rayaan was lying on his bed and looked at me with a tired, but happy face.

"I'm going home."

"Good for you, man!"

"Yeah, it's really happening," I said softly.

I could hardly believe the words coming out of my mouth, but it was true. They really said it. The day I had fantasized about for so long, dreamed about so often, had finally arrived. I felt lightheaded. It was really about to happen.

23

It was dead silent in the prison. I quietly said goodbye to Rayaan, who stayed in his bed. I stepped over the other inmates who were sleeping on the ground like snakes huddled together. I had nothing to pack, all I had to do was brush my teeth, put in my contact lenses, get dressed and fix my hair. I took along my suitcase and backpack, and I followed the guard toward the main entrance.

I heard nothing but the clacking sound of the guard's heels hitting the floor in front of me and the chirping of sparrows outside.

I'm going home. I'm going home. I'll see my mom again, and William and my dad, my brothers, everyone!

The butterflies in my stomach were going crazy.

In the prison's administration office, there stood three plain-clothes police officers with documents in their hands, ready to pick me up. The guard saluted them dutifully and handed me over. They asked some routine questions about who I was and whether the belongings they had were mine. I saw three phones, my old passport, a new emergency passport – arranged by the Dutch embassy at the last second –, my camera and my driving license. The same items they took away from me on the day I was arrested were lying right there as if time had stood still. A Nokia, Ericsson and Samsung phone. The camera with the pictures I had taken more than four and a half years ago. It was surreal seeing these things again.

I confirmed that they were mine. They nodded and asked me to sign a bunch of documents. They were written in French, so I read them carefully and then signed them.

"Ok, let's proceed to the police van now. The Dutch Royal Military Police are waiting for you at Casablanca airport."

I complied with their request and walked with them. They were formal but understanding, and didn't even handcuff me.

Fifteen minutes later we were standing in front of the main entrance to the airport. The door of the police van slid open. I got out with my suitcase and backpack, and walked inside with the three men. They left the van at the door with the lights flashing.

Although I was still being treated like a criminal, I was keenly aware of the freedom I suddenly had. Once inside the airport I couldn't believe my eyes. I walked among the people like a normal passenger. Women were walking right past me and I couldn't help but turn around every now and then.

It was on that airport that I had my first sense of freedom again. And oh, how sweet it was!

24

The officers took me to a separate department within Customs, where they handled all the formalities and officially handed me over to three men of the Dutch Royal Military Police. Just like back in prison, I served as a translator between the Dutch and Moroccan authorities.

The three Dutch officers were tall men, and wore tight black uniforms with vertical white stripes. They politely introduced themselves. Two of them were my age, the other seemed to be in his forties.

We had to check in at an ordinary airline desk, which was a little strange. Like a tourist with my backpack and suitcase full of letters, I stood there among all the other people who were completely unaware of everything I had been through.

The maximum weight for luggage was sixty-six pounds, but my suitcase weighed seventy-nine! So I had to open it right there on the spot and take some things out.

Everyone was watching with wide eyes when they noticed that the suitcase was filled to the brim with letters. The military police were amazed and asked what it was all for.

"Oh, but that's not all," I said with a happy face. "I have six more bags full of mail that are being sent to the Netherlands later on."

I was allowed to bring the extra thirteen pounds on board as a carry-on inside a plastic bag, together with my backpack.

After checking in, I was surrounded by three men in Armani suits, three police officers and a number of customs officers. Now I stood out. While waiting in the departure area, the other passengers were looking at me.

At our gate, a long line of passengers had formed at the entrance to the gangway, which was stuck to the plane like a huge leech. The flight attendant standing at the counter nodded to the men that accompanied me, and then looked at me. I smiled at her, but she didn't smile back. In the long row of passengers waiting to board, I saw several eyes staring at me. Some were standing on their toes to see what was going on.

So this must be how it feels when you're a celebrity walking through an airport.

To be honest, I really didn't enjoy it. I kept thinking that this entire circus around me was unnecessary. I wanted to tell them that this charade wasn't necessary at all, that they could just let me go. I wasn't a danger to anyone, I'm just a regular guy... An ordinary guy, who four-and-a-half years ago happened to be in the wrong place, at the wrong time, asking some armed customs officers what was going on.

The three military officers walked with me into the gangway. The police and customs officers stayed behind. The pilots and flight attendants kindly welcomed us. The plane was completely empty. We went to the back. They motioned that I could sit in a window seat. The oldest of the three officers sat down next to me, another sat in the row behind us, and the third one sat in the row next to us.

The passengers were safe.

Five minutes later, the other passengers came trickling in, each one of them taking the time to look in my direction. It was starting to irritate me, so I looked out the window and watched the bags pass by on luggage carts. I looked for my red suitcase. That was my biggest fear, losing my suitcase.

"Uh, sir? Sir?"

The officer sitting next to me tapped me lightly. I looked at him and then at the steward next to us. He was bent over in the aisle about to ask me a question.

"Yes?" I said.

"Are these people the police?" the Moroccan steward asked with a high pitched voice. He was a bit of a feminine type.

From what I remembered, this was typical for stewards.

"Yes!" I said sternly.

And I decided to play along.

"These men are indeed police officers," I continued. "And I'm the criminal!"

"Ooh!" the steward squealed and recoiled, throwing his hands in the air. "Okay, okay! Sorry for asking. Sorry!"

He turned around and walked away, hips-swaying.

"What did he ask?" the officer next to me asked.

"He asked if everything was to our liking," I said with a big smile, secretly enjoying this.

"Ah, okay, fine. Do you mind asking him for some water? I have a dry throat."

"Well, my guess is that he won't be coming back anytime soon."

25

For some reason, the men of the military police and I were waited on hand and foot during the flight. The flight attendants asked continuously if we needed anything, or if everything was okay. They looked first at the police men, and then at me. Every time, I smiled kindly. I liked this treatment as a VIC – *Very Important Criminal.* Well, why not?

During the flight I got to know my three companions. Of course, I began my story in early 2005, telling of how I was falsely accused and sentenced to ten years in prison. Naturally, they reacted with expressions of disbelief.

"Everyone says they're innocent."

Sigh.

"Yes, I know, but I truly am innocent."

I think the flight from Morocco to the Netherlands had

never gone by so quickly. Before we knew it, the plane was landing again. During the flight, I had told all the gory details of my story. Instead of three military policemen sitting upright and formal, the oldest sat sideways in his chair next to me, the policeman behind was intently hanging his face between the seats and the third leaned over to our side form the other row. They were all quiet and listened attentively to every detail of my story.

They especially thought the fact that I had asked at the gate of the packing station what was going on, was sufficient proof for themselves that I had nothing to do with it.

"If you did know..." the officer next to me began to say.

"...Yes, then I think I would have turned around and left," I finished his sentence. "But I didn't know, I just wanted to know what was going on."

"And the difference of five stamps in your passport, the twenty-two entry stamps and seventeen exit stamps, that wasn't the truth?" the officer behind me asked.

"You should have my passport with you, count them," I said.

I told them about the independent investigation by the trust lawyer from the Dutch Ministry of Foreign Affairs, who said that I "didn't even deserve a fine."

"Unbelievable", "bizarre", "do you really mean that?" were the responses they gave me. They just didn't know what to say.

"It really is all true..." I finally said.

During the landing, the three men were looking ahead, puzzled, as if they had just heard they were fired.

I looked out the window, smiling, and saw the familiar Dutch countryside. Polders in all shades of green, several lakes, winding rivers, straight ditches.

Schiphol Airport came into view. It was slightly cloudy and small drops of rain were splashing against the windows. Typical Dutch weather in a typical Dutch setting. Completely different from the withered brown sands of Morocco.

I'm home again. I'm going straight home. I can't believe this...

26

The landing went smoothly. After the aircraft had taxied to its place, we sat down until all the passengers had departed. Like an artist, I was taken out the back exit. I walked down a few steps and got into a van. At this point, I was under the impression I would get to go home right away.

After a minute ride, we arrived at the military police headquarters. The oldest of the three was my escort while the other two took my luggage. Another big guy, wearing a military police uniform with a shaved head came along as well. He ostentatiously "snapped" on some rubber gloves and said, "Well, boy, I'm gonna search you now!"

Holy shit! What's he searching me for?

I looked questioningly at my escort with a worried, but serious expression. He smiled at me.

"Is this really necessary?"

"Yes, I'm sorry, but would you please come over here? You can take off all of your clothes in that room."

Noooo, this can't be serious.

With sagging shoulders, I walked into the room.

Suddenly, the two police officers started laughing.

"No, man! We're just kidding! Come back here, I'm just gonna pat you down on top of your clothing."

For a moment, I still wasn't convinced, and then began to laugh along with them nervously.

"Really?"

"Yeah, we were just joking around with you."

27

Ever since last February, when I found out that I would be transferred to the Netherlands, I was being told that I could go home on the day of my transfer. William said that he would be waiting for me at Schiphol Airport. The Ministry of Justice and Foreign Affairs urged my mom to keep things quiet and simple. My friends had wanted so badly to welcome me with balloons, banners, cameras and even a marching band, but that kind of attention could jeopardize the ECJL procedure of other Dutch men – including Maurice's – who were still imprisoned in Morocco. If the Moroccan officials would see me coming home to a festival or party, they might feel disrespected. This could put a damper on all future transfers.

We kept our promise and William would be waiting impatiently, until the military police would let me go. During the flight, I had also told my company several times that I would be allowed to go home, but the military police knew nothing about it. They were supposed to receive the order as soon as we landed.

"Well, I'm sure you guys know all about it already," I said, delighted.

But unfortunately, rather than sleeping at home in my own bed, I would spend another night in a cell.

28

I told everyone how well the officers of the Dutch Royal Military Police had treated me. Bravo to them.

But I was ready to kill them when, after spending three long hours in the waiting room doing nothing, they told me that I wasn't going home.

"You will be transferred to Den Bosch[15]."

"That can't be!" I said, as my stomach turned in knots. I felt like someone had just punched me in the face and I wasn't ready for it. "The Ministry has been saying from the beginning that I would be allowed to go home today!"

"I'm sorry, Joseph, we are truly sorry for you, but these are our orders..."

I was silent. I didn't know what to say or do and I just stood there staring at the officer in silence. He looked back at me and I could see he genuinely felt sorry for me.

"You'll be picked up by some men with the Judicial Services Department in a minute. I really hope that you get to go home very soon."

"No, no, this can't be, I have to go home, I am going home. My best friend, William, he's here waiting for me. This is a mistake, really, they ... they...," I started stuttering. "They told me that I could go home. Please call the Ministry of Foreign Affairs, or Justice. Please call them, there's been a mistake."

I didn't get an answer, the only thing the officer said was "sorry". Then he closed the door.

Damn it! It can't be...! Why can't things go right for once?

I felt tears coming. My joy had been so intense, the desire for my homecoming was so strong... It only made my grief sweep over me faster.

There I was, in the holding cell, standing in front of a closed door yet again, with my eyes to the floor. I turned around and wiped away a few tears.

---

15. Capital of the Province of Brabant in the Netherlands.

29

"Keep holding on, my child and make yourself strong."

I quickly pulled myself together. I had already been through so much, I could deal with this too! There was one consolation: at least I was in the Netherlands.

But this thought, which had given me strength, also worried me. I thought of the judge here, and how he might decide that I should stay in prison for a few more months.

I paced the room. I sat on the benches, lied down and sat back up again. Time went by incredibly slow, until suddenly the door opened.

A dark man, uniformed in a white shirt and dark trousers, walked into the room. He wore earrings and had gum in his mouth which he chewed excessively. He looked down at his list and called my name.

"Joseph… Oubelkas?"

"Yes?"

"Are you coming?" he asked with a thick Amsterdam accent.

I got up and followed him. My suitcase and backpack were waiting to be loaded in the white prisoner van of the Judicial Services Department. The van, which had blacked-out windows, was waiting at the entrance to the military police office. I got in and saw three small cabins made of thick plexiglass, the back one slightly larger than the front two. In the back cabin, two men were sitting there, gazing apathetically. A dark man with a weathered face and a white boy wearing a cap. I could choose my seat and I chose the front cabin. I said nothing and sat down while the cabin was being locked.

Again, here I was, locked up.

In the corner I noticed a hidden camera and a speaker, from which I could hear the radio playing. Hearing the Dutch voices on 3FM radio[16] was surely a welcome sound!

The dark, uniformed man stepped in and started the van. He was accompanied by a colleague sitting in the passenger seat. I could hear them talking to each other.

I looked outside and was surprised how well I could see through the windows, whereas they looked so dark from the outside. I thought of William who was waiting for me, and my mom who would be at home awaiting my arrival together with my father, Fouza, my brothers and many others. They were probably wondering why I never showed up.

Soon. This can't take that long. Pretty soon I'll be home.

We drove toward the prison complex at Schiphol Airport. The infamous complex where that terrible fire occurred. Shivers ran down my spine when I saw those sad buildings, surrounded by fences and barbed wire. I thought of the poor men who couldn't escape and were burned alive like trapped rats. I couldn't believe such a thing had happened in the Netherlands...

I was deep in thought as we arrived at the registration area of the complex.

I overheard the bizarre conversation of the men from the Judicial Services Department.

"Hello, this is 3410, this is 3410, over!"

It was the same voice with the thick Amsterdam accent. I think they spoke into the radio. There wasn't a response.

"Hello! This is 3-4-1-0, this is 3-4-1-0!" he said distinctively louder.

Again, no response. Then I heard them talking to each other:

"Aren't we 3410? Or are we 4310 now?"

"I don't know, try 4310."

---

16. 3FM radio is a popular Dutch public radio station.

“This is 4310, do you hear me?”

Response.“Yes?” 4310, go ahead,” projected through the radio.

“Yes, we are standing by at the Schiphol complex right now waiting to drop some prisoners, but we were told that they weren’t registered by the lifeguard.”

Drop? Lifeguard? What were they talking about?

“One moment please 4310,” sounded through the radio again.

It was quiet.

Then the men began to joke...

“They better be registered, I wanna be home in time for dinner. I could eat a horse!” the one man said.

“They have to be, otherwise we’ll just handcuff ‘em to this lamp post here.”

They laughed.

“Or we’ll hang them from the highest tree!”

Again, laughter.

I couldn’t believe my ears. Didn’t they know that we could hear them? Or were they doing it on purpose? This was a big change from the polite, professional attitudes of the military police officers.

Finally, we were registered and told to get out. I stared at the two men. I wanted to tell them how funny they were, making their little jokes, but I stopped myself. They weren’t worth it.

We walked inside the complex and each one of us was placed in a separate cell. I asked several times for someone to call my mom and let her know that I wouldn’t be home. “One phone call, it’ll only take ten seconds, please?”

But every time they refused, telling me that it wasn’t allowed. This really pissed me off, why couldn’t they just call?

I knew that my mom, William and everyone else who were waiting for me would be worried.

After two hours in the small cramped cell without windows or daylight, the massive cell door opened and they put me back on a transport.

30

I was back in the van of the Judicial Services Department. The drivers were different from the jokers earlier. We drove to several prisons and every time, someone was "dropped off" at the "lifeguard" or picked up.

The sun came out from under the clouds and was shining brightly. With narrow eyes, I gazed at the outside world, which never felt closer than right now.

I saw people with happy faces riding their bikes, some with serious faces sitting in their cars. I wondered if any of these people truly realized how much they had to be thankful for. How much happiness is derived simply from living in freedom.

I looked out the window quietly, listening to 3FM's music and the Dutch singers touching my ears. The surroundings were so beautifully green. It surprised me again how clean the roads were, how orderly the traffic was here. I enjoyed the typical Dutch sky, an orange tint that always had many clouds as if they were pulled across the sky like a wool blanket.

"Those typical Joseph skies" as my mother once wrote.

In the evening, we drove on the A2 toward Den Bosch. At some point, I noticed the Amer power plant appearing on the horizon to my right. This was right next to my hometown, the station had been the backdrop of my life for years and years.

That's where I have to go... My home is there, within reach.

I'm here, mom, so near to you.

31

At the police station of Den Bosch, a kind officer was waiting for me. The van had already left again for the next address.

I followed the officer into the detention center, and politely asked if I could call my mom. "Please sir. She doesn't know where I am, and no one would let me call."

"Sure, but first let's put away your suitcase. You can take out anything you need for the night."

"It can stay closed," I said with a little smile. "All that's inside are letters from my mother."

The officer frowned, then smiled modestly.

"Maybe something else then?" he continued. "I need a moment to look in your backpack if that's okay."

"No problem," I said, handing it over to him.

"Okay, sure."

There was nothing in it that was forbidden. He only made me take the laces out of my shoes and remove my belt.

Déjà vu.

My mind raced back to Morocco, to the police station in Berkane, when I was asked to do the same thing. At that time I never could have imagined the things I was about to go through.

I did what I was kindly asked, and the officer then took me to a cell. He opened the thick, dull green door to a small, but very clean cell.

No cockroaches... No dozens of men... No smell...

There was a brick bed with a mattress, blanket, pillow and clean sheets. In the corner, I saw an aluminum toilet and sink. There was also a small brick table with a fixed seat. I sat down on the bed with my backpack next to me. The officer told me that I could call home in five minutes. The cell door closed and exactly five minutes later, he came back. I followed him to a separate room, holding up my pants with every step.

In the room was a table with four chairs and a normal phone. I sat down on a chair as the officer picked up the receiver and dialed a special code.

"Here you are" he handed me the phone. "Just dial your mother's number. Take your time. When you're done talking, just press this button." He pointed to a button on the phone and I nodded. I felt like telling him how much he reminded me of Chief Nordin, but I kept it to myself. Before I started dialing, he said that his orders were to bring me to the Palace of Justice the very next morning. There, I would be brought before the court.

My hand was shaking as I dialed the number. I began with 0031, but then realized that I didn't have to use the country code anymore.

I'm in the Netherlands. That's right. I'm in the Netherlands.

"Janny speaking," my mom answered.

"Mama, it's me!"

"Oh, Joseph! Finally, finally! Where are you? What is going on? We're terrified here."

"I'm in Den Bosch, in the detention center of the police station"

"In Den Bosch? What happens next?"

"Tomorrow morning I will be brought before the court."

"Okay, William and I will be there."

"How's William? Is he home yet?"

"Yes, he just arrived. He didn't know what to do anymore. Nobody said anything to us. We called the Ministry of Justice, the Ministry of Foreign Affairs and even journalists with the newspapers. No one could tell us anything. Your friends have been calling constantly. Everyone is worried. How are you now? Sorry for rambling from one thing to another, I'm just so glad to hear your voice!"

I laughed softly.

"Everything's okay, mom, I'm being treated well by the military police and the officers here have been very kind to me. It is also very clean and they're giving me something to eat."

"Oh, I'm glad, that's good to hear."

We chatted away for almost 45 minutes.

After we hung up, I "beeped" the police officer and he took me back to the cell, where I had a hot meal and some fruit. He gave me the weekly and daily newspapers. I got through about half of them, but I wasn't really in the mood to read.

"Is there anything else that you need?" the officer asked me.

I shook my head.

"Only my freedom..." I said, swallowing the lump in my throat.

32

Wednesday, June 17, 2009, day 1637.

That night in jail, I couldn't fall asleep. The picture of a screaming judge with a big gavel constantly flashed through my mind. I'm so afraid that he'll sentence me to another period of imprisonment.

"He still has to rehabilitate here, after such a lengthy prison term abroad," is the argument I was making up to myself.

I'm constantly tossing left to right in bed. I wonder how the guys in Morocco are doing. Will they talk about me? Will they take good care of Pipi? Will they think of me? I told everyone that I was going home, but I'm still imprisoned.

What will happen at the tribunal?

I'm thinking of my mom's voice over the phone. My sense of loss is now stronger than ever. I yearn for freedom, for my life.

It's so close now.

At 7:00 a.m. I'm already dressed. Thirty minutes later, a police officer opens my cell and kindly asks if I would like to take a shower.

Taking a shower?

That is what I want, especially after the past few days of transfers. I'm walking with the officer back to the showers and see four stalls. He is putting a white towel, washcloth and soap in my hands and I step into a stall. Next to me, someone is scrubbing himself extensively. I can see his face through the glass window of the door.

"Good morning!" the young man says cheerfully.

I am surprised by his cheerfulness and say "good morning" back. I'm looking around, still amazed at how clean and well-kept everything is. No dirty walls, no dirty floors, no dirty people, no mess, nothing. Everything is clean!

After showering, I have to return to my cell for a while. Later, I will be picked up by the same police officer from before. I think he's a little younger than me. While picking up my things, he asks what it was like in Morocco. We continue to talk, all the way to the police van, and throughout the trip to the tribunal until we get out.

Through a back entrance of the Palace of Justice, we enter a room, locked by a big solid rolling door. The young police officer is now briefly telling my story to some of his colleagues.

"You know what this guy has been through?... He just got back from Morocco, where he has been in several prisons for almost five years..."

The responses are nice to hear, from "you poor guy" to "you still are looking good."

My red suitcase and backpack are taken into a separate safe, and the young police officer hands me over to the staff of the tribunal.

"Good luck, Joseph. You will be all right!" he says, and he winks at me.

"Thanks!" I answer excitedly. The positive attention makes me feel good.

They put me in a cell and a friendly lady in uniform tells me that I have to wait for a little while, until I am called. It's a quarter to nine.

The cell has no windows and is soundproof. I can hear myself breathing. I shuffle my feet on the ground and I'm nervous for what is about to come. A fluorescent lamp colors the room yellow. The walls are plastered with text and writing, I'm trying to read everything. Here, there are no 2Pac slogans like *only God can judge me*, that I once read long ago in a public cell, far away from here. I keep hanging on an ingenious piece of text, "A.S.S.".

What was the meaning the author of this abbreviation would have thought of, with the obvious dots between the letters? "After Such Suffering?" Or "Alive So Secure?" I look at my watch for the umpteenth time.

Finally, the time has come.

It's a quarter past nine. The cell door opens. The woman in uniform is standing half hidden behind the door and tells me that I'm allowed to stand up. I stand up.

"You can come here," the woman says, smiling.

I feel a bit stupid that I kept standing there, so I carefully step out of the cell.

A man in a nice dark suit is walking toward me. He has an A4 sheet in his left hand. Two feet in front of me, he stops. The woman is still standing behind me, with the cell door crank in her hand.

"Mr. Oubelkas?" the man asks.

"Yes?"

"I'm Mr. Dadanski, the prosecutor." He reaches out.

"Nice to meet you," I say softly and shake his hand.

I look at him with my head bowed slightly, afraid of what he is going to say.

"Mr. Oubelkas, I have a letter in my hand."

He shows me the letter.

"It's a letter from the court with the order of release."

For a moment, it's quiet.

It doesn't really hit me what "the order of release" means.

"Mr. Oubelkas," I feel his hand on my shoulder. "You can go home."

Suddenly I look up, and I'm looking the smiling prosecutor right in the eye.

"What did you say? Are you serious? Can I go home? Really, I'm going home? "

The prosecutor is laughing.

"Yes, you may really go home. It's over."

Tears are jumping in my eyes. He said the words. The words: "It's over." He really said it.

It's over.

I'm still looking at the smiling prosecutor, then back at the woman behind me, who's also smiling. I don't know what to say or do, so I embrace the prosecutor.

The man in the suit wasn't expecting this reaction, but he answers the embrace willingly with a few pats on my back.

"Finally, finally! Thank you so much! I just don't know what to say!"

We let each other go calmly.

"My mom, William, they would be here, did you see them?" I'm asking, while wiping away my tears.

"Yes, they are upstairs, waiting for you in the lobby. Just go there."

Just go there.

He says it like it's the most normal thing in the world. So easy

... Those few words. Finally I may, finally, I can go to the people for whom I care so greatly...

My suitcase and backpack are brought in. They are handed to me by an employee who wishes me lots of luck.

With my red suitcase in hand and my backpack on, I walk up the stairs. With every step, I'm getting a better view of the lobby.

And then I see them sitting there.

My mom and William, side by side, on a plastic chair. They are looking ahead. For a moment, I'm standing on the stairs and see the profile of their faces.

Mom, William...

"MOM! WILLIAM!" I'm yelling and let my suitcase and backpack fall.

They turn to look at me.

"JOSEPH!" my mom and William call out at the same time.

While they are standing up, I run to them and everything seems to be set in slow motion. Mama with her smile, the smile that I have known since she picked me up from the nursery in Breda when I was a little boy, the smile that lets her shine so brightly. And William, my best friend since I was eight years old. There they are, with their arms wide open...

My safe haven, finally I'm back in my safe haven.

"Oh, Joseph, my child," my mom says, just before she takes me in her arms.

We are crying, just letting our tears flow. William puts his arms around my mom and me, buries his head between ours and also begins to cry. Here we are, the three of us, embracing each other in the large lobby of the Palace of Justice.

It's over.

It's finally over. Really over.

EPILOGUE

Day 1637, the day of my release, felt like a dream. And it will always feel that way. How I walked out of the Palace of Justice with my mom and William. How people on their bicycles were passing, laughing. How we got in the car and I couldn't believe how green the trees and meadows were, how clean the roads and how orderly everything was moving in traffic. It was fairylike weather. The sun was shining and the sky was bright blue with motionless white clouds scattered throughout.

For the entire drive home, William handed me his phone. Friends were calling constantly.

My mother and William told me that on Friday evening, a welcome-home party was organized for me. There would be a lot of friends and acquaintances who wanted to see me and speak with me again after so many years.

The way I felt when I got home was indescribable. How I hugged everyone, how everyone asked me all the ins and outs of my experience. I heard the voices echoing and I began to feel light-headed.

In the evening, my mom, William and I went to the polders in "the land of Heusden and Altena". We stood at the fence of a meadow and watched the cows grazing in peace. We enjoyed the sunset and the deep silence. Finally, I could look into the distance and watch the sun disappear beyond the horizon. The sky was a festival of colors. For a minute, I felt as though all of this beauty was organized especially for me and I felt a shiver of joy move through my body.

It was all just right. The day came together perfectly, like a beautiful puzzle. Until the moment my mom and I wished each other goodnight, and I was standing alone in my bedroom.

My bedroom, decorated to my wishes, the walls in orange and yellow tones. Pictures of sunsets were shining on the wall. It was exactly as I imagined. Even a little nicer. Oddly enough, I didn't feel strange in this new house at all. My mother brought out the heart and soul of her Norwegian wooden home.

I couldn't believe it was over. Really over.

I was exhausted from all the events of the day.

On the bed I saw a paper. I unfolded it. It was letter four hundred from my mom. I started reading and instinctively I remembered my first transfer from the prison of Berkane to the one in Taza. When I was handcuffed in the lattice cage of the transfer bus, reading one of the many wonderful letters she had written.

But that was history. Fortunately.

The only similarity to the situation back then, was that while I was reading the final letter from my mom, every now and then a big tear fell onto the paper.

Letter 400.

"Sweetheart, here it is: the final letter. Who would have thought that it would be four hundred letters, but I'm sure we all will get over it. We will become stronger from this whole tragedy. A lot has changed in your life and the amazing thing is that your character remained the same. You have proven yourself completely as a human being. Despite the hard life, you've won everything and lost nothing. You're wonderful, my son, keep it that way.

Life is drifting by, just like a murmuring brook in a forest early in the morning. Seasons pass, and trees lose their leaves. They will be bare, they will have knobs, and they will be green again. Everything seems so normal, but it isn't. Nothing should be taken for granted. Neither should freedom. Neither should health and love, like you said, the three pillars. Cherish them. Unbeknownst to you, your life has begun a new path. Put your shoulder to the wheel. You have gathered many experiences. Let yourself go with the flow of your new life. Think again of your dreams. Of course, not everything will be a bed of roses, but it's important that the theme of your life is one that gives you satisfaction, one that guides the way to your talents. It doesn't have to be earth-shattering things, but if there were one hundred other people who act like you, you would already be successful because you're leading by example. Like I once wrote to you, you always leave a trail of courage, joy, innocence and goodness in your path. The sense of beauty in your heart reflects a sense of beauty to others and because of you, they will experience the feeling of happiness. Therefore, the work you perform will be very important.

Try not to view the past as time lost, but use it to structure the rest of your life. Do your best to handle it in a positive way, because there is already enough destruction in the world. Let us not be a part of that, what do you say, boy? You never have to forget, you can't forget, but you can give it a place in your life. A place that takes away the rough edges and that will protect the useful, beautiful moments. And you will succeed, for it is inherent in man to forget the bad things and make the good things a little better than they were before.

I also hope, and this has great importance in life, that you can be gentle in your judgment of others and put things into perspective. Things are as they come. Build on your inner peace as much as possible. I believe this is the highest goal you can achieve as a human being: peace with yourself and with the world around you. This allows you to be good for one another. If everyone had this talent, the world would be a better place. I think we can achieve it.

I'm standing beside you, day after day, my son. If you notice anything different, even if it's only a bird's feather that you didn't see before, a leaf that swirls at your feet, or a daffodil, waving in the wind, know that this will always symbolize a special message from me.

I close my writings with the words that there will always be a light at the end of the tunnel, no matter how long the tunnel is.

The waves will break on the beach eternally, as long as you shall live, and beyond.

It's all a part of life.

Lots of love, mom. "

A WORD OF THANKS

Of course, I want to start by thanking my wonderful mother, who is so strong, both in character and as a person. She deserves great admiration. Every child would want for nothing with a mother like her and the love she gives has the power to overcome any situation.

Special thanks to William, for his precious friendship, and to my father and his lovely family, where my mother and I are always welcome "guests". Also my grandfather, for his support and beautiful handwritten letters.

Special thanks also goes to Angela, for everything she does for me, her commitment and her loving support.

A special thanks to the Bouhanou family, Husstege family, Van Ginkel family and Kuys family, for continually supporting my mom and me, to Peter from the fitness center Van Drunen, to Wilko and Joyce from the Wilko ruit firm, to Kees and his Jaguar Fresh Company team, to John and Theo from the @ Xit team, to all the employees of the Epafras Foundation and to the Franciscan Sisters in Breda, particularly Sr. Servatia († 1925-2011).

I also want to thank the following people who helped to create this book (in alphabetical order): Abdeljalil Kaddour, Alba Cuellar-Rojas, Ali Eddaoudi, Alex Timmermans, Andre Laarhoven, Anke Neutelings, Bart de Ruijter, Bart Vrijsen, Bas van Leijsen, Chris Nooijens, Damian Alcedo, Daniel Schoone, Ed and Mirjan Heijnen, Edward Zijlmans, Ellen van de Bovenkamp, Emre Kalkan, Ferda Göde, Henriëtte Balk, Hilde Baaij, Javelin Zwakhalen, Jean Paul Nelemans, Jeroen

de Bekker, Joep Rijk, John Sep, Leon van Gameren, Marin Hekman, Najet Assouiki, Nicole Andries, Nina van Ooyen, Olaf Harlaar, Paul de Groot, Suzie Angela and Ward Bergmans.
If I forgot to mention someone, don't worry, for your actions will never be forgotten.

Although some of the names have been changed, all of the characters in this story are real. I am grateful to everyone for the special moments we had together, in that cold world we all have known, and the friendships that were forged within it. Thank you Nordin, Karim, Soufian, Jeremy, Thomas, Younes, Rachid, Maurice and Fernando. In particular, I would like to thank Abderrahman (Abdul), whose actual name I have used. Abdul, rest in peace my friend. I still get tears in my eyes when I think of your sudden passing. The only justification I have, is that it was meant to be...

I would also like to thank all the people who took the time to think of me and left a message on www.freesef.com. Please know that I have read every word. The words were (and still are) of great importance to me, and I'm very grateful for that.

Not to mention Nika – thank you for lying next to me, purring so often to keep me company on my writing days, and Moesha, I'm glad you occasionally jumped in my lap, but you're still a fat cat. Odie, you were the sweetest cat in the world, but after twenty-three years, your body gave up in April 2012. Lotty, Musti and Cesar, you too rest in peace, I'm sorry I can't be there to pat you anymore. When I think of you, I think of Pipi and I hope she's doing well.
Finally, I would like to say that I hope that my experience, my story, can be an inspiration to those who are going through a

difficult time right now. I can tell you personally, you must be strong, you must remain steadfast in your pursuit to overcome.

Life has many barriers we must cross. Most of the time, a warning will precede them, but everyone stumbles at least once in their life on an invisible barrier. It is then that you must stand up and move on and see past the darkest clouds to a heavenly blue, with flowers blooming in all of their beauty.

I feel privileged and will remain grateful for the rest of my life, for the countless beautiful words in the many letters I have received from so many people. Without those letters, without the four hundred letters from my mother, this book would never have existed...

Thanks everyone. Thank you.

www.ingramcontent.com/pod-product-compliance
Ingram Content Group UK Ltd.
Pitfield, Milton Keynes, MK11 3LW, UK
UKHW041632190726
13854UKWH00006B/2450

9 789077 607831